Once Upon A Time In The East

Dave Rimmer

FOURTH ESTATE · *London*

First published in Great Britain in 1992 by
Fourth Estate Limited
289 Westbourne Grove
London W11 2QA

A catalogue record for this book is available from the British Library

ISBN 1-872180-48-5

Typeset by York House Ltd, London
Printed in Great Britain by Biddles Ltd, Guildford and King's Lynn

For
Ivan Jirous
whom I have never met
and to whom I was no help at all

and for
the Nevis Cadets
Marc, Callum & Seth
who all came to stay
while this baby was on the way

'I'm out for a good time – all the rest is propaganda.'
Saturday Night and Sunday Morning

Contents

1   Prologue: Once Upon A Time   1
2   The Museum of Hubris   5
3   Escape to West Berlin   19
4   Wallflower at the Bad Party   36
5   Passport to Pankow   62
6   Berlin Games   83
7   The Eastie Boys   112
8   'In the Mountains, There You Feel Free'   142
9   The Wall Totters   200
10   A Motor Tour of the Collapse of Communism   223
11   Epilogue: After the Fall   272
    Acknowledgements   278

I.
PROLOGUE:
ONCE UPON A TIME

O nce upon a time in East Slovakia, my three English travelling companions and I clambered out of hotel beds, nursed hangovers, stuffed belongings into bags and set out for a Sunday morning constitutional down a main street which was named, like main streets all over that part of the world at that particular point in history, after Vladimir Illich Lenin. It was a crisp, bright November morning in the town of Kosice. The skies were blue, the streets were thronging and the churches so packed their congregations spilled on to the pavements. Everything around was old and shabby: cracked paving-stones and subsiding kerbs, missing roof slates and grimy windows, pitted roads and peeling paintwork, slanting street signs and chipped façades. Down a sidestreet we came upon one small, unexpected patch of newness, gleaming out against the general disrepair: a Benetton shop. It seemed the most incredible thing, this tiny outpost of consumer capitalism, there below a red neon sign which strung its message across the rooftops: 'Czechoslovakia And The Soviet Union Together For All Eternity.'

Back at the hotel, we did our best to avoid the attentions of Stanley, who may or may not have been a secret policeman, bundled bags into the back of the car and set off for the nearby Hungarian border. It was a pleasant drive through green fields, with a line of low, brown hills to the

1

east. Somewhere beyond them was the Soviet frontier. After the light Hungarian control, we took a minor road that snaked through small, well-kept villages, booming Depeche Mode out of rolled-down windows and looking for somewhere to have a spot of Sunday lunch.

We pulled up at the Hotel Bodrog in the town of Saros-patak. The restaurant was decorated in slime green and diarrhoea brown with paper flowers and raffia bird-things pinned at intervals along the walls. Trevor, John and I pushed through a party of Russian tourists and found ourselves somewhere to sit. Moments later, Mark came dashing in after us, blue eyes bulging, waving a newspaper he'd picked up in the hotel lobby.

'You're not going to believe this!'

'We're not going to believe what, Mark?' asked Trevor wearily, motioning to the waiter for some menus.

'This!' he waved the newspaper around some more. 'Just listen, for Christ's sake.'

The paper was a day-old edition of the *Daily News*, a broadsheet compiled mainly from wire services and published by the Hungarian state in both English and German. Carefully holding it so that none of us could read over his shoulder and ruin the performance, Mark adopted a slow, portentous tone and began reading aloud:

'Symbol Of Division – Berlin Wall – Torn Down. In moves that cap one of the most, if not the most dramatic shift in post-war Europe, East Germany announced on Friday that its borders with West Germany are now open and the Communist Party declared itself in favour of "free, democratic, universal and secret elections".'

He stopped and looked up. We were silent, shattered, utterly speechless for once. Berlin was home. West Berlin. The Berlin Wall had fallen down. It was almost impossible to grasp the enormity of all that was implied in those six brief words. The Berlin Wall had fallen down. And with it had collapsed not only the boundaries of our daily life in Berlin, but also the whole international order which had shaped the world we grew up in.

'You're right,' I muttered. 'I can't believe it. Three days ago! The eyes of the world must have been on Berlin, the headlines must have been bouncing around the fucking globe, and there we were in what must have been one of the only countries in the world where it wasn't reported.'

'Heading straight,' added Mark, 'for one of the only other ones.'

'Just think, for the rest of our bloody lives people are going to be saying to us: "Hey, you lived in Berlin in 1989, didn't you? You must have been there on the day that –" "Fuck off, grandson!!"'

We didn't know whether to laugh or cry, whether to sing and shout or go outside and break something. On one level, we were simply angry, but it was hard to tell whether that anger was because we'd missed it or because it had happened at all. While most everyone else in the Western sector of the city had more or less ignored what was happening in East Berlin – couldn't really believe there was anything happening at all – we'd been making contacts and playing all sorts of games across the border. We had friends on both sides of the Wall, ways and means of moving things across it. Berlin was our playground and the division of the city was precisely what made it interesting. There on our doorstep had been the possibility of passing into another world. And now, with this one piece of news, it was suddenly all over for good.

It was also too late to go back. Our itinerary, agreed on after much debate a full two months before, dictated we spend that night in the small, wine-producing town of Tokaj. We couldn't have chosen a better place to emphasise our distance from the main action. We were even too early for the good local wine. In a bar like a tunnel we drank some sickly sweet variety, and then dawdled moodily down the one main street as a Russian Army convoy headed in the opposite direction. Eastwards, we noted. Back home, perhaps. Mark gave them a mock salute and muttered: 'Farewell, comrades.'

In the private guest house where we stayed, after much pantomime and ruffling of phrase books, we managed to get the couple who owned the place to let us join them in watching the television news, the better to get a grip on what might be happening back home. The pair of them sat stiffly on a furry ochre-coloured sofa, he in a Mickey Mouse t-shirt, she in a purple track-suit and curlers. On the wall behind them was a horrid painting of her looking about ten years younger, framed in a sylvan scene and wearing a red crimplene dress. Sort of Woolworth's realism. On the television was nothing but an interminable item about Hungarian pig-farming.

The next night we were in the considerably larger and marginally more interesting city of Debrecen, mentally preparing ourselves for the following day's foray into Ceauşescu's Romania. Said preparations involved a large meal, litres of beer and about three hash biscuits each. The hotel restaurant was a giant, once-grand affair with a huge domed ceiling, but only our table and one other were occupied. Despite a tendency to uncontrollable fits of giggling, we had successfully communicated our desire for pancakes served the English way with lemon and sugar, and now the inevitable gypsy violinist from the band in the corner was strolling our way with a snaggle-toothed smile. He hovered round our table for a minute and then, having finally decided what nationality he thought we were, broke into a spirited rendition of 'Somewhere Over The Rainbow'.

'No, no,' Trevor implored. 'Play something sad. Don't you realise we've just had our way of life taken from us?'

2.
THE MUSEUM OF HUBRIS

On one of my first visits to West Berlin, I'd dozed away some hours on the couch of a friend's apartment in the shadow of the Wall and there, perched recumbent on what was at the time the very perimeter of the Free World, dreamed one of those afternoon dreams that linger all the more vividly for being plunged back into the full light of day by a phone call or sudden knock on the door.

In this dream I was in a car, alone or with an anonymous other, aimlessly motoring around one of those nowhere areas of Kreuzberg which had the life carved out of them by a curve of the Wall. There was no other traffic, few shops, little colour, just dull rows of apartment blocks on an overcast afternoon. I wasn't really watching where we were going, my attention wandering haphazardly as the route took us through drab, deserted streets, turning here and turning there. But certain small details – the contour of a lamppost, the particular posture of the little green man at a light-controlled crossing – began adding up until I realised with a shock: we were now in the East.

Somehow, as we turned and turned again, we'd found a way through to the other side, crossed the Wall without noticing and ended in East Berlin. I was frightened. How were we going to get back? I had no idea what labyrinthine route had brought us here. Indeed, inattention seemed to have been the very key to finding the way and I knew somehow that the harder we tried the less likely it was that we would be able to retrace our steps. There was no Ariadne's thread, no trail of crumbs. We were lost, stranded without passports or visas on the wrong side of the city, the wrong side of the world. One could hardly stroll up to one of the heaviest, most carefully patrolled frontiers on the planet, buttonhole some uniformed pig of a guard and stammer hopefully:

'Er, look, you're not going to believe this, but . . . '

Which is where there was a knock at the door or a ring of the phone and I came to, startled and disturbed, in a scruffy Neukölln living room decorated with a constructivist mural and a dog-eared collection of 1950s black and white glamour photos, back in the Western world.

I had that dream in 1981. Over the years, as I carried on a protracted flirtation with Berlin before finally setting up house with the city, it stayed with me more clearly than any actual event of the visit which occasioned it. All sorts of things would nudge it back to mind, especially when I found myself in one of the areas where the action seemed to have taken place. In Kochstrasse, for example, once Berlin's Fleet Street, where the Axel Springer building towered over the Wall and produced several right-wing tabloids right up on the front line. Or over on the other side of Checkpoint Charlie, up Friedrichstrasse in the area around Stadtmitte U-Bahn, as central as its name implies, but for the last few decades stuck out on one end of an East Berlin underground line. And often it would creep back into consciousness crossing any main road in the East, when I stood at the kerb playing the obedient pedestrian waiting for the signal of the little green man, stockier and somehow more purposeful than his opposite number in the West.

So perfectly did the dream seem to sum something up that I often returned to it when discussing my fascination with the city. For me it had the force of a good anecdote, but recounted to others it invariably fell flat. Efforts to explain it met with nothing but polite nods, mild interest, the occasional attempt at amateur analysis. Slowly it sank in that the dream had stayed with me so long not because it conveyed anything of my experience of Berlin, rather because it offered some kind of clue as to the meaning of that experience, the roots of that fascination.

Across the corridor from my friend Mark's old flat in Kreuzberg used to live an old lady. Mark would help her carry her coal up the stairs. She'd been living in this house for most of her long life; she could remember the Kaiser and the First World War from the days when her mother carried the coal and she'd been too small to help. She'd been kept indoors as bullets flew in the streets outside during the 1918 revolution. With the mass inflation of the Weimar years she'd bought the coal with bales of nearly worthless Reichsmarks, and burned it all through the rise of Hitler, as communists from her staunchly red street fought it out with the Nazis on the next block. For the seven years of the Second World War she carried on lugging the coal, whenever it was available, then struggled to find anything at all to burn during the final bombardment of Berlin and the hardship that followed unconditional surrender. In 1948 the coal came in by air, and she got used to the constant noise overhead as British and American planes flew supplies into nearby Tempelhof airport during the blockade and airlift. She continued carrying her coal through the 1953 uprising in the East, the erection of the Wall in 1961, the terrorism of the 1970s, the winter of 1980–81 as the streets outside filled with rioting squatters, right until she died, in 1987, just two years too soon to see the Wall come back down again.

She had lived in a city that had been hit by just about everything the twentieth century could find to hurl at it: war, revolution, mass inflation, militarism, fascism, communism, systematic aerial bombardment, invasion, occupation, starvation, partition. The West Berlin she died in was a city in stasis, a little eddy cut off for several decades from the main current of European history.

Berlin was founded in 1237, its original centre an island in the Spree that is now known as Museum Island. A nice irony, I used to think. At the time of its 750th anniversary in 1987, Berlin had become a museum city, every twist of the Wall revealing another historical oddity. Giant railway terminals now lay derelict and overgrown because there was no longer anywhere for the lines to go. Teeming traffic intersections had become swathes of no man's land, strewn with barbed wire and dotted with watchtowers. Bridges on the border were painted one shade of olive green on the Western side, another on the Eastern, crossing stretches of water where only a line of marker buoys separated pleasure boats from patrol boats. And the biggest curiosity of all was the Wall itself, a political abstraction made implacably concrete, snaking a hundred miles or so around West Berlin and punctuated at intervals by checkpoints at which, for the investment of a short wait, a small fee and usually some uniformed abuse, one could step through to the nearest thing the real world could offer to an honest-to-God parallel universe. These were some of the weirdest tourist attractions on the planet: weird enough to lure many who didn't really know or care what it was they were gawping at, or how it had come about.

The tourists flowed to and from divided Berlin, ceaselessly circulating both halves of the museum city. Their routine fascination with the exhibits of the Cold War – decanting from tour coaches to mount observation platforms at Potsdamerplatz and feeling a little tingle of fear as they came so close to the threatening other, queuing up for the Checkpoint Charlie museum, wandering around Berlin Mitte wondering what they were looking at and how to spend the obligatory twenty-five marks they bought at the border – all this served to underline the biggest weirdness of it all: the utter normalisation of an utterly abnormal situation.

For the stranger to that situation, the most startling things about divided Berlin were precisely those points where municipal normality rubbed up against the stresses of the political situation. Say one wished to travel by public transport between Hallesches Tor in Kreuzberg and Lehrter Stadtbahnhof in the Tiergarten, a journey between two points in West Berlin. The quickest way to do this would have involved taking a U-Bahn train on line 6 in the direction of Tegel, pausing one stop later at Kochstrasse while the Western driver was replaced by an Eastern one and the station announcer declared: 'Letzter Bahnhof in Berlin-West'. You would then rattle along tunnels under East Berlin, through dead stations haunted by armed guards, and change at Friedrichstrasse, an Eastern station that had duty-free shops on the platforms and doubled as a border post. Without going through that border, simply negotiating a few tunnels and staircases patrolled by jack-booted Grenztruppen whose principal occupation seemed to be moving on the tramps who were always duty-free drunk, you would then get on an S-Bahn train and ride back out over a great stretch of no man's land and the Wall, emerging into the West near the Reichstag. There drivers would switch once again and, the final absurdity, you would maybe get busted by a Western plain-clothes customs official for having bought a bottle of Polish vodka or a carton of American cigarettes. In Berlin the grand conflict between East and West, Russia and America, communism and capitalism, had frozen solid around quotidian reality.

While the tourists picked their way around the debris of the Cold War, for most West Berliners the Wall was consigned firmly to the background of conscious life, shut out from any routine consideration. It was easily possible to go for days without travelling anywhere near it. It was equally possible to see it without ever really noticing it. And it was possible, indeed quite common, for West Berliners to live whole lives in their half of the city without ever once going over to the other side.

It would infuriate me whenever I ran into such people. Had they no curiosity? The same argument would inevitably ensue. They would dismiss my interest in the East as being a) purely voyeuristic, it being possible for me, an Englishman, to experience as exotic something that for Germans was merely sad and oppressive, and b) opportunistic, a cynical grabbing of the chance for a few cheap day trips in other people's misery. 'I wouldn't go over there,' one Berliner told me, 'like I wouldn't go to South Africa.' This was a particularly stupid comparison. It was not as if in visiting the East one was implicitly welcomed by a ruling élite that would benefit from your patronage. Quite the reverse. People who went over regularly and established any kind of unofficial contact with citizens of East Berlin were treated by the authorities as, at best, a nuisance and, at worst, a threat. I would counter that a) rather than pretending that East Berlin didn't exist, it was better to behave, as far as possible, as if it was the border that didn't exist and make the most of the possibilities for simple human contact across the Wall, and b) that to do this was nothing but a positive response to an essentially inhuman situation, perhaps, on the individual level, the only possible one.

'The East Germans have the real Wall to stop them travelling and meeting people,' I declared more than once. 'But people like you – you have a Wall in your heads.'

I found an echo of these words among the writings of Carl Gustav Jung. In his 1958 essay 'The Undiscovered Self', he wrote:

> It is quite natural that with the triumph of the Goddess of Reason a general neuroticizing of modern man should set in, a dissociation of personality analogous to the splitting of the world today by the Iron Curtain. This boundary line bristling with barbed wire runs through the psyche of modern man, no matter on which side he lives. And just as the typical neurotic is unconscious of his shadow side, so the normal individual, like the neurotic, sees his shadow in his neighbour or the man beyond the great divide. It has even become a political and social duty to apostrophize the capitalism of one and the communism of the other as the very devil, so as to fascinate the outward eye and prevent it from looking at the individual life within.

Elsewhere I'd read Jung – a native of neutral Switzerland yet part of the Germanic cultural complex – describing his paradoxical relief on learning that the First World War had broken out. Tragic though the news was, it nonetheless provided him with some explanation for the visions of continent-engulfing tides of blood which had been troubling him. It also, crucially – in terms of that particular strand of modern psychology Jung had begun unravelling

10

after his break with Freud – confirmed for him the importance of the connection between his inner life and the life
of his time, between events in the collective unconscious
and events in history. Jung was to spend the rest of his days
investigating the link between those two levels of
experience.

He claimed that 'as early as 1918, [he] noticed peculiar
disturbances in the psyches of [his] German patients that
could not be ascribed to their personal psychology'. These
disturbances were mythological motifs – what Jung called
archetypes – expressing violence, primitivity, cruelty.
Interviewed in the late 1930s, Jung diagnosed Germany –
late to nationhood, late to colonialism, beaten in the First
World War – as suffering from an inferiority complex.
Hitler as the longed-for saviour who would rescue Germany from the humiliation of Versailles, lead it to glory
and *Lebensraum*, was not so much statesman as medicine
man, ruling by revelation, less an individual than the
embodiment of a nation and its darkest desires.

'I take it to be literally true,' said Jung in 1939, 'that
[Hitler] has no personal friend. How can you talk intim-
ately with a nation? You can no more explain Hitler by the
personal approach than you can explain a great work of art
by examining the personality of the artist.' Hitler, walking
the way that providence dictated with the assurance of a
sleepwalker, was, as Jung described him on BBC radio in
1946, 'the most prodigious personification of all human
inferiorities. He was an utterly incapable, unadapted, irre-
sponsible, psychopathic personality, full of empty, infantile
fantasies, but cursed with the intuition of a rat or a gutter-
snipe. He represented the shadow, the inferior part of
everybody's personality.'

What Jung termed the shadow is the dark side in all of us,
his idea of shadow projection the mechanism by which
whatever we don't like or can't accept about ourselves is
perceived elsewhere. Instead of dealing with our own
shortcomings, we find them in others, and thus achieve
some kind of unstable absolution. This can work on the
level of individual relationships – watch any couple battling
it out – just as it can on the level of international relation-

ships – listen to any two nations having a tiff. Whenever people feel themselves threatened by villains, it's a sure sign that they're frightened of the villains in themselves.

An essential part of what Jung called the process of individuation – the progress towards consciousness and psychic wholeness in the individual – is precisely a coming to terms with this villain within. This is of course a more or less Manichean idea, in which good and evil are locked in perpetual conflict as parts of a dualistic whole. Nazism too was a Manichean system, the supposed goodness of the Aryan master race existing in distinction to the evil of the Jewish–Bolshevik conspiracy for world domination (a perfect piece of shadow projection, given that world domination was hardly the farthest thing from Hitler's mind).

From a Jungian point of view, the inability to deal with the shadow has always been Germany's problem. Looking for cultural clues one could turn up several: the triumph of the forces of darkness in the myth of Wotan; the dichotomy and act of classical hubris dramatised in Goethe's Faust; the insanely lucid poetry of poor old Nietzsche, gazing into the abyss as the abyss gazed also into him. The upsurge of Nazism was the phenomenon of a nation possessed by its own cruel and destructive demons, projecting the shadow at its heart on to Jews and Poles, Russians and gypsies and villains all around. This was the sin of hubris on a globally disastrous scale.

All the other explanations for Nazism – as Hitler fooling the entire German people through brute force of charisma; as the last resort of bourgeois monopoly capitalism; as an extreme reaction to the Bolshevist threat; as the non-communist side to the leaden coin of totalitarianism; as an outgrowth of a deeply ingrained German desire for order – stop somewhere short of explaining Auschwitz. And even after Germany was defeated and the death camps closed down and Europe lay everywhere in ruins, still this question of the shadow remained. Within a few years of the end of the war the archetype had burst its banks, carved a new channel for itself and then frozen over to become the Cold War. In the diplomatic run-up to the 1948 Berlin blockade, Eisenhower's political adviser on German Affairs commented that 'the Soviet government (like the Nazi government) charges the other person with those things it itself intends to do'. Germany, divided now into East and West, embodied a local form of what was now a global antagonism. And Berlin, the city that had aspired to become the centre of the world and was torn asunder by the very consequences of that ambition, instead became a museum of hubris.

One of Jung's last pieces of writing was his essay in the book *Man and his Symbols*. On the page opposite a picture of the Berlin Wall, concrete and barbed wire iced over on a winter's day, he returned to the theme of the world dissociated like a neurotic, the Iron Curtain the symbolic line of division.

> Western man, becoming aware of the aggressive will to power in the East, sees himself forced to take extraordinary measures of defence, at the same time as he prides himself on his virtue and good intentions. What he fails to see is that it is his own vices, which he has covered up by good international manners, that are thrown back in his face by the communist world, shamelessly and methodically. What the West has tolerated, but secretly and with a slight sense of shame (the diplomatic lie, systematic deception, veiled threats), comes back into the open and in full measure from the East and ties us up in neurotic knots. It is the face of his own evil shadow that grins at Western man from the other side of the Iron Curtain.

Which is where it began to dawn on me what the dream was all about.

On a simple level, my fascination with Berlin needed little explanation. I was born a decade after the end of World War Two, but in my Newcastle childhood it was still all around me. My parents had both come of age during The War, as it was invariably called, and despite many bad memories it was also associated for both of them with the paradise of innocence preceding the Fall into adulthood and responsibility. In one room upstairs lived a grandfather who had got a blighty in the trenches of the Great War – the other one – and in the attic stood a chest of drawers with a top dented by falling masonry during the Battle of Britain. I knew that a friend of my parents who jumped at sudden noises was held to do so because of experiences in a prisoner-of-war camp.

Sunday afternoon television was always showing patriotic war films full of snarling Nazis and honest, stiff-upper-lipped British. We read comics where Germans shouted 'Himmel!', 'Donner und Blitzen!' and 'Achtung, die Englander!' – 'die' always being understood to rhyme with 'pie'. In a patch of trees near the house where I grew up (known by us children, in another legacy of Empire, as 'The Plantation') we would play Gerries and English, make shooting noises as we pointed sticks at each other and compete to see who could clutch his chest, keel over and die the most convincingly. For Christmas my brother and I would often get model aeroplane kits, though I was utterly useless at assembling them and usually persuaded my dad to do it for me. From those and plenty of Biggles books I learnt all about Hurricanes and Messerschmitts and Lancasters and Wellingtons and Stukas, but mostly about Spitfires, in the servicing of whose radio equipment my father had spent a quiet war on country aerodromes. Sometimes, when a model was past its prime, my brother and I would take it out into the back yard, stuff it with cotton wool, soak it all with white spirit from a shelf in the garage, apply a match and dance with glee around the resulting conflagration.

Later, when I was nine or ten, The War was replaced by the Cold War in our private mythology. Someone took me to see *From Russia With Love* and I had read every Ian Fleming book by the age of eleven. The airwaves were full of spy programmes. A few years ago I found an old army surplus gas mask bag I had used to carry my things around in as a child. On the flap I had scrawled 'Danger Man', 'The Avengers', '007', 'Napoleon Solo' and drawn, as a centre-piece, a fairly meticulous 'Man From U.N.C.L.E.' logo. *Man From U.N.C.L.E.* was on just after my wolf cub pack finished its Thursday meetings, and I can remember the speed with which every boy raced home to catch it. Even the girls in my class used to sing a song about Ilya Kuryakin to the tune of the Rolling Stones' *Satisfaction* ('We can't get no Kuryakin/We don't want no Napoleon Solo'). I bought an U.N.C.L.E. badge, wrote off to the *Radio Times* for an U.N.C.L.E. membership card, saved up my pocket money for an U.N.C.L.E. gun and went off to primary school wearing it proudly in a makeshift shoulder holster. I remember once trying to make out that my father was a spy by telling a friend that he worked for 'Social Security'. I thought the word 'security' would do the trick but my friend wasn't taken in (half the fathers in the area worked at the nearby DHSS Central Office) and got his own back by observing, cruelly, that though I might have a shoulder holster, real spies certainly didn't wear short trousers.

In my street we organised ourselves into rival gangs with suitably acronymic titles and set about producing 'information'. My headquarters was in my parents' attic with the bomb-damaged chest, where I used to sit inventing codes, drawing badges and guns and miniature radios and maps of secret installations. The rival gang's HQ was in a garden shed over the back lane, where they used to sit with codes and badges and maps of their own. In what I now recognise as a classic espionage manoeuvre, my brother and I staged a falling-out. He pretended to go off and join their gang and, when the moment was ripe one light summer evening, hurled all their information out of the window to where I was waiting below with an open hold-all.

It was the perfect heist, glorious victory . . . except the two gangs promptly dissolved into one and there was no game any more. I can remember how, as we all cycled around together that night, unsure how to enjoy ourselves in the sudden cessation of hostilities, I was suffused with something of the same sense of paradoxical disappointment that I was to feel decades later when the real Cold War fell in upon itself.

For the post-hippie, pre-punk teenagers of my glam generation in the early 1970s, Berlin was further parcelled in mystique by the relevant novels of Christopher Isherwood, which had in turn been brought to our attention by Bob Fosse's movie *Cabaret*. I still know nearly every number by heart from the parents-away-for-the-weekend parties where the soundtrack would get played back to back with Lou Reed's 'Berlin' album and whatever was current by Roxy Music or David Bowie. When Bowie and Iggy Pop moved to West Berlin a few years later and started singing about this city of nightclubbing, bright white clubbing, the gaudy wrapping was complete.

Berlin offered in one neat package an evocation of both childhood games and teenage fascinations, all tied up in the related notions of a supposed decadence sanctioned in literature, film and pop music and the possibility of dallying, even dancing, with the devil. Whether that devil wore a bible-black swastika or a blood-red star, it all added up to the same thing. Berlin in some senses represented the Enemy – an enemy that one had almost grown to feel comfortable with. This was a constant subtext to one's experience of a city where the war and its consequences were quite literally all around. With my reading of Jung I realised that buried in all the images of the opponent from two world wars, embedded in the landscape of all those old secret agent thrillers, was something deeper yet. What the dream indicated was that going over to the other side of the Wall was in some sense connected with travelling into another part of one's own nature. For me, as for many others brought up in a culture which had encouraged all that was liberal, spendthrift and hedonistic, the East was fascinating because it challenged that part of me which was correspondingly furtive, austere and authoritarian.

I found, in turn, an echo of those thoughts in the writings of Václav Havel, a citizen of the other side, of what he called 'the post-totalitarian system'. In his essay 'The Power of the Powerless' written a decade or so before events were to hand him the presidency of his country, he said:

> In highly simplified terms it could be said that the post-totalitarian system has been built on foundations laid by the historical encounter between dictatorship and the consumer society. Is it not true that the far-reaching adaptability to living a lie and the effortless spread of

social auto-totality have some connection with the general unwillingness of consumption-oriented people to sacrifice some material certainties for the sake of their own spiritual and moral integrity? With their willingness to surrender higher values when faced with the trivializing temptations of modern civilization? With their vulnerability to the attractions of mass indifference? And in the end, is not the greyness and emptiness of life in the post-totalitarian system only an inflated caricature of modern life in general? And do we not in fact stand (although in the external measures of civilization we are far behind) as a kind of warning to the West, revealing to it its own latent tendencies?

Certainly, the more one explored the situation, the more it became clear that in divided Berlin, as in divided Europe, the two sides were very far from being the implacable foes of populist rhetoric. Rather, East and West were distorting mirror images of each other, the worst of each reflected in its opposite, the Wall not so much a boundary as a looking-glass which could be passed through into a wonderland where one would encounter the most familiar things, utterly transformed by context. In this sense, Berlin offered a city-sized version of one of the oldest symbols of all, that of the paradoxical unity in opposites.

The Wall, as is well known, was covered with graffiti. Along great stretches, particularly near the city centre and around Kreuzberg, words and pictures were sprayed with can, daubed with paintpot and brush. Laid and overlaid in great confusion were expressions of every political hue, of every philosophical persuasion, of every degree of seriousness and inanity. Jostling for space were base sexual suggestions, exultant dreams, mechanical slogans, daft jokes, statements of surreal intent, protests about conditions in both East and West, and lots of names. Names in German and names in Turkish, names in neat block capitals and names in hunched-up hip hop scrawl, names of tourists and soldiers and lovers. There were obscure cartoons, arcane diagrams, expressionistic clouds of spraycan colour, crude representations of genitalia, bold political

17

icons in blacks, reds and greens, and a host of paintings of doors and gates and holes and ladders offering imaginary ways through to the other side of this vast free canvas.

Somewhere on the Wall, probably in Kreuzberg though I know it only from a postcard I bought in a newsagent and pinned above my desk, was a painting of the two halves of Berlin, the West coloured white with a black spot in the top quarter, the East shaded black with a white spot in the lower quarter. Gripping the edges of the Western half, either holding it in place or tearing it away, were hands on the ends of arms whose red, white and blue cuffs indicated their American nationality. Clutching the Eastern half were hands that were obviously Russian. Underneath all this was lettered:

'YIN/YANG? BANG!!!'

3.
ESCAPE TO WEST BERLIN

'You can never run away from your problems. Whether you like it or not, you end up packing them in your suitcase and hauling them with you wherever you go.'

So friends have told me. So have I told myself. But after more than ten years in London, a lot of cutting and running finally came down to the fact that I'd come to find the city virtually uninhabitable. My stay there had coincided with the reign of Mrs Thatcher. There had been privatisation, deregulation, a Big Bang, a crash and several kinds of boom. The credit boom, the retail boom. It was all up for sale – past, present and future. The houses of finance paid the piper, the advertising agencies called the tune. Greed was good. Executive toys – Filofaxes, cellnet phones – were the cult objects of the day. Share issues became a national pastime. Everything had a price but nothing had a value. People began basing their self-esteem not on doing anything good or honest or useful, but simply on how clever they were with their money – which bugged me, of course, because I was useless with mine.

The property boom. That was the worst of the lot. Londoners jabbered on about it the whole time. Where do you live? How much did you pay? Oh yes and of course it's doubled in value since we bought it and so convenient for that nice new Sainsbury's. Whenever two Londoners got together they'd immediately start on about bargain basements and up-and-coming areas. The property boom, the property boom. It was an irresistible force. Some of my best friends clung on to their inexpensive council flats but bought houses, filled them up with cheap furniture, rented them to strangers and became absentee landlords. Increasing numbers of people took to living in cardboard boxes just round the corner from my favourite nightclub. Sometimes I'd walk past them in my designer trousers and feel a wave both of sorrow and of fear. There but for the grace of God.

No, it wasn't just a matter of greed or self-esteem. It was getting hard to survive if you didn't play the game. Housing was the key. If you failed to flag down the property bandwagon at a time you could afford a ticket, the thing would go rumbling off into the distance without you. The longer you waited, the more money you'd have to amass to catch up. It helped if you had been lucky or clever enough to have sorted out and clung on to a piece of the city's shrinking stock of secure, cheap housing – London's tatty licensed squats, exclusive housing associations, hard-to-let council flats with shit on the stairs – sad relics all of a vanishing order. But otherwise you were fucked. Either working four days a week just to meet the mortgage repayments on some tiny conversion or else condemned to run in ever-decreasing circles around rented rooms you could be kicked out of at a moment's notice.

By early 1988 I had reached the end of the line. History, it seemed, was squeezing me out. There was no middle ground left in London, no place to retreat and lick your wounds. I had just moved house for the fourteenth time in thirteen years, a process made increasingly complex by the fact that I worked at home. I had made the mistake of moving in with a lover who decided to terminate the relationship as soon as I'd put up shelves and unpacked my books. Now I would have to move again. For better or worse I'd gambled what little I had on a couple of abortive writing projects and let the Thatcherite gravy train roll on by. The boom was dying to a distant echo and I had nothing left to show for it but a pile of debts. All I could do was carry on writing but there was nowhere I felt settled enough to write, no money to go out and find somewhere, no way to earn money without writing. The whole of my life had been tied up in a single knot. The end of that relationship provided the single, sharp tug which was all that it took to unravel everything.

I sank to a near suicidal state. I never actually tried to kill myself, never even got around to a morbid inventory of methods, but I'd descended to a level of bleak, drizzling misery where the idea of taking my own life – dropping in as it often did when I surveyed an apparently insuperable mountain of problems – had come to be the only thought that lent me any comfort. The gloom had been gathering for months, maybe for years. It had, in effect, crept up on me. It took a couple of friends to kick me up the arse before I could see how far I had withdrawn, how deep I was drifting. Once I did, I started trying to swim for the surface.

And then everything got harder. And harder. I couldn't answer the phone without bursting into tears. I couldn't concentrate to read a book. I couldn't write down anything but the contents of the incessant mad conversation I was now having with myself damn near twenty-four hours a day. My brain would just never shut the fuck up. I'd drink myself to sleep in the early hours and then a couple of hours later wake right back up again, crying before I could even remember just what I was crying about.

All I had to do was pull myself together. Of course. That was all. It was as simple as crossing the road.

Then came a morning when I was forced to realise that maybe even that was now beyond me.

The night before I'd been out with my girlfriend. Sally was her name. By this point she was spending most of her time with a new lover – it was all I could do to stop her bringing him back to our house – but on this evening we were 'trying'. In other words Sally had agreed to go out so I couldn't accuse her of 'not making an effort'. From club to club, I trudged in her wake, clutching pathetically at any scrap of affection. She was irritable and impatient, talking to anyone she met rather than deal with the difficulty I had become. We'd ended up at the Dakota Bar in Heaven. She, her back to me, was being chatted up by someone much younger and prettier and happier than me. I stood further down the bar, staring bleakly about. This was where we'd met, almost exactly a year before, and gone back to her place and talked until way past dawn. Something finally broke when that memory came. I snapped a goodbye and strode off alone, knowing it was over for good.

I got home somehow and spent the rest of the night working on a review of a word processor for a computer magazine. In my jangled state, this light task turned into hours of pure black agony and ended up full of *non sequiturs* and spelling mistakes. The pain had become almost physical: clutching at my ribs, making it hard to breathe. I kept rising from my desk and stamping around the room, willing it to leave me alone long enough to string a few simple sentences together. The next morning I went to deliver the piece. For years I'd been negotiating all the various situations into which professional freelancing can hurl one, handling all the people who needed handling to get the job commissioned, executed, delivered, paid for. That day I found myself on the verge of tears in the middle of a routine conversation with an editor. I gabbled the encounter to a hasty close and virtually ran out of the door, unable to trust myself even to say goodbye without somehow fucking it up.

Half an hour later I was hurrying up Baker Street. At the corner of Marylebone Road I was just too distracted, too wrapped up in my internal monologue, to interpret the lights at the pedestrian crossing. I dithered nervously at the kerb, stepped off it, back on to it and then off it again straight into four lanes of traffic accelerating west on amber. I just managed to stumble back on to the pavement, clutching at a lamppost as the angry horn of a very close brush indeed dopplered away down the road beside me.

Staring shaken at the traffic, I realised I was still flirting with suicide. This is how it happens, I thought. There's no need for the bottle of pills, the razor blade in the bathtub. You just get yourself so wound up inside that you cease to be able to negotiate those basic urban functions the poorest fool can handle simple as breathing and – bang – suddenly you're blood and bone in the middle of another central London traffic incident. Get off the street, I told myself. It would be better to get off the street. I stopped a taxi and sought refuge at a friend's flat for the afternoon.

Later, when I felt brave enough to go home, I took the first small step Eastwards. It was, in its way, one of the hardest things I've ever done in my life. I'd already decided to get out of town for a while. No peace of mind, no part of my London life that wasn't also part of the problem: doing a runner seemed the only option. I'd settled on Berlin, a city I knew well, as destination. Now I simply had to gather enough strength to juggle the finances, tie up the loose ends, make the purchases, arrange the transport. The first task was to ring Liverpool Street station. I made a list of everything I needed to know, scared that otherwise I'd mess it up. Price of an ordinary second class return to Berlin? With a sleeper, if the overland part is at night? Times of departure and arrival? Cost of sending a trunk separately? Arrangements for that?

The street outside was dark and quiet. Around me the silent house seemed to breathe, the atmosphere thick with the fallout of my fissured relationship. No place like home. There was a dead Armagnac bottle lying on its side by the foot of the desk and, over by the door, a blade and a mirror. The desk lamp cast the only light in the room on to week-old coffee cups, ashtrays overflowing with cigarette butts and roaches. My books stood to attention in the shadows on the walls. I scanned the list. It seemed to cover everything. There was no excuse to delay the moment of action any longer. I looked at the phone for a long, long moment, then reached over to pick up the receiver.

In those days the East began at the Hook of Holland. You crossed the North Sea, cleared Dutch controls and walked out on to the station platform to find a string of East German rolling stock, nicely drab and dilapidated next to local trains in gleaming kingfisher colours. This was the North-West Express, a slim tendril of the communist world which, twice every twenty-four hours, would slither all the way out to this western edge of the continent. There was just enough on board to stir something in the soul of the Cold War romantic. In the dingy Mitropa car you could order an East German breakfast of hard bread, pale cheese and bitter coffee from a menu printed on some smudgily antiquated duplicating machine. You'd sprinkle salt on your far-too-soft boiled egg from an orange plastic cruet and watch Holland passing primly by through windows framed with grimy lace.

There is, God knows, little enough about the Netherlands to ignite the imagination of the traveller. Policeman on a bicycle, flowers in the window, good morning Mr Edam, why good morning Mrs Gouda, round goes the windmill, ding dong goes the happy red fire engine. The eery flatness. It's as though God, having created the rest of the world, spent a relaxing Sunday afternoon going over this part of Creation with a giant lawn roller. Next to this great safe garden suburb of a country, even Russian instructions not to flush toilet when train is standing at station came as something of a thrill. Not that West Germany was immediately any more interesting. On the border the train would pause in some small town and you'd be forced to wonder whether you were still in Holland or had already crossed over into Germany. Sometimes no border officials ever appeared. A branch of C&A was the only landmark. You could have been anywhere in Northern capitalist Europe.

It wasn't until mid-afternoon, when the train reached Helmstedt, that the fun and games began. After the tedious haul across the Federal Republic, here the train would pause and take on East German officials. Outside, a watchtower or two rose above what appeared to be a great, brown slagheap. Border guards came into the carriage bearing trays with shoulder straps – much like those of cinema ice-cream salespeople, except in place of popcorn and ices they'd be full of rubber stamps, rule books and blank transit visas, and instead of a shaded bulb to illuminate the wares, they'd have a little UV light to show up any hidden marks some colleague might previously have placed on your documents. In contrast to Dutch and West

German officials, their uniforms looked immediately Eastern: everything synthetic; drab shirts that ended in waistbands instead of tucking into trousers; duck-bill caps which, instead of being pulled down menacingly over the eyes, were pushed to a highly unlikely angle on the back of the head, peak tilting up at about forty-five degrees. The uniforms were in greys and greens, with big black boots and stars on the shoulder boards and shining red and silver cap badges featuring the East German hammer and compass. The officials in them rarely looked comfortable. The guys with the trays, who were the first to control you, were almost invariably young and a little flustered. You noticed their pale, unshaven faces as they examined your passport photo, then stared into your eyes for a long moment, then back at the pass, then back to your eyes again – always twice like that. Once they conceded you were what your papers claimed you were – sometimes this would involve both flipping through their rule book and using the UV on a few pages of your passport – they'd stamp about ten bits of paper, scribble down your details, then hand back your pass along with a transit visa covered, like a banknote, in little curly patterns that would be hard to forge.

Soon came other officials, older and gruffer, who would demand to see your ticket, or simply bark a few questions and look at you suspiciously. On a train like this, with rights of access to West Berlin guaranteed by hard-won treaties, it was all little more than a formality, but the elaborate protocol, the rigorous controls, were meant to leave you in no doubt as to whose jurisdiction you were now passing under. You're here on sufferance, chum, said the manner of these officials. Never forget that this is a serious border, a veritabie rift in the continent. We've graciously allowed you over to our side of it now. Better believe the rules are different.

The point was emphasised by the corridor the train would now be inching through, barbed wire to left and right, tall grey lamps standing every few yards. Presently it stopped at Marienborn on the other side. After squeaky clean West Germany you'd notice how much shabbier everything looked. Outside was a hard currency Intershop.

There were no branches of C&A here, would be none for over a hundred miles, and then only in the fortified outpost of capitalism that was West Berlin. No passengers waited on the platform, only more guards, some of whom would lead Alsatian dogs to sniff along the underside of the carriages. The station was sealed off from the outside world by a grey wall topped with more barbed wire. The guys with the trays would march off to unload their intelligence in spartan offices, the occasional passenger would slip off to the Intershop for coffee or cigarettes, and finally, after what always seemed an unreasonably long wait, the train would crawl off to traverse the Zone.

If you arrived in West Berlin by air it was possible to miss the point completely. Just as New York or London yield none of their glamour until long after touchdown at JFK or Heathrow, so the experience of flying into the sleepy West Berlin airport of Tegel offered no hint of the city's tense situation. Maybe travellers would notice that they couldn't fly in by Lufthansa, only on carriers from the Allied countries; maybe also that along the air corridor over the Zone the plane would be flying at about a third of normal cruising height – a hangover from the days when the rules were negotiated and unpressurised airliners couldn't venture much higher. The astute observer, looking down over the East German landscape on a rare clear day, might even notice the effect collectivisation of agriculture had on patterns of land use.

But the Inter-German Border, as the Allies used to call it, looked like nothing from the air. I never once managed to spot it flying in from the West. Coming down low into Tegel, it was possible to catch a glimpse of the Wall, if you knew where to look. And then it was gone as you descended over lakes, forest, neat red-roofed housing laid out around inner courtyards, tree-lined avenues ploughed by cream double-deckers. Finally you emerged from your antiseptic aircraft into a bright, efficient airport where the uniformed officials gave you a minimum of fuss. It could have been any normal city.

Not so coming in by road or rail. On the journey along the transit routes you were accompanied by a perceptible

26

heightening of tension. Berliners were used to it, but West Germans would often get a little edgy. I once hitched a ride out of Berlin with a woman on her way back to Cologne. For the whole 188 kilometres between one border post and the other, this woman was a bag of nerves: speeding up and slowing down, swerving between dawdling Trabants, careering from one lane to the other, torn between anxiety about lingering too long in this dreadful place and fear of being stopped for speeding by disagreeable Volkspolizei. The minute we emerged into the West at Helmstedt she was calm again – right after pointing out how, on a little fringe of the DDR just beyond their border controls, three armed soldiers guarded two dungareed workmen who were cutting the grass, just yards away from the freedom to choose between C&A and Benetton.

I was no stranger to the train. On my first trip this way, eight years before, I'd hung out of the window all the way across the Zone, fascinated by any glimpse of smoking factories, seedy farmhouses, funny little cars at level crossings. We'd stopped briefly in Magdeburg, the only town of any consequence between the border and Berlin. It was rush-hour. Over the heads of the guards blocking off our train from the others in the station, I watched local commuters and noted the Eastern cut of imitation leather jackets, the stiffly shaped briefcases, the peculiar design of their double-decker trains: my first glimpse of communist life.

But on that grey morning just before Easter 1988 I was content to let the sights pass by and tried to read something a friend had recommended, a Jungian analysis of *Tristan and Isolde*. This was heavy going, not only intellectually but also in the remorseless way it seemed to detail so much I was going through. From time to time I would squeeze out a long, slow sigh and peer at the window, seeing nothing but the distance I was putting between myself and all that had wounded and defeated me in London. When, finally – after another round with the East German officials, another slow slide through a walled-in corridor – the train parted the Curtain at Griebnitzsee and emerged into West

Berlin, arrival brought with it a relief wholly unrelated to having passed through the East. I was escaping from London. This was all that counted.

Mark was there to meet me at the Zoo station. A diminutive Mancunian, then just into his thirties yet still looking like he'd barely started shaving, Mark had big baby blue eyes and an austere short back and sides that suggested the 1930s or 1940s. Together with a penchant for dressing in a collage of the assorted militaria he devoted great energy to collecting, this could add up to what Mark himself admitted was a slightly 'dodgy' impression. Sometimes he'd appear completely costumed as a Russian soldier or East German border guard. Riding his mountain bike he might sport jodhpurs and jackboots. Yet he never looked even remotely macho. A mutual friend once described him affectionately as a 'sort of Third Reich version of George Formby' and Mark would laugh at this while reserving a fierce temper for any who dared seriously suggest that he might be a Nazi. Usually his outfits were a real mixture of Allied and Axis, East and West, past and present. That day at the station, smiling to see me, removing a leather glove to shake my hand, he wore a grey Luftwaffe flying jacket and a US Army camouflage cap. Often he didn't look military at all, just sort of vaguely old-fashioned in a smart yet still faintly 'dodgy' kind of way. Mark could coyly justify his taste on practical grounds – the clothes he wore were cheap, hardwearing, immune to the built-in obsolescence of more fickle fashions – but it was essentially a game he was playing. Mark's was a natural but carefully nurtured eccentricity, a meticulously crafted and highly individual 'look'. It made him one of the best-dressed people in town.

By then he'd been living in Berlin for ten years or so. I'd known him for about six of those. He used to play a guitar, painted camouflage colours, in a band with an even older friend of mine. These days he pieced together a living out of odd jobs – some graphic work, occasional research for visiting British media, a regular gig as a club doorman, film extra work. (His look was perfect for the kind of movies people came to Berlin to shoot.) One time he researched for the writer Steven Poliakoff who was setting a story in

East Berlin. Mark worked hard and eventually the finished screenplay (destined never to go into production) arrived so he could check it for factual inaccuracies. Pencil in hand, he flipped the pages with growing consternation. It wasn't just that the story was crap. In it there appeared one character, a funny little Mancunian who wore a lot of militaria . . . and was gay.

If people didn't think Mark was a Nazi, they'd often mistake him for a friend of Dorothy's. This he didn't mind, but it showed up a narrow-mindedness equal to the assumption that if he dressed the way he did he must spend his spare time making lampshades out of human skin – or that if he didn't, then he shouldn't dress that way. Just by being himself, Mark had a way of bringing out the hypocrisy in people's cultural prejudices. Once, passing through the West section of Friedrichstrasse station and looking only slightly more dodgy than usual, he was stopped by two East German Grenztruppen with their jackboots and jodhpurs and guns and epaulettes. In that hollow tone of moral superiority adopted by officials of the DDR, they demanded to know why he was wearing a 'fascistic-militaristic' outfit. Mark would quake with fear when confronted by any kind of uniformed authority figure but then would laugh about it afterwards. He liked to be scared.

I went to Copenhagen with him one weekend on a train that took us transit through the DDR to Warnemünde on the Baltic. Twenty minutes into our journey, the first East German border guard came into our carriage at Friedrichstrasse, took one look at Mark's brand new US Army rucksack, closed all the curtains to hide the scene from the East German citizens on the opposite platform, and set about searching us. Mark went rigid. Under his Luftwaffe jacket and US Army pullover you could just see peeping out the insipid green collar of an East German army shirt. Had the guard noticed this and investigated further, any pretence of innocence as to the possession of this highly illegal item would instantly have been negated by the discovery that Mark was also wearing East German army epaulettes, an East German army tie and an East German army officer's belt. Caught with that lot they could send you away for impersonating a soldier, spying, smuggling, God knew what else. Luckily the guard was too preoccupied with the rucksack. He pulled out some olive green sachets of peanut butter – part of some US Army field rations a tame GI friend had given us – and kneaded them suspiciously as if he thought they might contain plastic explosive.

'Where did you get this?'

'Camping shop, camping shop,' Mark assured him.

Then, raising an eyebrow, the guard held up a pair of khaki gaiters which, it being June, Mark had brought along to go with a pair of baggy Rommel shorts.

'They're, like, to keep the sand from getting in the top of your boots,' Mark explained helpfully, as if it were common knowledge that Denmark was as sandy as the Sahara.

'Thank God he didn't see the shirt,' he breathed when we were alone again.

I observed that it had been the sheerest lunacy to wear it in the first place. What was more, we were certain to be controlled by the East Germans at least three more times before we were safely back home.

'Thing was,' Mark started to laugh, 'I didn't have any other clean shirts.'

The day I arrived in Berlin we took a taxi back to Mark's place: a stinking hole in Kreuzberg 61. He'd lived there for eight years and it was a cause of general astonishment that he'd stuck it so long. It consisted of one small room facing on to a sunless back yard, a kitchen that was nothing more than a cubby-hole and a shared toilet on a dingy staircase outside. Every conceivable corner of these already cramped lodgings was filled up with junk. Shelves were stacked with disco singles and classical LPs, videos of war movies, British sitcoms, episodes of *Stingray* and *Thunderbirds*. Old issues of *Private Eye*, *Viz*, *Smash Hits*, *Bravo* and aircraft-spotter magazines stood in teetering piles on the floor. Bits and pieces of a hundred army uniforms – Russian hats and Czech jackets and East German trousers and American shirts – were piled into and all around one large, ugly wardrobe. The only other furnishings there was space for were a couple of old armchairs, a coffee table (occupied by a half-finished model dalek) and a sofa that unfolded into an almost supernaturally uncomfortable bed. On the floor by the front door were scores of returnable bottles that went on accumulating until some visiting Czech, desperate for hard currency, spent a day lugging them all to the supermarket. To get to the 'kitchen' you'd have to edge around a mountain bike that Mark loved too much to leave outside. Every window ledge, every surface, was covered with ornaments, badges, pamphlets, watches, toy soldiers, packs of cards, pots of paint, tools, old picture frames, secondhand photo albums – the whole mess gathering a thick, furry layer of dust and grime. But none of this caught your eye first. That honour fell to the scores of plastic model aeroplanes, lovingly assembled and suspended from the ceiling in one great, chaotic Second World War dogfight.

For three days I sat around in this mess. Added to the indigenous confusion, my suitcase, trunk and computer barely left room for us both to stand up at the same time. I supposedly had a flat of my own but the key was in the possession of some minor pop star who was currently touring West Germany. Occasionally I heard news of its whereabouts. It was appearing in Frankfurt. It was being interviewed in Bochum. It was recording a cable TV show in Munich. Arrangements were complicated by having to go long-distance through Sally. Every conversation was strained and bitter and she talked to me as though I were a child. I couldn't wait for the moment when I would no longer have to speak to her and tried to distract myself by listening to Kraftwerk and Beethoven, watching old episodes of *Monty Python* and *Blackadder*. It felt like I still hadn't arrived yet, as if I never would, as if I was condemned to hang forever in the air like one of Mark's model aeroplanes. These I would lean back and gaze up at from time to time – that was a Hurricane, that a Wellington, over there an ME-109 – amazed I could still recognise so many.

On the fourth day my luck began to turn. I'd tracked down another old Berlin friend who'd been out of town since my arrival and set off to walk round and see her. In the dark of a chilly mid-evening, I marched down Geneisenaustrasse and swerved through the crowd of punks on the corner, ignoring their efforts to tap me for small change. Along the Mehringdamm, light gleamed out of closed secondhand stores, dingy bars, too-bright kebab shops, the businesses tapering off as the avenue rose to the Platz der Luftbrücke. There I paused. Over the road stood the main entrance to Tempelhof airport, one of the largest buildings in the world. Latterly this had been a US Air Force base, but the sign in cold blue light over the doors still proclaimed its old role: that of Berlin's civil Zentralflughafen. From somewhere on the vast roof behind, a searchlight swept in regular passes across the sky, a finger of light that seemed to motion paternally over the entire neighbourhood.

My friend Elisabeth lived on that triangle of land, defined by three railway tracks, known as the Schöneberger Insel. I found her in the kitchen, cooking spaghetti for a new boyfriend called Peter. I was still in a state where any innocent enquiry after my health was liable to unleash a torrent of words instead of the usual ritual responses. Elisabeth was in any case curious. Soon they had heard everything. I knew she'd had her share of heartbreak and pain – the last time I'd been in town, her relationship with the singer Nick Cave had just broken up. This had scarred her deeply. Probably Peter had scars of his own. By the time I'd finished my story, maybe twenty minutes after walking through the door, he was already speaking up.

'I'm moving to West Germany on Friday. You can have my flat if you like. Do you want to go over and see it now?'

Much later, unexpectedly equipped with somewhere to live, I set off to walk back to Mark's and came to a crossing where the man was red. In Germany it was illegal to cross on red. Whereas in Britain you are taught to watch out for traffic, in Germany you are taught to obey the signal. Even on a totally empty street you are expected to wait for the man to turn green. Disobey and you can get fined on the spot. Normally, unless there was a cop about, I would flout this rule at every opportunity. This was surprisingly difficult. The impulse to submit to regimentation is so strong that unless you were concentrating you'd end up pausing automatically with all the other pedestrians. Resistance to this impulse is in turn what makes any Englishman, schooled extensively in the Green Cross Code and determined to prove his natural disrespect for petty authority, determined to walk straight on. But all that week, mindful of my near accident in Baker Street, I had been giving in to the pressure to pause.

An old man with a dog stood waiting at the opposite kerb. There was absolutely no traffic in any direction. I paused for a second and then shrugged and smiled to myself and, with a new feeling of confidence, set off against the lights.

'*Halt, halt!*' the guy with the dog started shouting. '*Das Licht ist rot! Das Licht ist rot!*'

'*Englander,*' I told him when I reached the other side. There was still no traffic. You couldn't even hear a car.

The old man glared at me angrily, maybe somewhat resentfully, the way people can be when someone gets away with something they can't bring themselves to do.

One morning the doorbell rang. I edged around the bike, stepped over the empty bottles and opened the door to see a dangerous-looking character with a long, curving scar dimpling his right cheek, beady brown eyes that glinted with mischief. The cast of his jowly features seemed insolent at first, fading to merely cheeky as he leered and spoke a greeting.

'Hallo. I'm Trevor. You must be Dave. Heard you were coming. Is that bastard Mark about?'

I had also heard about him. Trevor was a native of the Essex blockhead belt. Paunchy and with a knack for wearing clothes that could make the most immaculately tailored item look like some moth-eaten rag from a secondhand shop, he was that most dangerous of creatures: a hooligan with a brain. The tale of how he received his scar was instructive. Trevor had been in Weymouth with his mates, was drunk and leaning up against a bar. The man on the next stool was bothering him. Trevor told him to fuck off and that he'd better watch it because he, Trevor, was a black belt karate expert. The man kept on bothering him. Trevor, who knew as much about karate as he did about

Egyptian hieroglyphics, then tried to poke the man's eyes out. The man stood up. He was big and had tattoos. He grabbed Trevor's lapels with one hand and threw him crashing against the wall, selected a bottle with the other, smashed it against the bar and, still holding Trevor pinned like a butterfly, brought the jagged edge sweeping up and across his face. Then he let go and Trevor collapsed to a bloody heap on the floor.

If someone asked about the scar he'd shrug and tell this story utterly deadpan. Like, I do stupid things but hey what the fuck, I can live with the consequences. This invariably had any audience, like Trevor that Weymouth night, in stitches. He could be charming when he felt like it – there were times when this was all that saved him – but stirring up trouble was his speciality. He'd grab a mundane situation by the scruff of the neck and send it careering off in some unexpected hazardous direction. When on the rampage, his sense of humour was reckless by any standards, and took that very English form of pushing a joke and pushing a joke until his adversary of the moment ceased to find it amusing. Only at that point would Trevor really get into it. That he could neither hold his drink nor fight worth a damn simply added an entertaining touch of danger to the proceedings. He was well known in Berlin: partly because his behaviour was so obnoxious, partly because he and his wife Anne edited a scurrilous fanzine called *Ich und Mein Staubsauger* (Me and My Vacuum Cleaner) that sold a couple of thousand copies every month by hurling invective at anyone in town they felt like insulting.

That morning, Trevor had a bewildered-looking Czech called Marek in tow. This was Marek's first trip over the Curtain and Trevor, having just returned from his first visit to Prague, was amusing himself by trying to give his guest the most lurid impression of decadent Berlin. Trevor had taken him to the food hall at Ka De We, Berlin's version of Harrods, where was to be found a display of capitalist excess that even I found overpowering. That night they dined on shark steak, Trevor feigning that this was a normal Western meal. Marek, a scruffy geologist, didn't know what to make of anything. He sniffed around Mark's room, clearly unable to believe that this appalling squalor was really how anyone would live in the affluent West, and enquired if Mark's collection contained any porn videos. The next day Trevor would sate his interest in pornography for good by taking him to some really hardcore show. Marek, I think to his surprise, found himself seriously shocked.

Trevor wanted Marek out of his hair for a while and dumped him on us for the afternoon. He was bursting with questions. Settling on the sofa, he turned to me. So I had just arrived from England? And what did I think of Margaret Thatcher? I took a deep breath and started to answer.

He added: 'Of course, we all support her.'

Belziger Strasse was a quiet Schöneberg street. At one end it emerged on to John F. Kennedy Platz, where the US President of the same name had once famously declared: 'Ich bin ein Berliner'. At the other end it came out on Hauptstrasse, opposite the house where David Bowie and Iggy Pop had lived in the late 1970s. In between the two was my new flat. A long way down the status ladder, on the first floor of a staircase off the second backyard, it was still a good few rungs up from Mark's place, with a bath and a couple of radiators. There was a cramped but functional kitchen and a long room that was dark at one end even when a rare shaft of sunlight overcame all obstacles and shone through the single window at the other. Furnishings comprised a table, a chair, a bed, some inadequate shelving, a big old tiled oven, bare floorboards painted grey and lots of empty space.

On Good Friday evening, Trevor and Mark helped me carry my things over there. Over Easter weekend the house was still. I sorted my things out, sat and listened to sad music, looked out at the bare tree in the yard. All was quiet on the Western front. I had escaped.

4.
WALLFLOWER AT THE BAD PARTY

People who'd never been there expected West Berlin to be claustrophobic. Certainly there were many West Germans who didn't feel comfortable cut off from family and friends by the hostile expanse of the East. But unless they were in Berlin to dodge the draft, they usually didn't stick around. Certainly, too, it could be oppressive for native Berliners who'd grown up when the city was whole. They'd remember what was down that street they could no longer walk along, were acquainted with the lie of the land behind the Curtain.

And for those of us who knew neighbourhoods near the Wall only from the Western side, there could be something disturbing in the way it affected your sense of spatial mapping. In the years before I moved to Berlin, over repeated visits to a friend's place on the Kreuzberg/ Neukölln border, in a block that backed on to the Wall, I came to know his locality well. But as you neared the concrete barrier – running along the side of some roads, sharply blocking off others – a big blank space loomed in that spot, somewhere in the back of your mind, where you log the layout of familiar streets. I often sat in my friend's apartment, closed my eyes and felt the proximity of this *terra incognita* – just over in, yes, that direction – and wondered just exactly what was there. I peered from local observation platforms, watching the guards in the towers watching me, but couldn't see much more than the tops of houses beyond the tank traps, dog runs and floodlit reaches of raked gravel. Often I pored over street plans and considered going over just to check out the area immediately behind the house – a round trip that would have taken a couple of hours to travel a couple of hundred yards.

According to the only street maps you could purchase on the other side, beyond their city boundaries lay nothing but featureless white space. This void was labelled 'Berlin (West)'. To anyone in the Eastern half of the city, the message was clear enough: Don't even think about it.

But claustrophobic? Maybe if there'd been a Berlin Ceiling as well as a Berlin Wall. Since the tides of history had swept around it in the late 1940s, especially since the East Germans had erected such an effective flood barrier on 13 August 1961, West Berlin had essentially been an island, and was no more claustrophobic than any other island. It wasn't that you couldn't get off it, just that the mainland was a fair old haul away. Though the city was now isolated from its immediate hinterland, it was still possible to procure a visa and voyage in the grey surrounding seas. Perhaps it would have been a nicer island if you could have gazed out from open shores on to Euclidean horizons instead of being caught up short by the grim geometry of watchtowers, barbed wire and barricades, but away from the edge West Berlin felt like a surprisingly roomy city. People lived in big apartments with high ceilings. The streets were wide, straight and thinly trafficked for a metropolis of over two million people – a pleasing side-effect of there being no far-flung suburbs to motor in from, nowhere for any through traffic to go. Berlin has many trees, much water. Within the confines of the West you could still hike for miles through forests of pine – although chances were you'd come on some GIs playing war games. You could also take a two-hour boat trip through a system of open lakes, and in certain places, where the border lay just on the other side of the channel and a stretch of water was all that separated you from the East, West Berlin could even for a moment feel like an island of the more conventional kind.

As is conventional, islands have their castaways. This one was full of them. West Berlin teemed with people on the run from unhappy lives elsewhere. On the face of it, this was an odd city to escape to: encircled not only by the Wall but also by around half a million Russian and East German troops who could easily have overrun the place any time they felt like it – so long as they didn't mind starting World War Three. Not everyone could take the idea of living in a geopolitical flashpoint and the inward flow of exiles had long been balanced by an outward flow of escapees. But curious corners exert their own fascination and if the city's unique situation repelled some, it also attracted many others. The Federal government poured in funds to bolster the city's attractions. Wages were higher than in West Germany, housing cheaper, cultural activities subsidised. There were plenty of opportunities to study, casual work wasn't too difficult to find. The Wall might cage you in, but the enclosure it defined was more playpen than prison.

On to the island streamed the exiles. They came as draft dodgers to escape a spell in the West German Bundeswehr – because of the city's occupied status, West Berliners were exempt from national service. They came as refugees from the political systems in East Germany, Poland or Romania – because of West Berlin's role as symbolic Free City, there were no visa restrictions for visitors from Eastern Europe. They came as *Gastarbeiter* to escape the severity and poverty of life in Yugoslavia or Turkey – after Istanbul and Ankara, West Berlin was the world's third largest Turkish city. They came as students to escape the stuffiness of small-town family life in Hessen or Swabia – West Berlin embodied the myth of bright lights and big city, supposed capital of decadence and nightlife.

And yes, they came looking for somewhere to piece it all back together again. I was certainly not alone in this. Sometimes it seemed that everyone I met described a journey that began at some emotional upheaval.

The peace of Easter weekend soon proved but an interlude. As the city stepped back into its normal daily rhythm, as the inhabitants of my staircase drifted back across the transit routes from family get-togethers in West Germany, so the background noises of my new situation began to take up their refrain. First, striking a discord to underpin the whole daytime soundtrack, came the screeching of an electric saw from a workshop across the yard. This began at seven in the morning. It was soon joined by the beating of hammer on metal, the harsh crackle of welding gear right below my window. I peeked out into the yard and saw an enormous man working on the wreck of an old Mercedes. Bearded and begoggled, he looked like a barbarian from Nordic myth and turned out to be my downstairs neighbour, a secondhand-computer salesman.

I'd no sooner registered his noise when a muffled Scorpions record began wailing through the wall from a flat on the adjoining staircase. This had the sole merit of almost drowning out the screeching saw. I checked the window again and caught a glimpse of a heavy metal kid with long hair, faded denims and a bum-fluff moustache. A little later, from a window way above, a tune by Leather Nun began laying down an ugly counterpoint. This, as I soon found out, was Olga, bass player with a band called The Lolitas. Finally, picking up in the foreground of this caco-phony, a new rhythm began to beat out through the ceiling, rattling my windows with every stroke: the distinctive thud-ding of metal-tipped cowboy boots on bare floorboards as my upstairs neighbour trod from bed to kitchen, kitchen to bed. She turned out to be a journalism student called Ellen who spent her time painting, studying the occult and hanging around with boys from rock groups. Ellen was destined never to finish her degree. Very few of the stu-dents I met in West Berlin ever finished their degrees.

At night the screeching saw fell silent but the music usually got even louder. From time to time someone would snap and start screaming from their window. The offend-ing party would then start shouting back. This would carry on late into the night. Apart from Olga and Ellen, my staircase also housed a small-time booking agent who dealt with rock acts like Nikki Sudden and Crime And The City Solution; a couple of aspiring artists who dressed in black, painted everything in their apartment grey and worked on huge monochrome canvases; and an assortment of rebellious students who worked in local bars like the Rössli or Turbine. Every last one of them had a collection of loud and angry records. Very few of them retired before four.

The only one who kept normal hours was the computer salesman. It was obviously a struggle. Around nine o'clock one Saturday morning, the fellow finally cracked. He opened his windows wide, cranked his system up to a volume if not actually sufficient to wake the dead, then certainly loud enough to rouse all those near corpses for whom the morning after would more properly arrive sometime in late afternoon and then, an act which on grounds of taste alone surely upset all the others in the house, began playing Chris de Burgh records. Windows started slamming open, voices were raised in protest. The heavy metal kid kept the coolest head. He leaned way out from his kitchen window and, demonstrating a steady aim which evoked the admiration of all, emptied a large pot of water and old spaghetti through the top of the computer salesman's window.

The silence was sudden and absolute. A few startled pigeons took flight. Seconds later, dripping wet and flushed with rage, the computer salesman appeared in the yard, still in his dressing gown, some strands of spaghetti lodged in his beard. He looked left and right, unsure from just which window the torrent had sprung, then ran upstairs and started hammering on doors. No one was fool enough to open up. Eventually, still with no idea whom he ought to be strangling, the salesman retreated to his coffee and boiled egg. Quiet reigned again – for the next couple of hours.

Soon I was fighting back with my own desert island selection of Jimmy Jam and Terry Lewis, early acid house, old Beatles records, Shostakovich. Mark turned up one day with a gift of some leads that connected my small but deadly ghetto blaster to some formidable speakers Peter had left in the flat. After that I was a match for any of them.

Armed with a set of familiar barpersons and doorpeople in the shape of my new neighbours, I set about exploring the local nightlife. The district of Schöneberg is located, both geographically and psychologically, halfway between the smart West end of Charlottenburg and the punky ghetto of Kreuzberg. This suited me fine. At night the streets played their cards close to their chest. Trees lined avenues that here and there opened on to squares with fountains. Blank terraces of rebuilt Berlin apartments were irregularly punctuated by buildings that had retained their ornate pre-war façades. If you didn't know otherwise, it would be hard to guess that discreetly dotted about these apparently peaceful streets, often behind unmarked doors and rarely lit up to look like anything special outside, were some of the most fashionable dives in the city.

They were mostly small places. The earliest anywhere seemed to close was around four in the morning, some simply stayed open until the last reveller had staggered on home. At weekends this could be any time up until noon the next day. Top of the scale in Schöneberg was the Pinguin Club, a German idea of an American cocktail bar run by an avuncular old anarchist named Volker and decked out with film stills, 1950s advertising, mirror balls and old US car number plates. The crowd here was mixed and, by Berlin standards, almost elegant. Not only the best bar but the one nearest to my flat, this soon became my local. At the other extreme was Ex 'n' Pop: peeling wallpaper, bar staff who smashed the empties with a petulant air and dank back rooms which were used sometimes for sex, more often for the ingestion of speed or smack. The clientele here was self-consciously 'underground' and among them was usually to be found the odd member of Einstürzende Neubauten, and other examples of what passed for pop stars in West Berlin.

In between those two extremes were places like the Rössli Bar, owned by a couple of Swiss guys, where people in denim and black leather drank bourbon to old Johnny Cash records below a wall-sized papier mâché mock-up of the Alps. There was another, known only by its address in Zossener Strasse, where little rivulets of water ran along grooves cut into the stone bar, light was cast from giant glowing eyeballs and people drank while perching in tree-

41

things constructed from scaffolding and netting. The latest-running was Krik, which didn't seem to open till around 3 a.m. or so and didn't really get going until much later than that. Here you would find washed up all the detritus of the night. That ravaged-looking blonde at the bar was earlier sipping a marguerita on the next stool at Cabeza Blanca. The guys in the corner were the same ones who'd been sarcastically demanding more Paul McCartney records in Domina. Those two drag queens on the dance floor – the tall thin white one and the small fat bald black one with the moustache – they'd sashayed past you arm in arm as you lurched out of the Havana Club.

And when you finally tired, you could walk home through a city just stretching and waking, the lights outside newsagents and bakeries gleaming against grey morning, buy some rolls for breakfast on the way and drift off into the land of nod while the rest of the world brushed its teeth and hurried off to work.

The British abroad inevitably run amok when released from the fetters of pub opening hours. I was no exception. In my first restless weeks in West Berlin, I worked my way around all the bars. But what would have been a welcome release on a short holiday quickly began to curdle into stupefying routine. Nothing much was really going on in these places. The music was always too loud to talk over. No one even seemed to laugh much. Late one Saturday night in a place called Turbine, I paused on the way in and scanned the eyes of the crowd. It struck me right then that what I had hitherto taken for an overly studied Berlin cool was actually nothing more than a veneer on simple boredom. And gazing longer into those dull, dead eyes, I began to discern my own reflection.

One evening I ended up in the Dschungel. Located behind an unmarked door in Nurnberger Strasse, this club had been on the go since the days when Bowie lived in the city. People would point out the balcony table where he used to sit, watching the crowd below through mirrors mounted at angles on the mezzanine. The decor hadn't changed at all since then – there were pillars with mirror tiles, a couple of weedy fountains. I'd been visiting Dschun-

gel on and off for the best part of a decade but for some
reason never quite felt comfortable in there. That night I
wandered around and ended up among the crowd at the
edge of the dance floor, just watching the dancing, listening
to what the DJ was playing – when someone knocked my
hat off my head.

Nothing is more annoying than when someone messes
with your hat. The trick is to keep your equilibrium. This
hat was a dark blue flat-brimmed affair that made me look
like a priest and in Berlin often attracted this kind of
unwelcome attention. Whoever it was this time just flicked
the brim up at the back so it fell down over my eyes. I
tensed a little but simply restored the thing. The guy
flicked it off again. I still didn't look around, just replaced it
once more at the appropriate angle. Then the guy knocked
it off for the third time and I completely lost my temper.
Big mistake. I wheeled round and snarled at him, some
ugly guy with hard eyes and a moustache who looked like
an off-duty policeman. I think I also grabbed the lapel of
his brown leather jacket. Next I knew, I was being hauled
across the room and crunched against a shelf where
dancers could leave their drinks. It left me with a cracked
rib that made laughing, coughing or breathing deeply
painful for a month or more. The honeymoon with Berlin
nightlife was definitely over.

By day I was exploring a different city. This one was made
up of broad, straight avenues peopled by solid citizens who
went off to work for the *Wirtschaftswunder* at seven or eight
in the morning, knocked off at three or four in the afternoon and somehow got all their consuming done before six
on weekdays or lunchtime on Saturdays. While the night
took whatever shape it pleased, the opening hours for
daytime business were strictly circumscribed.

Mark lent me a bicycle. West Berlin was perfect for
cycling: flat and cross-hatched with bicycle lanes, parks to
cut through, canal paths to follow, plenty of strange
corners to discover. On Sunday afternoons, one section of
the Tiergarten turned into a giant Turkish barbecue. Fami-
lies set up their picnic chairs, gathered around charcoal

grills and sometimes roasted whole goats on spits. Turkish music ululated from a hundred cheap ghetto blasters while a pall of smoke and smell of burning meat wafted across the park. Turning into Truman Plaza, shopping area for the US forces, was like suddenly stumbling out of Germany straight into Hicktown, Ohio. People stocked up on Oreos and El Paso Taco Sauce at the PX, slapped down quarters for a Double Whopper or Baskin Robbins Rocky Road to go, picked up *People* magazine at the Stars & Stripes bookstore. At the Outpost cinema everyone stood for the 'Star Spangled Banner' (accompanied by a morale-boosting montage of American military might) before settling down to munch salted popcorn through the latest Schwarzenegger picture.

One evening Mark and I accompanied Trevor and his cricket team to a match at the Gatow RAF base. Inside, for pounds and pence, but only to anyone with military ID, the NAAFI shop sold Marmite and chocolate digestive biscuits, PG Tips teabags and tins of Heinz baked beans. Between the innings, the RAF team served sandwiches of processed cheese on sliced white Sunblest with tepid orange squash to wash them down. Listening to the thwack of bat on ball as the RAF hit Trevor's bowling all over the ground, it seemed that here was some corner of a foreign field that would be, forever, England.

Over in the East Berlin suburb of Karlshorst, location of the Soviet military command, could be found the Russian equivalent. Down Fritz-Schmenkel Strasse, uniformed officers hurried on by. Soldiers' wives toted string bags of bread wrapped in old newsprint, bottles of sterilised carrots and peas. Cyrillic signs marked drab and windowless shops, grass grew through cracks in the kerb. Down at the end stood the former school where unconditional surrender had been signed in 1945. Now it was a museum testifying somewhat dourly to the heroic struggle of the Soviet army against fascist military aggression.

Mark and I pedalled all over West Berlin that summer of 1988. On sunny days Mark usually wore his Rommel shorts, gaiters, and a little pair of Latin dictator sunglasses. Bent over the handlebars, skinny white legs pedalling away, he looked years younger than he really was. Though firmly on the threshold of his fourth decade, Mark still clung tight to his boyhood. It was infectious, this boyish-ness. We started playing a bicycle game. Mark or I would ease up behind the other and try, with a sudden burst of energy, to gather enough speed to freewheel by, legs motionless and head tipped back in mock disdain for the other's puny efforts and inferior machine. If in front, the trick was to listen for the other's approach, carefully judge the moment and speed up just enough to leave him falter-ing behind, all effort expended in vain. Leapfrogging thus across the city on lengthening summer days, we juddered down cobbled back-streets, swept across open squares, got chased by dogs as we sped through the woods by a lake. The sun and the sights and the exercise began to work a healing effect. I was rediscovering my capacity for play.

One afternoon I left my apartment to go to the super-market on Hauptstrasse. Normally it was a pleasant enough stroll up leafy Akazienstrasse, but that day I turned the corner into a street choked with police. Their vans were parked along both sides. Uniformed officers were flagging down cars, blocking both pavements, stopping and search-ing every single pedestrian. Unnerved, it took me a second to remember this was the first day of the World Bank conference in Berlin. I watched solid citizens being asked to turn out their shopping bags, mentally ran through the contents of my pockets and realised that although there was nothing in them that there shouldn't be, there also wasn't something there that should be. It was a minor irritation of living in Berlin that you were obliged by law to carry a piece of ID at all times. I never bothered. For a second I considered turning round and going back for my passport, decided this would look suspicious enough to invite unwelcome scrutiny, sighed and walked on.

'I am a tourist,' I told the cop who stopped me, making out that my inadequate German was even worse than it was. 'My passport is in the place where I am staying.'

But the cop didn't care about ID. He merely expressed polite curiosity as to what there might be in my pockets.

I turned them out for him: a pen, keys, cigarettes, a throwaway lighter and some coins with which I intended to purchase bread and milk. No bombs, no bullets. Nothing that would worry any World Banker, save perhaps the pronounced lack of funds. The cop waved me on. At the corner of Hauptstrasse it got even more intense. Off into the distance in every direction receded great long lines of parked green police vans. Down the middle of the road stood dozens of police bikes, their riders trying to look cool and macho in ugly bright green leather jump suits. The pavements were clogged with cops dawdling, cops coagulating in bunches, cops standing round and looking gruff but sort of aimless.

This was clearly not a moment to cross on red. I started counting the vans and got up to thirty or so – not even half of them – before the lights changed and everybody else stepped into the road. Surrounded by so many uniforms, I was suddenly nervous of standing alone at the kerb, even though, as far as I knew, not crossing on green was no kind of offence. I followed the crowd and ducked into the shop. This was the biggest police operation I had ever seen in a street – miles out of any World Banker's way – where there was no demonstration, no passing royal motorcade, nothing else happening at all. The point was that they were treating the whole city as a potential demonstration, every last passer-by as a possible terrorist. By the time I re-emerged with my modest purchases, the streets were already emptying of uniforms, the vans and motorcycles moving off to control some new location.

'Being controlled.' This was the idiom. Say you caught the U-Bahn without buying a ticket. Easy enough to do. Tempting, even. There were no automatic barriers, no ticket collectors, nothing to stop you just stepping straight on to a train. Not only did this save the flat fare of DM2.70, there was also a certain pleasure in having flouted another German regulation – a dodge, you told yourself, for which the locals were plainly just too timid and obedient. So you rattled through the tunnels, checking your reflection in the window opposite, childishly proud of having bucked the system in this elementary fashion.

But suddenly the carriage might fill with bright blue uniforms – maybe fifteen or twenty of them. *Kontrolleure*, they were called – controllers. Sometimes they came singly and in plain clothes. What you had hitherto taken for an ordinary passenger would suddenly wheel round, whip a badge from a bomber jacket, bark at someone to take their feet off the seat and generally reveal themselves to be a secret agent of the BVG – the West Berlin public transport authority. But the uniformed gangs were more common. You could often spot the waiting thin blue line as the train drew into a station, but it was still hard to tell whether to sit tight or leg it. Sometimes they stayed on the platform, sometimes they climbed on to the train. Once on board, this gang would demand your travel documents. To no avail might you shrug and speak English, affecting incomprehension. These people had heard it all before. Next thing you were frogmarched off the train and into a little office on the platform. Details of your ID were recorded and filed. A spot fine lightened your wallet by the sum of DM60. For you the ride is over, Tommy. *Du bist kontrolliert worden –* you have been controlled.

Germans and expats alike translated the idiom thus. 'I was controlled yesterday,' someone would moan. Or as a German once put it to me: 'In London they control you on the way out.' At first it sounded strange. I was struck by the macabre comedy of the phrase, evoking visions of electrodes to the head, fiendish ticket collectors directing your movements with some kind of joystick. Stop on the red man, cross on the green. You are being controlled, you are being controlled.

But in divided Berlin one was soon using the phrase like a native, broadening out as it did to encompass any kind of brush with uniformed authority. In this, as in no other field of human endeavour, the city excelled. On each side of the Wall lined up parallel armies of officialdom, all just waiting to control you. There were ticket collectors and traffic wardens. There were border guards and customs officials. There was every imaginable kind of police. You could be shot for going over the Wall. You could be reprimanded for marooning hedgehogs on Peacock Island. And at every point on the continuum between lurked officials empowered, in their various ways, to stop you, search you, detain you, question you, examine your documents, fine you on the spot, move you on or stop you smoking.

And those were just the local authorities. Matters were further complicated by the Four Power status of divided Berlin. Though on an everyday basis this mattered little, technically the whole place was still under Allied control. The West Berlin Senat, along with the police it administered, had only that authority delegated to it by the Allied Kommandatura. Servicepeople of the British, American, French and Russian armed forces were exempt from local laws, couldn't be busted by any Berlin cop, East or West. Even as an Allied citizen in Berlin, utterly unconnected with the military, it was possible, if arrested, to elect to be handed over to the military police. Possible, but scarcely sensible. I heard of one Englishman, under the influence and driving somewhat dodgily in the British sector, who was stopped by German police. He refused to acknowledge their authority, stood firm on his rights as a subject of Her Majesty the Queen – and when the British MPs finally came to collect him, got badly beaten up for having wasted their time.

The thing was, in West Berlin no one had any rights – or at least no rights that couldn't be taken away, worked around or simply ignored if it suited the Allies. The Four Powers ruled by virtue of military conquest, not by consent of the governed. The Allies were accountable to no one, could act unhindered by any constitution. They could look over any laws passed in Bonn before deciding whether to allow them in Berlin. They could censor mail, tap telephones, jail anyone who criticised them, throw away the key. Up until the early 1980s, practically all of the 1938 Nazi penal code – albeit in 'de-Nazified' form – was still on the books in West Berlin. Meanwhile, to pass a new law the Allies simply had to write it down on a piece of paper, hand that piece of paper to the Mayor and – hey presto – whatever was written on it henceforth became 'law'.

In practice, of course, the Allies were quite restrained in their use of these powers. The occasional residents' association might find itself with no court to appeal to when the British or Americans decided to build a shooting range near their nice suburban homes. The anarchist groups of Kreuzberg might find a few more of their phones tapped than usual when, say, Reagan came to visit. But it had been many years since the Allies exercised their power (to cite laws still in force up until the mid-1980s) to incarcerate anyone for not carrying identity papers or to carry out the death sentence on anyone who physically (i.e. with force of arms) attacked them. Hostilities between the Allies and Germany had after all officially ended way back in 1951. West Berlin was functionally, if not technically, now part of the territory of a friendly power. The only reason the Allies were still there and these old laws still in force, was because, since the Blockade and Airlift and the 1948 Russian walk-out from the Kommandatura, the status of territory under military occupation was the only thing that stopped West Berlin from being swallowed by the East.

And herein lay one of the central paradoxes of Berlin. It was more than the irony of powers so dictatorial existing in the West to keep it 'safe for democracy'. Over on the other side of the Wall, the legal shape of things in East Berlin formed a neat mirror image. Though the original 1949 version had been steadily toughened up in successive amendments, the constitution of the German Democratic Republic still theoretically guaranteed its citizens freedom of speech, freedom of the press, the right to peaceful assembly and the right of association. Trouble was, these rights could only be exercised 'in accordance with the spirit and aims of this constitution' or 'within the framework of the principles and aims of this constitution'. Given the pride of constitutional place reserved for 'the leading role of the SED [i.e. the Communists]', this effectively meant 'at the discretion of the Politbüro'.

In other words, forget all about freedom of speech. While it existed (more or less) in the West, it wasn't guaranteed. While it was guaranteed (sort of) in the East, it didn't exist. While the Western authorities kept on hand drastic powers that were rarely exercised, the Eastern authorities kept on the books basic freedoms that were seldom allowed. On neither side were 'rights' really rights. Despite the righteous clichés attached to its role as global symbol, the yin-yang city resisted black and white distinctions. Freedom was more complicated than the distance between one side of the Wall and the other. In East or in West, it was nothing more than the distance between power and policy, between what the authorities wanted to do, and what the authorities could do if they wanted.

That night of the World Bank conference, I climbed on my bicycle and set off up Goltzstrasse. I was escorted the whole distance by a police van in front and a police van behind. There were few pedestrians about. Other green and white police vehicles, their windows armoured with metal mesh, lay in wait down side streets. A few faces peered from the picture window of Café M, a location where people usually sat to be seen, never to see out. At Winterfeldplatz I normally went up on the pavement by the church and cut across the square. Tonight that space was filled with still more waiting vans. Sticking to the traffic regulations with exaggerated care, my escort and I followed the one-way system round to the other side. The cops joined their colleagues in the square. I continued up Maasenstrasse, past the end of the street where Christopher Isherwood used to live, and turned the corner into Nollendorfplatz.

Earlier that evening units of riot police and GSG para-militaries had forced an anti-World Bank demonstration out of the Ku'Damm, past the Gedächtniskirche and along Tauentzienstrasse before cornering all the participants in this square. The rioters had long since fled or been arrested, but the place still swarmed with police in helmets. Windows had been pushed out by the crush outside Café Swing. The occasional puddle of vomit testified to the fact that gas had been used. I locked my bike against a lamppost outside the Metropol and looked over the scene. Here William Bradshaw in *Mr Norris Changes Trains* had listened to Goebbels on a radio horn, announcing that Germany was awake. Here Len Deighton had concluded his *Game, Set*

& Match trilogy with an unlikely shootout on the overhead railway. And here, that night, I had to go to work.

Money had been tight ever since the last of my meagre initial funds had been dribbled away in bars and clubs. Since then I'd been taking any odd job that came along: painting a sign outside a theatre, selling t-shirts at Pink Floyd and Michael Jackson concerts, playing a snap-happy paparazzo in a sketch for children's television. None of them paid very much but I eked out just enough to get by. Whenever I got a little money I'd rush out to buy rice and lentils, pasta and tins of tomatoes – cheap food that wouldn't go off – and maybe stock up on duty-free cigarettes at the Friedrichstrasse Intershop. When I was feeling especially flush, I might allow myself the treat of cycling over to the English secondhand bookshop on Sesenheimer Strasse and purchasing a couple of paperbacks.

The Loft on Nollendorfplatz provided the closest I had found to regular work. A first-floor annexe to the Metropol disco, this was the best small-to-medium concert venue in Berlin. Once or twice a fortnight I might earn DM50 for filling in on the door when one of the regulars couldn't work. This was nicely humbling. In London I had been the kind of music journalist who swans around fashionable backstage areas. Here in Berlin the lowliest no-hope support bands were now elbowing me to one side. I often failed to recognise even the headliners – rock bands usually, guitars and tough poses, not my cup of tea – and would embarrass everyone by demanding to see their tickets as they arrived for the performance.

Otherwise I tore tickets and rubber-stamped wrists, searched leather jackets for cans of beer, listened to whiny sob stories about why some punk simply had to be let in for nothing, tried to prevent people from just charging in, took a lot of abuse. Mark had been working the door of the Loft for years, often dressed up in an East German border guard uniform. It amused him to see me on the job too. 'Dave Rimmer, controlling people, brilliant!' To lighten the hours of toil, we developed another game. I'd long been thinking of an SF story about Fashion Police who busted you for wearing the wrong clothes. The idea suited Berlin perfectly. Not only was it the world capital of controlling, it was also a horribly vivid nightmare of implausible hair-styles, drab or else violently mismatched colours, too-tight trousers, ugly footwear, silly details and ill-advised facial hair. West Berlin begged for draconian measures in defence of good taste. So Mark and I started playing *Modepolizei*.

There were specific *Modepolizei* offences. Scruffy trainers with a dinner suit – Gross Dereliction Of Detail. Bunch of people in leather jackets and Palestinian guerilla scarves – Conspiracy To Commit A Cliché. Yet another set of black denims and little round spectacles – Grievous Lack Of Imagination. Those orange rayon monstrosities ballooning over a pair of brown and cream platform boots – Wearing Of Flares In A Public Place. There was a table of automatic spot fines. Large round glasses with funny-coloured frames – DM10. Leather Donny Osmond cap – DM15. Lurex Donny Osmond cap – DM20. Cowboy boots with fake fur sewn on – DM25. Skin-tight jeans in fake animal- or snake-skin pattern – DM30. As above but in fluorescent colours – DM35. Sunglasses at night – DM50. Gold and turquoise paisley one-piece skintight leotard on a fat, bald man – throw away the key. Persistent offenders to be incarcerated for self-criticism.

It wasn't just the individual items. West Berliners had a knack for fitting things together in especially vile combinations, every component looking as though it had been plucked from a different costume. Like cowboy hat with feathers in it, large yellow ad-agency spectacles, red hooded t-shirt, tweed maths teacher sports jacket with suede elbow patches, lilac track suit bottoms tucked into light brown Robin Hood boots. And even then it wasn't just the combinations, but the attitude that went with them. Such outfits presumably represented a groping after some kind of irony and a dash of humour might indeed have seasoned one of these combinations to the point where it became forgivable. But no, you'd see somebody got up in a blue baseball cap with glittery red star-shaped sunglasses balanced on the peak, green schoolboy blazer, beige shirt with funny duffels, fraying cut-off denim shorts, psychedelic stockings and lace-up patent leather knee boots, striding around with head held condescendingly high, obviously convinced they were the coolest thing in Christendom.

'You know,' I sighed as the audience trooped in one night. 'Sometimes I wish they'd all go back to wearing pointy Prussian helmets.'

But such combinations were only common exceptions to a rule that was otherwise basic black in general, black leather in particular. Black leather trousers landed a *Modepolizei* spot fine of DM60 but the offence was so widespread as to make this virtually unenforceable. Not everyone wore them all the time but every West Berliner seemed to have a pair tucked away somewhere. It wasn't just the Kreuzberg punks or the Charlottenburg art set. My newsagent wore black leather trousers. One of the clerks in my bank wore black leather trousers. The barmaid in the prolo pub on the corner with too much make-up and a sweatshirt with snarling leopard picked out in gold and silver sequins, wore black leather trousers.

They made thin legs look like shiny, brittle sticks; fat legs bulge like overstuffed black puddings. They were almost invariably held up with studded belts and all too often matched with black leather jackets though they might sometimes protrude from beneath a smart designer blazer or drab winter anorak. Purists completed the picture with skull rings and black tooled cowboy boots with metal chains on them. But whoever was wearing them, however they were worn, black leather trousers never seemed to transcend their substance, never blended neatly into a larger look, never became anything more or less than their stiff and shiny selves.

It would have been damned hard to wear them ironically, had anyone ever tried. What statements they made – about rebellion, about sexuality – were blunt and literal. Their meaning in Berlin resided partly in the city's long-standing, though scarcely still justified, reputation for decadence. In so far as decadent Berlin existed at all, it was being kept alive by the steady immigration of draft dodgers and students from small towns in West Germany, eager for a taste of what they imagined to be big city life. The colour black has been associated with the classical notion of decadence since the turn of the century. Other relevant cultural connotations are clear enough: black is the colour of nihilism, negation, the night, absence, austerity, despair and death. Black means evil and extremes, the colour of both anarchism and fascism.

Whatever goes for black goes double for black leather, which ever since Marlon Brando in *The Wild Ones* has been the official uniform of the rebel without a cause. It also carries a hint of sado-masochism and deviant sex. Black leather trousers come off as being just that little bit more decadent than black leather jackets. If you're thin (if you aren't thin you should never dream of wearing them) they make you look even thinner and can lend the wearer a look associated with the abuse of heroin and long ago (1973) termed 'elegantly wasted' by one Nick Kent writing of one Keith Richards, both of them veteran black leather trouser men.

Kreuzberg 36 was the black leather trouser heartland, packed with junkies and punks, artists and students. It was also packed with Turks, and was in this sense a double ghetto, though unemployed black leather rebels and immigrant Balkan guest workers didn't mix very much. Formally a central inner city district, Kreuzberg had been closed in on two sides by the Wall and stranded out at one end of U-Bahn Line One and had been the dissident part of town since the squatting movement took off in the late 1970s, a safe little corner in which to play at being revolutionaries. Attitudes there were hard. Say you tried to open a nice vegetarian restaurant, a little upmarket perhaps. Somebody would probably firebomb it. Black leather Kreuzbergers would only accept a properly scruffy place to eat or drink. Never mind that the owners of a dive like Madonna on Weiner Strasse were probably coining enough to drive around in Porsches. If it looked the part then it would gull the locals.

Kreuzberg politics had little to do with the art of the possible. They wouldn't be content, say, just to squat a house, keep their heads down and negotiate to be allowed to stay. No, they'd immediately hang out banners imploring workers of the world to unite and kill all fascist pigs. Once the fascist pigs duly turned up in force, the squatters would then set to with bricks and petrol bombs. It seemed that confrontation – always heavy-handed on both sides of the law – was the most important thing. Violence was not a means to an end, but, whether the participants realised it or not, some kind of end in itself.

At the age when Mark and I had been playing Japs and Commandos in the woods, German children of my generation had barely heard there had been a war at all. I discussed this once with my friend Thekla, then a science student at the Technical University, and she ended up taking a straw poll of her all-female volleyball team – all born in the late 1950s or early 1960s – on how and when they learnt about Nazism. In their schools it seemed either to have been badly taught or never to have been taught at all. When one of them had seen a Nazi uniform in an old family photograph, or heard some dreadful story and started asking questions, excuses would usually fly quicker than explanations. Their parents often pretended they'd known nothing about any atrocities, flew into a blind rage whenever the subject was mentioned, muttered: *'Das war damals so, man darf ihnen das nicht vorwerfen'* – That's how it was in those days and no one can blame you for it. One of Thekla's team had first heard this line at the age of five, the only reply when she saw a swastika somewhere and asked her mother what it was. Another one hadn't even seen a swastika until she was seventeen. Some had parents who still spoke admiringly of Hitler, others remembered hearing tales of 'poor' Germans and 'wicked' Poles. Such recollections as their parents voiced were mostly nostalgic, of friendships and roughing it through hard times. Only a couple had parents or teachers who'd given honest answers to their questions. Most had put together the pieces themselves in adolescence.

I remember how I learnt about sex: an embarrassed talk from my father when I was too young properly to understand what he was on about, a couple of rather ludicrous biology lessons, the fitting-together of some unlikely-sounding details culled from playground chatter. Imagine learning of the Holocaust this way. Imagine a loss of innocence compounded by the sudden stark understanding of your parents' or grandparents' complicity in all the death and brutality of the Third Reich. Imagine the generation gap that results. Hence petrol bombs and black leather trousers. Hence the imagery of death and darkness. Hence the ugly music in dingy bars. It was exactly the kind of thing an angry teenager would run upstairs and play at full volume to piss off his parents. The games being played out in Kreuzberg were adolescent games, confrontation with father as much as with fatherland.

On arrival in Kreuzberg you were always greeted by beggars. Punks and hippies hovered around every station exit, open-palmed and aggressive, demanding that you part with some small change. Their attitude was that they were entitled to your money, that you owed them a living simply because of what they were. It was as if they considered themselves secular equivalents of, say, Buddhist monks begging in India – that you should keep them alive because of the spirit they represented. Although in straight political terms the Kreuzberg community had long since ceased to represent anything but themselves, the way black leather trousers had broadened out to become a cross-city, cross-cultural item did suggest a glimmer of truth in this attitude.

Though it carried echoes of America – West Berlin rebels often seemed to be living in a Lower East Side of the imagination – this was a style that had deep roots in Germany. Among the memorabilia in the Pinguin Club there was a picture of The Beatles in Hamburg. John, Paul and George stood on a St Pauli rooftop in black leather jackets, black t-shirts, black jeans tucked into ornate cowboy boots. They'd picked up the style from Astrid Kirchherr, an art student who had become Stu Sutcliffe's girlfriend and was also responsible for what became known as the Beatle Haircut. This photograph was probably taken on their first visit. On the second one she introduced them to black leather trousers.

I liked this photo, often looked at it, and on any night of the week you could glance around the bar and see one or two people dressed exactly the same way. The fact that the style was around three decades on just underlined my dislike of it. Black leather trousers were another exhibit in the museum city – a city that by the late 1980s was living on its reputation and very little else.

As spring slid into summer, as doors and windows opened to greet the weather, the noise around my apartment grew louder and louder. One day I was woken by shouts and banging as early morning workmen erected scaffolding outside my window. They were going to strip and repaint the façade. All day I struggled to muster concentration in the midst of this redoubled commotion. The workmen went home in late afternoon. There was an hour or two's respite, then music and the sounds of communal merry-making began booming down from Olga the bass player's flat. She was having a party.

I'd been invited so I looked in. Cowboy boots thudded in rhythm to heavy swamp rock. People smoked and swigged beer from the bottle. Faces were closed to me, huddled in local intrigue. I couldn't find anywhere to sit, any safe corner in which to stand and adjust. I paced the length of the room and then started walking back. It wasn't just my still lamentable German, though that didn't help an already shaky self-confidence. It wasn't just my still nervy state after London, though that hardly helped me to feel at home. The truth was, I just didn't feel comfortable in this scene. I shuffled round the edges of the party feeling sorry for myself, then ducked back out to go for a bike ride.

First I went to see if Trevor was in. He and his family lived on the ground floor of a grey-blue block of flats, just round the corner from a long shit-brown one. It was an ugly but interesting location. Off in one direction, the Yorckstrasse whisked traffic under the series of bridges that once carried trains south from the Anhalter and Potsdamer stations. As part of his plan for the capital of the new Germanic empire, Hitler had planned to rip out these tracks, build an immense avenue along the space thus freed

and stud a tyrannical skyline with outsize ceremonial struc-
tures. A triumphal arch would have towered three times
the height of the one in Paris. A new chancellery would
have required visiting diplomats to take a chastening
quarter-mile hike once inside the building. A new Führer's
palace was to be no less than 150 times the size of Bis-
marck's old residence. The most bombastic scheme of all
was for a monstrous domed meeting hall. This would have
held 180,000 people, with room for a cool million in the
yawning square outside. The copper dome, 825 feet in
diameter, big enough for clouds to have formed inside,
gathering a greenish patina as it oxidised with age, would
have loomed over the city like a small mountain. Albert
Speer used to butter Hitler up by showing him sketches of
how magnificent their buildings, especially designed so as
to decay picturesquely, would have looked after genera-
tions of neglect. Long after the Thousand Year Reich had
been consigned to ancient history books, their ruins would
continue to awe the populations of the future.

But ruins, of course, came way ahead of schedule. By
May 1945 Berlin had been reduced to 25 million cubic
metres of rubble – enough, once usable bricks had been
sifted out and the rest eventually piled up, to give the city
seven small new hills. The area of the railway tracks,
abandoned not for grand new avenues but because they
now went no further than the Wall, had slowly choked up
with weeds. The only piece of totalitarian architecture to
pierce an otherwise uneventful skyline was the Fernsehturm – Television Tower – over in the East. Round where
Trevor lived, as in so many areas on both sides of the Wall,
there was nothing but these cheap post-war flat blocks, as
dull and unremarkable as the lives one imagined went on
inside them.

By day these buildings looked soggy in the rain. By night
windows flickered with the light from identically tuned
televisions. Just over Potsdamer Strasse, where the now
demolished Sportpalast had once rumbled with exhor-
tations to total war, now stood a block where the post-war
architects had actually managed to blend their work in with
the surroundings. The concrete stump of an old Nazi flak

tower over the road was virtually indistinguishable in style
from the brutalist machines-for-living-in which straddled
the road to rest across the top of it. I walked past that
bunker scores of times without even noticing it was there. It
had never seemed anything but a natural part of the
structure. Yet history was the only thing that made this
ugliness special. The worst excesses of Berlin were easily
matched by sections of my home town, by bombed-out then
rebuilt sections of towns all over Europe. The only truly
remarkable piece of post-war town planning in Berlin was
the scheme, most radical and brutalist of them all, that
carved the city into two unequal halves.

Trevor wasn't in so I cycled on towards Kreuzberg. It was
a fine evening and there were people out everywhere,
sitting at cafés, sunning themselves on canal banks, leaning
over balconies, playing football down dead-end streets. I
cut through a park by a canal. The Wall ran down the
opposite bank, leaving a thin strip of overgrown no man's
land on which children played with bows and arrows,
hippies with bongos and guitars. A solemn-faced German
couple in tight striped trousers went through a series of
slow Tai Chi exercises. A Turkish couple on a bench held
hands and watched them, smiling. Outside a squatted
house, maybe a dozen punks brawled and spat beer on the
pavement.

As I worked my way round the edge of what had once
been Görlitzer Bahnhof, I remembered that an acquaintance called Kerstin lived nearby. I'd first met her in East
Berlin maybe four years before. Since then she'd married a
Swedish guy, been allowed to emigrate, had hated Stockholm and left her husband to move back to Berlin. Now she
was a West Berliner with a well-paid job at Siemens. A few
months before I had seen her in London.

Kerstin knew I was in Berlin but was unnerved to see me
on her doorstep. She invited me in and offered beer,
carefully dividing one bottle between two glasses, then sat
down and fidgeted on the other side of the room. I resolved
not to stay very long. Her small flat was anonymous and
antiseptic, like a hotel room. Everything in it was new and
decisively Western, items unobtainable in her previous life:

a wall-to-wall grey carpet, lots of black and chrome furniture, the full range of sleek audiovisual gadgetry. The only personal touch, the only things that couldn't have come out of a catalogue, were a few photos pinned above the CD player. These were pictures of Kerstin and her friends at parties and concerts back East, back in the old days. Everyone was smiling and laughing, but the pictures looked forlorn on the wall. That life, those relationships, were gone. She had swapped them for the furnishings among which she and her mementoes now looked so uncomfortable.

I left as soon as I had finished my beer and cycled on into the dying light. A woman sat knitting on the balcony of a house daubed with murals, strung with political banners and flying a black and red anarchist flag from the chimney. People waved agendas at a meeting in some community café. At the Schlesisches Tor I pulled up and sighed. 'The Silesian Gate'. In English it sounded romantic. This was one of my favourite spots in all Berlin, perhaps in all of Europe. For a distance of just a few hundreds yards, the border ran down the River Spree. The Oberbaumbrücke, a crossing for pedestrians, bristled with towers and barbed wire and checkpoints. On the water below, white swans and grey East German gunboats glided by.

I locked my bike to some railings and sat down on the riverbank, listening to the voices of the Turkish fishermen, thinking about Kerstin's photos and the party I had left. In teenage years my group of friends had gone to every party we could find. We didn't really care if it was a good party or a bad party. If it was a good party, then great. If it was a bad party, we'd have a good time taking the piss out of it. West Berlin, I decided, was a bad party. This was the only way to approach the city. In Kreuzberg the party was one of those cheap affairs, all the furniture moved out, bare floorboards, red light bulbs, beer finished long ago, everyone shoving shoulder to shoulder as music plays too distorted to enjoy, too loud to talk over. In Schöneberg the party was a gathering of trendy students. Better music, sharper clothes, maybe a little food on the kitchen table. Lots of angry, arrogant young things taking themselves and their games just that little bit too seriously as they pose in anticipation of glorious deeds to come. In Charlottenburg the party was older, full of gallery owners in velvet jackets sipping fine wine and laughing politely at each other's jokes. The guests have money and a certain elegance, but are bored and used up their imagination long ago. In the outlying districts the party was a suburban barbecue, the neighbours over on a Sunday afternoon, lots of dull talk about cars and washing machines, whatever was on the telly last night.

The sun was dipping right down to the West. Buildings on the Eastern side were briefly bathed in red. This was a quiet corner of West Berlin but I could hear traffic on the other side. A busy road ran along the opposite bank, hidden from view by the Wall. Over in the distance to my left stood the Fernsehturm on Alexanderplatz, the glass ball on its flaring concrete spike glinting in the last of the light. Suddenly I longed to be in the other half of the city. If bad parties were the game, just think how much worse they would be over there.

5.
PASSPORT TO PANKOW

The ways through to other worlds have traditionally been strange and obscure: down a deep rabbit hole, through an old wardrobe, staring in a mirror until it shimmers and dissolves. Often they allow only one-way traffic. Usually they are accessible only to a privileged few. There are sound reasons for this. Wonderland, open to all, would soon cease to inspire any wonder. The next you know, there'd be package tourists everywhere and some food combine opening a canning plant for mock turtle soup. Within divided Berlin, the right of passage through the Wall between the worlds depended on the possession of a magical item: any kind of passport except an East German one. Moving West to East, your papers would eventually see you through but you had to be back by the witching hour or you'd be turned into a pumpkin. A DDR pass worked the opposite effect. It prevented you from crossing unless you managed to get rid of it. You might then pass West but were condemned to remain there for ever and ever.

For Brits like me there were many obstacles but few real problems. Non-Germans could use only two crossing places. Checkpoint Charlie catered for foreigners, the diplomatic corps and Allied military. Friedrichstrasse station controlled the passage of every kind of civilian: West German, East German, non-German and Berliner. If your chosen route was Charlie, you'd surface from Kochstrasse U-Bahn, push through the inevitable knot of tourists outside the escape museum, stroll uncontrolled past both the Western military checkpoint in the middle of the road and the small wooden hut where a couple of bored West German police staffed a counter, then push through more tourists taking pictures of each other in front of the sign that many apparently dared not pass: 'You are leaving the American sector'.

Here the boundary between Americans and Russians, Germany and Germany, the Berlin districts of Kreuzberg and Mitte, was a thin white line across the road. You stepped right over it: back foot coming up in the West, front foot padding down in the East. The Wall stretched away to either side. Ahead were watchtowers, armed guards, barbed wire, iron gates, descending barriers, slalom barriers, speed bumps, prefabricated buildings and numbered lanes directing traffic under a flat metal roof that made the whole thing look like a fortified filling station. Dotted lines on the tarmac steered you towards a squat grey structure on the right: the control point for pedestrians.

When going over by Friedrichstrasse station, you'd breach the Wall by bridge or tunnel from any one of five directions, pass through a couple of dim ghost stations and get off at the interchange which lent the border post its name – geographically in the East but still on the Western side of controls. Signs directed you along grubby subterranean corridors, past duty-free shops, up and down staircases to the *Grenzübergangstelle* – the border-over-walkplace. This was a large room tiled in mildew colours, blocked off with a row of wood veneer cubicles, lit by harsh fluorescents. Stencilled wooden signs sorted you into queues by citizenship: West Berliners here, West Germans there. The shortest line was always that for East Germans. The longest was usually the one we had to join, that for 'citizens of other states'.

Once you'd inched your way into the uncomfortably narrow cubicle at the head of the queue, you slid your passport over the top of a high counter and under the glass partition which separated you from the guard on duty. He'd sweep it over to his side, do the look-at-you-twice bit, then glance up at the angled mirror behind you to check you weren't concealing anything just out of his line of sight. Beneath his counter, he'd shuffle your papers around for a while, shine lights on them, deploy a rubber stamp or two. You slid five marks over. He slid back your passport along with a day visa. This looked much like a transit visa but was backed with a map of the East Berlin U- and S-Bahn network, the contours of its validity in space.

On the buzz of an electronic lock you pushed open a metal door and stepped through to an area where piles of foreign currency declaration forms, printed on paper one grade up from everyday toilet roll, sat waiting on wood-style shelves. You were expected to fill these out yourself – a few broken pencils dangled on pieces of string – and this was supposed to stop you changing any money on the black market. As an elementary precaution, we filled out these forms only when directly ordered. If they ever did ask, we'd fill one out with meticulous honesty and simply throw the thing away later. Currency declaration form? I'm afraid no one told us we had to do one of those.

Next stop was a little glass cubicle where you would hand over twenty-five hard West marks and receive twenty-five soft East marks in return. In terms of exchange value, this was ruinous. On the black market or in a Western bank you could get up to eight times the official one-to-one rate. In terms of entertainment value, the notes at least looked the part of 'funny money'. They were small and long, more on the dimensions of king-size Rizlas than of honest, square deal banknotes, decorated with pictures of Marx and Clara Zetkin, rows of combine harvesters and proudly smoking factories. They were also usually freshly minted, which aided the impression of some useless vouchers they'd just knocked off to screw you for a bit of hard currency.

Occasionally customs would then let you walk straight through. This was more common in busy Friedrichstrasse and we favoured the station for that reason. In another little wood-style cubicle you might have to empty your pockets, count out your currency. Woe betide the innocent traveller who had earlier bought East marks in a Western bank. Anything more than the obligatory twenty-five marks added up to instant trouble. A thick roll could get you a prison sentence. A first offence with a modest amount would usually add up to a strip search, a long wait in a holding cell, a warning lecture, your money confiscated, a boot back Westwards and a mark on your passport that would stop you getting in again.

They demanded to know the purpose of your visit, feeling down the seams of your clothing for sewn-in *Schwarzgeld* or concealed James Bond-style equipment. They looked out for Western books and magazines or anything that appeared to be a present for one of their citizens. A punnet of strawberries, perhaps. Some flowers. An arcane Western consumer durable that couldn't be of any use on a simple day out. They would then grill you about who you were going to see, demand names and addresses. With anything heftier than a bunch of grapes, it was hard to pretend that you were just seeing someone you met last time in Alexanderplatz.

Most guards were unfailingly rude, some clearly smouldering with a barely suppressed rage. You could read the resentment in their faces as they eyed the lustrous Western consumer items in the luggage of even the poorest, items that were otherwise out of their reach. Like uniformed officials the world over, they would loose the frustrations of their own lives in making a hearty meal from their little slice of authority. Probably it was even expected of them. Although the DDR government always had uses for your hard currency, the procedure was made deliberately unwelcoming to discourage you from going through it too often. Many undoubtedly were deterred, but for the Cold War romantic it was all fun and games.

Mark, for example, was perversely proud of having once incurred the ultimate indignity. They had found a skeleton key in his bag. Mark stuttered out the unlikely truth: having misplaced the lone set of keys to his flat, this was the only way he could get back in. The guards were unimpressed. At best this guy must be a burglar, at worst a spy or saboteur. Mark always carried a small Czechoslovakian olive drab knapsack, neatly buckled and packed with his survival kit: a camouflage wallet, a camouflage pen, camouflage notebook, sunglasses, screwdriver for tightening sunglasses, paper handkerchiefs, bottle opener, penknife, aspirin, tape measure. The guard unpacked it slowly, subjecting each item to practised suspicion, then ordered Mark to undress. When the last shred of clothing had yielded nothing of interest, a special operative was summoned. This expert was a pimply youth, the lowest of the low, the man with the worst job in the checkpoint. While the officer hung gingerly around the other end of the room, drumming his fingers as he pretended to be absorbed by whatever he could see through the tatty lace curtains, the bottom inspector carefully parted Mark's buttocks and shone a special flashlight into the orifice thus revealed. He rose after a moment, pronouncing it uncluttered by anything that shouldn't be there, and sloped off to deploy his skills elsewhere. The officer flew into a rage. Surely he could nail Mark for something. He prowled around the table where Mark's things were all laid out. Hah! He snatched up the camouflage pen and, hands shaking, frantically pulled it apart. Nothing came out but lots of ink. Biting back frustration, he threw the pieces on the table.

'You are free,' he told Mark, 'to enter the German Democratic Republic.'

Customs was the last obstacle, save a guy with a gun who watched as you pushed open the final door. At Friedrichstrasse you emerged into a busy station hall; at Charlie into a street which, in later years, sported a sign with happy cartoon bear declaring: *'Berlin grüsst seine Gäste'* – Berlin greets its guests. Although once, having overslept, I made it from bed to East Berlin in thirty-five minutes flat, the transition would usually have lasted between one and two hours. Outside you'd breathe a deep sigh of relief and notice a distinct new odour in the air. Acrid, a little musty. The aroma, as Mark always put it, of 'Trabant exhaust and cabbage farts'. It was the scent of the East.

This was the normal way through, but we had discovered a means to bypass all that rigmarole.

On 22 October 1961, back when the Wall was but a few weeks old, one Allan Lightner, then the senior American civilian official in Berlin, tried to drive through Checkpoint Charlie. He was on his way to see an experimental Czech theatre company but instead found himself main actor in a more serious drama. East German officials stopped the car and asked to see his passport. According to the theory of the situation, the Americans recognising neither the DDR diplomatically nor East Berlin as a part of the DDR, the car's US licence plates should have been identification enough. Lightner refused to show his passport. The East Germans refused to let him proceed. Lightner demanded that a Soviet officer be brought to the scene. No such officer was summoned. Lightner tried to accelerate on through. He was slowed by barriers and his car surrounded. The East Germans told him that no matter how long he sat there, unless he showed his passport they would not let him through.

He sat there long enough for word to get to General Clay, who sent out an infantry platoon, four tanks and two armoured personnel carriers. After further argument with the border guards, still insisting that all civilians must show identity papers when entering the DDR, two squads of American infantry, rifles at the ready, took position around Lightner's car and slowly escorted him across the border. This time the East German guards stepped back. Lightner drove a couple of blocks, came back, and then tried to repeat the manoeuvre without the escort. The guards stopped him again. Once more the US soldiers came forward, once more the guards grudgingly let them through.

In the following days, the situation began to escalate. Clay sent further probes across the border. Soviet armour was drawn up on the other side of Charlie. Nose to nose in the same Berlin street, across the white line of the sector border, American and Soviet tanks faced each other off. Journalists crowded on the Western side and the world watched, anxious and perplexed. Why all this fuss about showing a passport? Was it really worth risking World War

Three? The Americans and Russians began to ask the same question. The tanks rumbled back to their respective barracks, the world retreated from the brink of war and, in time, a compromise was reached. Allied civilian officials would show their passports, but only to prove that they didn't have to show them. The result was a loophole in the regulations. Allied citizens, as long as they were not registered as residents of Berlin, could pass the border unmolested when provided with a military escort.

Mark had met a GI at the Loft, name of Buttle, a gawky southern boy who worked as some kind of chaplain's assistant. Naive but good-hearted and a fan of the kind of guitar bands who played at the Loft, Buttle knew enough to understand the value of befriending your local club doorman. Observing Mark's taste for militaria, he began turning up with presents: a camouflage cap, a case of MREs (Meals-Ready-to-Eat – US Army field rations), sundry badges and insignia. Soon we got to know him better, which is how Trevor, Buttle the GI and I came to be standing one Saturday morning in the Allied Powers' hut on the Western side of Charlie – the one you normally walked straight by – being briefed by an American Military Policeman.

The MP had a strong, square military jaw and clear, blue military eyes. His delivery was practised and precise. We would all remain in the vehicle and Buttle must sit 'in a position of modified attention' while going through the checkpoint. Car windows must be kept tightly closed. When the East German guard approached the vehicle, Trevor and I must hold up to the window only the front and first few pages of our passports. We must not show him any further pages. Once on the other side, we were not to acknowledge the authority of any East German police officer or official. Travelling under the protection of Uncle Sam in the Soviet Sector of Occupied Berlin we would answer only to officers of the Soviet Army. If we got into any trouble, the MP would come over personally to sort things out.

Trouble? That sounded like an open invitation to start some. The idea that the US Military Police might come and bail out the likes of Trevor and me was so ludicrous I had to struggle to keep a straight face.

Back in the car, Buttle put on a tape of the Dead Kennedies. This, he claimed, was to baffle special microphones used to monitor conversations in cars. We followed a lane marked out for diplomatic and military and pulled up before the final gate. In the next lane a guard wheeled a mirror under a civilian Volkswagen passing the other way, just making sure there were no illegal emigrants clinging on down there. Buttle assumed his 'position of modified attention': he sat very straight and stared unwaveringly ahead. A guard came to the car and took down the licence number, peered through the windows to scribble details from Trevor's passport and mine. We didn't have to pay any money, we didn't have to take any shit. It was such a simple joy to keep them at a distance that holding up that passport felt like holding up two defiant fingers. After the briefest of waits, they opened up the barrier and waved us through.

The day that lay before us promised to be an interesting one. Popular Düsseldorf fun-punk group Die Toten Hosen – The Dead Trousers – had recently played a benefit for Trevor's magazine, *Ich und Mein Staubsauger*. As agreed payment for this, Trevor, with the help of Mark and various contacts over the Wall, had organised them an unofficial – which was to say, illegal – appearance in East Berlin. Much of the necessary equipment had been sorted in the East. The guitars were in the boot of Buttle's car – along with copies of the *Staubsauger*, wads of black market money and a great quantity of the finest hash biscuits. The concert was taking place at a church in Pankow. Mark, who couldn't cross with Buttle because of the resident's stamp in his passport (Trevor's was in his old passport, I hadn't been in Berlin long enough to bother getting one yet) had taken the normal route over the border and would meet us later outside Pankow U-Bahn station.

We drove up Friedrichstrasse, past the brand new Grand Hotel. Up Unter den Linden, past the guards prancing their ironical goose-step outside the Memorial to Victims of Fascism and Militarism. We crossed over Museum Island

and paused at lights outside the smoked glass Palast Hotel. Roadsigns indicated routes to Prague and Warsaw, the Fernsehturm towered ahead like a giant children's toy. The difference between East and West was more than the new smell in the air, more than the drabber clothes, the Russian-style uniforms, the paler complexions and the dated-looking cars. Here in the centre of town the whole deployment of space was different. In part this was because the area had always been the administrative hub of the city. Avenues were grander here than elsewhere, great institutional buildings had lined them proud and pompous. Many museums and ministries, cathedrals and theatres, stood pristine again after painstaking restoration. But in deciding how to fill the bombed-out gaps, Stalinist planning had lent the old Prussian centre an even more authoritarian air. Alexanderplatz stretched away to clean, modernist horizons on which surviving old buildings – the Red Town Hall, the Marienkirche – looked like museum exhibits plonked down into a void. The concrete hotels, shops and apartment blocks that surrounded it were lifeless and monolithic. Avenues like Grüner Strasse, apparently wide enough to accommodate whole tank battalions, were eerily empty of traffic. We drove on up towards Pankow, through the relatively picturesque district of Prenzlauerberg, bumping along Schönhauser Allee under the elevated train line. The road had been surfaced sometime in the last few decades but in most places had now worn back through to the cobbles below. The car rocked and juddered, Buttle cursing communism and all its works for the effects on his suspension. To either side were poky shops, simply labelled according to the products purveyed. Shoes. Stationery. Ironware.

On a normal day's visit to East Berlin, you never quite escaped what Mark called the 'Escape From Colditz' feeling. In the uneasy silence of an East Berlin bus or train, no one talking to anyone else, you often did feel like some thinly disguised impostor travelling on false papers. It was like spending all day with that irrational surge of guilt you feel on passing a policeman in the street. While in the West I would deliberately cross on red wherever possible, in the

East I felt constrained to wait patiently for green on empty roads.

But this time it was different. Somewhere towards Pankow, we took a wrong turning. Buttle and Trevor argued over a map: there seemed to be only one solution. 'Hold on to your hats,' said Buttle, and I sat back to savour the rush as he steered the wrong way down a one-way street. Buttle leaned on the horn. Trabants and Wartburgs careered out of the way. As we swerved through the on-coming traffic, I burst out laughing as I realised we were exempt. In a car full of drugs and rock and roll equipment, breaking every traffic regulation on the books in the middle of a stern communist capital, we were immune to authority. We zig-zagged out of the one-way street, careered across several lanes of traffic and seemed to hit about five gees as Buttle hauled us round a hair-raisingly tight U-turn. Five minutes later, a cop on a corner spotted our licence plates and ceremoniously stopped all traffic to let us pass. Buttle saluted as we rolled on by.

Our friend Torsten, the younger brother of Kerstin who had moved West, lived near Pankow Town Hall in a ramshackle version of the street I inhabited back West – a mixture of old and new tenement buildings, restored and original façades. The hall was tatty, the yard overgrown. He and his wife Tina had a comfortable flat in the back house, the door marked with a sticker advertising Trevor's magazine. Torsten sent the occasional article or cartoon West and distributed copies informally through friends in the East. We lugged a bundle of the new issue up the stairs and brought back down a box full of Eastern bits and pieces. Torsten came with us as we scouted various restaurants, looking to book a table for thirty or so. Trevor, nominally respectable in a shirt and tie, went into each place accompanied by Buttle in his Class B uniform. When we finally found room enough at the Haus Budapest on Karl Marx Allee, they were expecting a party of respectable folk.

Torsten sat with me in the back. He had a kind of washed-out look: hair bleached light, pale skin that had obviously never seen strong sunshine, pale blue eyes that gave little away but seemed to take everything in. Like most young East Germans I got to know, he was always very quiet. This was not a society that rewarded the loudmouth. Generally he radiated an almost preternatural cool but on rare occasions, among company he trusted, this could suddenly fall away to reveal a spitting resentment of the DDR and the life to which, at the age of twenty-one, it seemed to have confined him.

Since the age of fourteen it had been his intention to get out. He and a football friend used to fantasise about playing for VFB Stuttgart. It wasn't that they were especial fans of that team, or even that they knew very much about Stuttgart the town, but on the map it looked like a reasonable destination: near the Black Forest, far enough south to be a bit warmer than chilly Berlin. They pored over maps a lot in these years. Would the Hungary–Austria border be the best one to go over? Maybe they should try escaping from Bulgaria to Greece. Wherever it might be, they resolved to cross the Curtain by the age of eighteen.

They kept the idea to themselves, of course. 'At school,' Torsten remembered, 'you could never just open your mouth and say what you were thinking. Everybody knew what was going on but no one would speak about it. School was so much politics, even though by the 1980s no one in the DDR still believed in socialism. You learnt so much about fascism and you looked around and saw everything was just the same.'

Instead of the Hitler Youth, the DDR had the Free German Youth – the *Freie Deutsche Jugend* or FDJ – enthusiastically present at every official function, chanting slogans and waving banners, wearing their royal blue shirts. Up until his early teens Torsten had been a keen member of these Stalinist boy scouts. You were encouraged to join, a lot of your political education came this way, active membership was a good first step on the ladder of political conformity. Having been a star member, Torsten was up for a place on the step beyond that: entry into one of the *Erweitere Oberschulen* – 'extended schools' – providing special education for political high-flyers. But by that time he no longer wanted any part of the FDJ and carefully pondered how to get out without jeopardising his school place. He solved the problem by starting a photographic club. This still counted for political brownie points, and he could develop his snapshots for free. A new boy at the extended school, he sneaked a look in the class register. Apart from names and marks, this also recorded parents' occupations. Torsten was staggered to see that practically every one of his fellow pupils had a father listed as working in the MDI – nominally the Interior Ministry but also the usual euphemism for the Ministry for State Security. He was surrounded by the children of secret policemen, and had even less idea than usual just who he could trust.

Round about this time, he went to his first punk concert. This was an earlier Toten Hosen show, organised by Mark and Torsten's sister Kerstin at a church in Rummelsberg. The event was small but exciting enough to lend Torsten a new sense of identity. He cut and coloured his hair, dug around for clothes that could be adapted for a punk look, starting hanging around with others who chose to do the same.

In the West punk had long degenerated into an essentially conservative series of motions to go through: you occupied these social spaces, wore those trousers, listened to this music. It was less a bold stance than a set of lifestyle options and attracted the attention of the authorities only if you chose to challenge them directly, by hurling a brick at a policeman or something. Otherwise, though it might prove difficult to find gainful employment with a fluorescent pink mohican and ten rings in your nose, you were pretty much left alone. In the East, it was harder. The social spaces were tightly controlled, the music available only on Western radio and the production of bondage trousers unlikely to be contemplated by any bureaucrat working on the next five-year plan for clothing. As a stance it was harder still. Just to cut and colour your hair implied insult to a system in which power was maintained by insisting that you go through the motions.

For Torsten, trouble came quickly. He and his friends were controlled on the street by Vopos, the people's police, their pockets emptied, their identities checked and recorded. A few days later a cop was knocking on his door. What had he been doing with these people? Relax, have a cigarette, tell us all about it. As a token of resistance, Torsten wouldn't let him in the flat. Instead they sat talking on the stairs. After an hour of carefully modulated, ever-so-friendly conversation, the cop suddenly produced a declaration for Torsten to sign. It denounced his friends, said he wouldn't ever see them again. Torsten refused to touch it. Soon he was being invited to pop down to the police station with his mother. She said she couldn't see her son had done anything wrong. The declaration remained unsigned. Next Torsten was summoned before the director of his extended school. A hard-line political careerist, she scanned the report on her desk. Well, what *had* he been doing with these people? Torsten thought fast. His punk look was recognisable to fellow travellers but vague enough for what the CIA call 'plausible deniability'. He hadn't actually been with them, he said. He'd just been walking down the same street and, before he knew what was happening, why, there he was being controlled with all these punks.

She believed him. And that, for the time being, was that — except that by the tender age of sixteen Torsten had already learnt how to dissemble in all public situations, scheme to outwit the authorities, think on his feet, dodge through the loopholes, handle low-level interrogations and lie his way out of trouble. More than anything on the extended school curriculum, this was a suitable education for life on the margins of the DDR.

He left school at eighteen and considered his options. The first thing to deal with was national service. It was possible, though frowned upon, to declare yourself a paci-fist and serve as a 'working soldier' without bearing arms. They'd bundle you off to dig ditches or something. He should have done this while still at school but older friends advised him that such a show of political faint-heartedness was followed, sure as night follows day, by a sharp down-grading of academic results. Torsten was still thinking about getting out. Who'd read between those particular lines once he was in the West? They'd just think he was stupid. But now, his qualifications secure, he made the declaration. He was called in to see an officer who spoke of terrible experiences in a British internment camp after the war, impressed on him the grave importance of bearing arms for socialism. Torsten was more impressed by the news that he wouldn't be called up until the age of twenty-six. He felt sure he'd be long gone by then.

Next came finding a job, it being illegal to be unemployed in the DDR. They offered him a start in a television factory – shifts on a conveyor belt, evening classes to become a radio technician, excellent opportunities for socialist career advancement. This sounded too much like hard work so Torsten applied to become a bus driver. A driving licence, he'd decided, would be useful in the West, but through normal channels it took years to get one. This way he'd jump the queue and be paid for it too. After two years on the buses he switched to a job driving a hospital van. It wasn't just the change from shiftwork. East Berlin had a severe shortage of bus drivers. If he stayed in that job the authorities might be less inclined to lose him.

By now Torsten had officially applied to emigrate. Plans to steal over the Hungarian border had been put to one side, partly because he had met and married Tina, partly because his sister Kerstin had met and married a Swede. She was waiting for permission to join him in Stockholm and if her brother did a runner then they'd never let her go. Torsten was sick of waiting. He'd planned to move Westwards with his life still in front of him; now he felt time was running out. Kerstin was finally allowed out. A new law scheduled for 1987 promised to make the process of emigration even more difficult. So, on 31 December 1986, Torsten and Tina took a deep breath, delivered their deposition to Pankow Town Hall, and carefully crossed their fingers.

They knew it could take years, if indeed it ever happened. In the meantime: no privileges, no perks, no socialist career advancement, no new flat. At worst they could expect a prison sentence; at best a host of bureaucratic obstructions on every level of daily life. A few months later they were summoned for an interview. It was all very

75

friendly. Why on earth did they want to leave the DDR? Oh, they had nothing against the place, just fancied trying their luck in a different country. Well, they were sorry to inform them that there was no law that said they could do that. Unfortunately it just wasn't possible to be a citizen of the German Democratic Republic and run off to live somewhere else. Oh yes it was, said Torsten, struggling to keep things non-political, his sister was still an East German citizen and she was now living in Stockholm. Oh no it wasn't, said the bureaucrats, and they were afraid that was all there was to it.

Later Torsten and Tina tried to renounce their citizenship. They were told that wasn't possible either. Letter followed letter, interview followed interview, some of them friendly, some of them not. When they stopped getting any replies at all, they started going to the office without appointments. Each time they were kept waiting for hours before being given a brush-off. Eventually they were forbidden to come back again, threatened with prison if they ever so much as darkened the doorstep of Pankow Town Hall. Their mail began to arrive erratically: no letters for a month, then a dozen on one day. Their flat was subjected to searches they were obviously meant to notice. They'd come back home to find the door not locked properly, a light or two left on, some things in a drawer rearranged.

Torsten had ceased to care. He'd come to conclude that, short of taking a running jump over what the authorities on his side were pleased to call the Anti-Fascist Protection Barrier, a spell in prison was his only route West. Maybe the East would kick him out, maybe Bonn would buy him out. He felt like nothing he did now was going to worsen his situation, so why not get a little reckless? He left copies of the *Staubsauger* lying around the flat where the next searching Stasi would come across them. In 1987, when I was a visiting journalist, he'd allowed me to interview him for a Western magazine, knowing the secret police surveyed them all. Just a week or two ago, aware that Buttle would be driving his boss there that afternoon, he hung around outside the US Ambassador's residence and, in this presumably well-monitored location, engaged his good friend the GI in a chat and gave him a package to pass on to his sister. Buttle had been terrified. What did Torsten think he was doing? Torsten just shrugged. And this day, four years after his sister had helped organise the first illegal Toten Hosen concert, he had helped organise the second one.

Mark was waiting outside a Delikat shop that offered East German 'luxury' goods. In the window were packets of 'Ronhill' cigarettes, bottles of anaemic-looking liquid labelled 'Scotch Whisky' with a picture of a cowboy and a cactus. Torsten slipped off to the church and some last-minute arrangements. The rest of us had time to spare and chose to spend it in a bar up the road. We took over the whole of the back room, quaffing East German beer and oily schnapps. At one table were members of the Toten Hosen, resplendent in the kind of clothes from which they derived their name: lime green nylon trousers with capacious flares, bright orange jackets with tapered waists and lapels wide enough to land a plane on, lurid yellow crimplene shirts with fluttering wing collars – everything cheap and nasty, outdated and in sickening colours.

On a table in the other corner, Trevor, Mark and I were ribbing Buttle about his job as a chaplain's assistant.

'Do you have, like, a camouflage Bible?'

'A ruggedised crucifix?'

'Holy water field rations?'

'Hey – dehydrated holy water.'

'Yeah, just add water and – holy water.'

'I think that's called a blessing.'

'Buttle,' said Trevor, 'do you have to run round chanting every morning, like in *Full Metal Jacket*?'

'Cadences? Sure, we do those every day.'

'Like what?'

'Yeah, do one for us.'

Buttle announced that his favourite was one from the Airborne Infantry and launched loudly into the following refrain:

'Airborne, Airborne Infantry,
All I ever want to be.
All I ever want to see,
Is bodies, bodies, bodies.'

'Hardly suitable for a chaplain's assistant,' I said.

I scribbled notes on a beermat, writing around the edges of a bright red Berliner bear who cheerily hefted a big tray of beers.

'OK Buttle, here's one for you:
Chaplain's, Chaplain's assistant,
Camouflage bible in my hand.
I'm a holy god squad guy,
Look my enemy in the eye.
No matter how much he fights and shrieks,
I still turn the other cheek.'

There was already a crowd in the playground by the church, milling about between swings and sandpit. The punks at the Toten Hosen's *Staubsauger* benefit back West had been rude and unruly, shoving past you and snarling like they'd heard punks were supposed to behave. This Eastern bunch was different. In the absence of any retailers catering to their trade, their outfits had been cobbled together from many sources: things friends or relatives had sent over from the West, items from Eastern shops that had been taken in or dyed black. The punky look achieved was more subdued than that in the West. Leather jackets were less elaborate, hair coloured quiet red or subtle blond instead of violent green or purple. The mood was friendly, almost gentle, tinged with a sharp note of apprehension. Everyone clustered naturally into protective groups. Breath steamed on cold air as people glanced around a little nervously. There was absolutely no guarantee that the police wouldn't arrive any minute and break up the illegal assembly.

The support was an East Berlin group called Die Vision. I'd just shaken hands with their lead singer, Geier, a sharp-featured, beady-eyed youth who'd somewhere got hold of an American baseball cap, when the minister from the church stepped up to the microphone. He was portly and earnest-looking, with a full bushy beard. His announcement was grave: although Die Vision would presently appear, 'because of the ice age that is now covering East Germany' he could not allow the Toten Hosen to perform.

There were one or two weak shouts of protest, trailing

off quickly into sullen silence. Otherwise, scarcely a murmur. An air of resignation settled on the company. You could feel it falling, like the first few flakes of snow that now began to spill from the sky. The concert had an alibi of sorts. It was supposed to be, of all things, a benefit for Romania. The idea had made Mark and me laugh. Although it was heartening that they cared and understood enough – certainly more than most in the West – to extend the limits of their own protest, what the hell could this bunch of irregulars and misfits, on an only slightly longer lead than those terrorised by Ceauşescu, do for the people of Romania? Their impotence was emphasised as, into the silence, the minister began to intone a prayer for that nation. The odd shaved head was bowed, people fidgeted on the fringe of the crowd. Two hundred punks praying in a sandpit, in the last of the April snow. It was a strange congregation.

Die Vision were well-meaning but couldn't play for toffee. The Eastern punks watched loyally but with less than total excitement. One of the few groups they were ordinarily allowed to see, this was really nothing special. Halfway through their set, I got too cold to stand around any longer and went back with Buttle to warm up in the car. The GI intrigued me. At times he seemed a lawless hooligan in uniform, at others a fine, upstanding soldier. Maybe the two weren't that incompatible. He told me that back in North Carolina he'd been stocking produce in a supermarket. Through the army he would now get a chance to study.

'It means a lot of pain and bullshit to get there,' he sighed. 'But I'll get there.'

Up until now he had been a curiosity, but here Buttle suddenly became human to me. Yes, here's another one, just dealing with his own pain and bullshit.

Trevor and Torsten had an idea. How about if the Toten Hosen played, but pretended to be some band from, say, Dresden? Everyone would know who they were but, in the event of trouble, the minister could pretend he had been fooled. The strategy was agreed, word was whispered through the crowd. The atmosphere crackled as bad humours began to lift, surging into a tingling charge of

79

excitement when Toten Hosen duly took the stage. In the elemental spirit of punk – no future perhaps, but at least a party in the present – the crowd began to dance out their rage and resignation. The punks pogoed in the sandpit as more light snow began to swirl. Curious faces appeared on the balconies of nearby blocks of flats.

Toten Hosen were one of the better German groups: their attitude an earthy irreverence, their repertoire a mix of their own songs and old German *Schlager* anthems, their strength that they took nothing too seriously. The high point came when the band put down their instruments and singer Campino led the crowd through an a capella rendition of their song 'Bis zum bitteren Ende'. Gentle at the beginning, soaring into a rousingly sentimental chorus, the song seemed to unite all present in one touching, bittersweet moment.

Later, at the appointed hour, we all converged upon the Haus Budapest: the two bands, their friends, organisers from both sides and their friends too. It was a smart place, full of guzzling party functionaries. The whole day would have been worth it for their expressions alone when thirty Eastern punks and Western weirdos hove into view and took their places at the biggest, longest, most centrally-situated table in the room. Some sputtered out their Hawaii Toast, others frowned in deep distress. Their digestion was not improved by the crowd of Toten Hosen fans who, despite all efforts to throw them off, had kept on our tail and now gathered outside. They sang and they chanted, and then abruptly scattered into the night just before the police arrived.

I'd been drinking and eating hash biscuits all day and was now almost too out of it to take anything in. I remember staring at a slimy fried egg that sat on top of boiled potatoes and some warmed-up processed beans and carrots. This was the vegetarian speciality. At one point I stumbled through the disapproving faces of the crowd to take a piss in the toilet. Bright disco lights seemed to pulsate up the water pipe in front of me. As midnight approached, everyone said thank you to everyone else, the huge bill was settled with black market money and the party dispersed as we Westerners prepared to hop back home.

The lights were going out on Karl Marx Allee. Trevor decided to relieve himself against the wall before getting into the car. Some passers-by stopped and voiced objection. Trevor, in three carefully chosen words, not only requested them to leave him alone but further alleged they had an attitude problem dating back to around 1933. The citizens puffed up in righteously redoubled anger. Trevor zipped up and, with his unfailing instinct for pushing a thing too far, serenaded them with excerpts from the Horst Wessel song.

'Get in the car, will you, Trevor?'

Now he was singing the communist Solidarity Song, an anthem of the current regime. '*Vorwärts, und nicht vergessen* . . .' Having called them Nazis, he was now extending this opinion to cover the whole Marxist-Leninist establishment.

'Trevor, will you get into this fucking car?'

It looked like a fight, or maybe some kind of citizens' arrest, until Buttle – the one member of the party who had stayed sober – stepped between the warring parties, apologised most sincerely for his colleague's lamentable behaviour and cuffed the still singing Trevor into the car. It was almost midnight. We would have to hurry.

'God, Trevor. That was really over the top.'

I didn't know whether to laugh or be disgusted. Hanging round with Trevor, this was a common mixture of emotions.

We raced round the fountain at Strausberger Platz, shot the lights at the intersection with Karl Liebknecht Strasse. Days in East Berlin would always end this way: a dash to the border through a city closing down for the night. Mark was dropped off at Friedrichstrasse, joined the crowd slowly filing in to the checkpoint. Buttle drove the few blocks to Charlie. Getting out with Uncle Sam was as simple as waking from a dream. The East German guards shone flashlights through the windows. Trevor and I held up our passports again. An American MP waved us down at the Allied checkpoint and asked the ritual question:

'Run into any trouble over there?'

'No,' said Buttle, and we were back in the West.

From the dark of East Berlin we emerged blinking into the light. Just as the East seemed strange and unfamiliar when you first stepped over, by the time you passed back through the looking-glass the West had acquired an alien aspect. The colours were now too bright, the cars too smart, the cigarette machines stocked with an unnecessary profusion of brands. Bars and restaurants were still open. There were people on the streets. While East Berlin finally got rid of its guests and shuffled off to bed, West Berlin had a hot cup of coffee or some powder up the nose and prepared to party on all night. It was Saturday. I had a couple of invitations in my pocket. As we waited for Mark in a pizza place near Charlie, I felt myself gaining a second wind.

Trevor and Buttle went straight home but Mark and I carried on for most of the night: dancing to old James Brown records at a party in a disused S-Bahn station, failing miserably to make the right sort of conversation at a classic Charlottenburg bad party full of velvet-jacketed academics from the Max Planck Institute, and finally dancing some more at the Metropol disco until the crowd began to thin. On the corner where our ways diverged, we stopped and shook hands, as much in congratulation as farewell. Few people in the world, we told each other, could have had as much fun as we had that day. The smile on Mark's face lit up brighter than the lights of the taxi rank across the road. For me it was a turning-point: the moment where the mood I'd brought from London began to dissolve and dispel. I walked back home across Winterfeldt-platz as the birds began to sing.

6.
BERLIN GAMES

 re we allowed to go in that place?'
A   It was mid-evening in Andrews Barracks, Dahlem, built in the bad old days as a training camp for cadets in the SS Leibstandarte Adolf Hitler, now the place that maybe a third of West Berlin's American enlisted men called home. Mark and I had come down here with Spud and Salman – two more GIs we had met through Buttle – and been amazed at how easy it proved to get in. The guard on duty seemed half asleep, barely glanced at our papers as he waved us by. Had we been Russian spies or the treacherous beneficiaries of Libyan gold, cultivating military contacts in pursuit of dark designs, we could have been up to absolutely anything. As innocent civilians motivated by nothing more sinister than idle curiosity, we had merely peered around our friends' spartan accommodation. Mark had been much taken by a camouflage bedspread and had opened negotiations for a pair of patent leather US Army shoes. Now I was being drawn by a sign which promised, in dim red neon, 'Annexe Bar'.

'I guess so,' Spud gave a little nervous laugh. 'I'm not sure I'd recommend it, though.'

'I never go in there,' Salman shuddered slightly at the thought. 'Full of cowboys.'

'And German hookers,' Spud added.

'Well,' I said, 'if German hookers can go in then so can we.'

There was a dispute at the door over whether Mark and I would have to pay, how many dollars it might cost. A small gang of cowboys came to check out the commotion. They stood there in ten gallon hats, plaid shirts, jeans and tooled leather boots. Mark and I were subjected to a long, slow look up and down until one of them finally drawled his verdict:

'Probably Brits.'

I confirmed their diagnosis with a nod of mock regret. Got it in one, my dear chaps. I'm afraid we're jolly old 'Brits', don't you know. Satisfied, they swaggered back into the fray.

Inside, it was ugly. We took a table in the middle, drank a beer and chewed on a plate of nachos, microwave-fresh and smothered in cheese with the taste and consistency of molten plastic. At one end of the room was a bar, at the other a country and western disco. All around us on the tables in between went on much jockeying for position between cowboys and German girls. All the men were dressed like the guys at the door. Some had gunbelts and fancy leather holsters containing what were presumably replica pistols. When one of them left the premises with a girl or walked over to the bar, he would imitate, imperfectly, the gait of a man who has spent all day on horseback.

'Just look at them all,' said Mark. 'I had a cowboy outfit like that when I was about seven years old.'

'And of course you've never worn a funny outfit since,' I said.

Over on the dance floor, two dozen cowboys moved in meticulous formation. They'd all throw a hand up in the air, step in one direction, hunker down in unison, pop up again, step back, swivel ninety degrees and then repeat the manoeuvre. At the climax of the evening's entertainment, the DJ span Lee Greenwood's 'Proud To Be An American'. The cowboys ceased dancing, put down bottles of beer, paused in all dealings with German girls. To the last man, they all stood to attention. Hats were removed and clutched to hearts, burning lighters were held aloft.

'Ah'm proud to be n'Merican, cuz at least ah know ah'm free . . . '

One of the cowboys had neglected to remove his hat. Another swiped it from his head. Show some respect, soldier. German girls looked on in admiration as still the lighters were upraised, even as they sputtered burning fuel on horny hands. Salman and Spud hunched in palpable embarrassment. I didn't dare catch Mark's eye in case we burst into giggles and wound up getting stomped.

'Well, what did you think of that place?' Salman asked me as we stepped outside.

'I have to say, it makes me proud not to be an American.'

Salman looked pained. 'It makes me sick to be one.'

Salman wasn't actually sure that he was an American. He'd been born in East Africa and spent much of his childhood in Pakistan before emigrating to California with his mother. His father still lived in Tanzania and for this reason Salman was classed a security risk. Once or twice, getting into arguments around the barracks, he found himself blurting: 'The trouble with you Americans . . . ' It was clear he fitted in really badly. Not many GIs subscribed to *Granta* and the *New York Review of Books* or spent idle hours on field exercises getting through Proust and Dickens. Among NCOs and fellow soldiers, whose concerns embraced nothing more literary than the magazine of the World Wrestling Federation, he was held to be something of a nancy boy. About one hour of his day was spent being the medic he had trained to be. The rest of the time he was sweeping floors or cleaning toilets. If there was ever any dumb extra detail to be done then the sergeant would inevitably pick Salman for the job.

He had enlisted in a fit of madness. Literally so, it seemed. There had been an affair with an older woman which involved six months of motel-hopping up and down the West Coast. A large sum of money, expected daily by his lover as the settlement for some lawsuit, never arrived. They scrounged around for cash, Salman ringing his mother and maintaining the fiction that he was safe in college at Santa Cruz. He left his passport behind in one motel they'd had to exit without paying; soon after that, his lover left him. Salman went to pieces. For a month or two, he odd-jobbed around the States in a daze until one day he woke up to find himself in the middle of US Army basic training at Fort Leonard Wood, Missouri – an institution known to all who passed through its clutches as 'Fort Lost In The Woods'.

There were consolations. He was able to travel on an Army ID card and eventually wangle a new passport. Like Buttle, he would also get money to study. He knew Berlin was a prime posting and did his best to make the most of it. But though Salman's morale was never high, though he was as comfortable in the US Army as a siamese cat among a pack of pit bull terriers, in one respect he was typical.

It was the fashion among American soldiers to develop a broad and bulky musculature that distinguished them immediately from the more wiry British or sadly skinny Russians. While uniforms seemed to hang off the scrawny Soviets who guarded their memorial on the Strasse Des 17 Juni, GIs wore their shirts just a little too small, muscles straining at the buttons as they showed off their 'definition'. Because his bookish ways meant everyone expected him to be a wimp and a fuck-up, Salman too had spent long hours in the gym and his muscles bulged with the best of them.

Spud was the same, but for different reasons. He pumped iron and swallowed steroids because, he said, 'it makes me feel like a man'. This was obviously something he had trouble with. For the last six years every ounce of his sexual energy had been focused on an unreceptive girl next door in his home town of Battlecreek, Michigan. She even came out to live in Berlin for a while, but continued to deflect his advances. It drove Spud to distraction. Why did she come to Berlin if she wasn't interested? Why was she tormenting him so? He redoubled his regimen in the gym and took up writing bad poetry.

One obsession followed another. First it was Hemingway. This led on to bullfighting. Spud, who had never seen a bullfight in his life, would unfold tiresome and entirely unoriginal theories on the refinements of this activity.

After failing to get leave in time to visit the bull run at
Pamplona, he picked up a copy of Camus' *The Rebel* and
spent the subsequent weeks instructing all he encountered:
'You gotta commit existential soo-ee-cide.' His next fixation
was *Apocalypse Now*. Spud taped the soundtrack from the
video and played it over and over in the car, memorising all
the dialogue. He bought a Doors CD and then, on learning
the origin of their name, a copy of Huxley's *Doors of
Perception*. 'You gotta open the doors, man,' became his new
catch-phrase and he started eating huge quantities of acid.
Salman sometimes joined him. It was the only recreational
drug that wouldn't show up if Uncle Sam tested their urine.

Spud was like a cartoon character: always too loud, too
insistent, trumpeting the results of his latest enthusiasm,
larger than life and twice as tiring. Although a good-
hearted guy – he often turned up bashful at my door to
drop off some small gift: a jar of Marmite from the NAAFI,
some chocolate chip cookies from the PX, a carton of duty-
free Luckies – he barged through most situations with all
the sensitivity of a rampaging rhino. One time I heard him
comfort a jilted lover, trembling on the edge of tears, with
the words: 'Hey, cheer up. You should feel glad you
weren't born in a communist country.'

Though he considered himself something of a rebel and
was far from being typical cannon fodder, Spud was in
most respects a loyal soldier. He'd joined the army and
chanted 'bodies, bodies, bodies' through eight weeks of
Airborne training because he'd been attracted to the activity of jumping out of aeroplanes – the better, perhaps, to
demonstrate his manhood to the girl next door. Instead he
ended up an NCO in Intelligence, pushing papers around
a desk and occasionally 'showing the flag' by driving a
vehicle around East Berlin. He would park near a railway
line in Karlshorst and count all the trains that went by.

The GIs were encouraged to go East in their off-duty
hours. They were forbidden to fraternise with the locals,
shouldn't make themselves too conspicuous and must
remember that at all times they were ambassadors for their
country. But on the other hand, with East marks easily
purchased at the bank in Truman Plaza, they could do their

Christmas shopping on the cheap, and eat out for a fraction of what it might cost in the West. For individual soldiers, it was a simple perk of the posting. For the military, it bolstered routine assertions of precious rights of access under the Four Power agreements. And if East Germans and Soviets seeing well-fed Western soldiers freely crossing the border and spending loads of cash was also a subtly destabilising piece of propaganda, then this too was fine as far as the Western Allies were concerned.

It was a godsend not just for Mark, Trevor and me, but also for our friends in the East. After the exploratory foray for the Toten Hosen concert, there were no holds barred. We could take over anything we wanted. We could bring almost anything back. Just about the only item we couldn't whisk across the border – the MP at Charlie would sometimes open the boot of the car just to make sure one wasn't crouching in there – was an emigrating East German citizen.

This had opened up a whole new set of possibilities. First and foremost there was shopping. Even without wads of black market money to spend, shops throughout the East were fascinating. Forget the treasures of antiquity in the Pergamon Museum – the bas-reliefs of the ancient Pergamon Altar, the glazed blue splendour of the Babylonian Ishtar Gate. These were much less absorbing than the contents of the Centrum department store on Alexanderplatz. The intricacies of the East German economy filled every nook and cranny of its 15,000 square metre shopping area with items strange and wondrous to behold. Which concatenation of planning committees, for example, ever decided that among the priorities of industry in a socialist state of workers and farmers should be small foam rubber flowers, affixed to a loop of knicker elastic, which looped round the spout of your teapot to catch the drips? Which Five Year Plan had organised the production, distribution and exchange of orange plastic travelling egg kits: handy moulded boxes that clipped together and contained a mini-cruet set, a pair of small spoons and dual indentations for the transport of two nourishing hard-boiled eggs? Pricing was also unfathomable. While in the profit-motivated West things either came in round numbers, or else a sucker figure hovering just below one – 19 marks and 95 pfennigs – in the centrally planned East everything was priced with a bureaucratic pedantry. Tags of 1 mark and 65 pfennigs, 3 marks and 35 pfennigs, 10 marks and 10 pfennigs – fixed prices always printed on the packaging or the item itself – reflected economic considerations that were boggling to construe. Or else they were a simple con trick: figures plucked from the air that simply looked like the results of painstaking calculation.

To the strains of unlikely socialist muzak – 'The Internationale' and other communist favourites interpreted in the manner of James Last and his Orchestra – we would amuse ourselves exploring Centrum's many departments. Each began with a queue. It was forbidden to look around without the regulation wire or plastic basket in hand – assistants shooed you back out if you dared enter a department without one. These baskets were typically in short supply. So first you stood in line, waiting for a departing shopper to leave theirs behind.

The household department was always an absorbing place to begin. Clutching your first basket of the day, you could mull over the merits of strange tongs and spare bottle tops; capacious bins of rubber rings to seal jars they had long run out of; cheap alloy pans that probably poisoned any water boiled in them; cutlery so light it might float; a profusion of egg-piercers; kidney-shaped lunch boxes in a hammered metal finish; meat tenderisers in three sizes; collapsible cups that always collapsed when full; foam rubber off-cuts in every shape, size and colour but with no clearly discernible use. Brightly moulded plastic was the 'in' material. From it were crafted blue and yellow egg cups in the shape of happy chickens; pink or green thermometers in the shape of fish; endless variations on the cruet theme; plant holders in a brown macramé style; socialist tupperware containers; bumper packs of grey 'universal clips'; rotating biscuit moulds that saved labour by pressing out shapes in the manner of a miniature garden roller.

The order of items often reflected patterns of production rather than consumption. The stationery department stocked everything to do with paper. Coffee filters co-habited with yellowing and over-absorbent writing pads. Scratchy toilet rolls rubbed against paper red flags. Sturdy pieces of cardboard bearing the emblems of FDJ and SED were stacked up next to old black and white postcards of kittens, flowers and the interior of the Palast der Republik. The inevitable cheap plastic surfaced as flimsy portfolios with implausible binding mechanisms and identity card holders that were always in stock.

The souvenir stall opposite the entrance was of course packed with curiosities. Tassled needle and thread containers, the lid a tawdry thimble, bore views of the Brandenburg Gate and the legend *'Berlin – Haupstadt der DDR'*. There were many keepsakes of the Fernsehturm, that great socialist landmark and supposed source of civic pride, whose outline formed the 'i' in 'Berlin' on all Eastern tourist information. Its image was stamped on key-rings and wallets, pictured on postcards from every conceivable angle. Colourful arrays of cocktail sticks, dangly silver plastic brooches, bottle openers that were hard to grip and sets of children's wooden blocks were all formed to resemble its ball-and-spike shape.

Upstairs in hardware were piled heaps of obscure spare parts that could never have added up to any whole: odd configurations of piping, supplementary cupboard doors. You could embellish your bathroom with a variety of plastic objects: translucent brown toilet seats, magnetic soap holders in a streamline design, toothbrushes whose gum-lacerating bristles were part of a single moulded plastic body. For the DIY or wine enthusiast, there were screwdrivers that would bend and twist, corkscrews that unwound.

The clothes department was a rustle of artificial fabrics, a wash of insipid hues. Bargain bins brimmed over with lurid plastic 'fashion hats', every last one of them in size 62. There was an extensive range of anoraks in beige and grey-blue, sheeny ties, nylon shirts and fluffy fake fur headgear. Among the toys were poorly moulded plastic soldiers that always fell over; inaccurate models of T-34 tanks and Skoda cars remotely controlled at the end of low-tech lengths of wire; ten-piece jigsaws featuring scenes from life in the Nationalvolksarmee; big furry bananas with smiley faces.

A small computer department stocked primitive but expensive 'Robotron' machines, heavy in weight and light in memory, along with antiquated software and BASIC programming manuals. On the very top floor was the clock department, sparsely stocked with brown plastic pocket watches; elaborately ugly fake wood cuckoo clocks; outrageously priced single function digital watches; industrial-size alarm clocks whose tick alone could wake the dead; exorbitant 'luxury' gents' watches in a Rolex style whose metal finish reacted with sweat and made your wrist go green.

There was a word for all this stuff, a word for all these poorly made and oddly designed things. It was a simple word, a pithy word, a word that summed every last plastic cruet set and spare bathroom cupboard door.

The word was crap.

We loved crap. We gorged on it. We became connoisseurs. There was something unfailingly funny about being so poor in the West, yet, through several quirks of geo-political circumstance, having so much money to spend in the East, and then there being so little to spend it on save official portraits of Erich Honecker and cardboard dice beakers glued round with poorly registered scenes of old Berlin. After a week of pain and bullshit in West Berlin, we all found it exhilarating to sift through this pitiful rubbish, contemplate its absurdities, and now and then, with a smile and a thrill of victory, actually turn up something that we wanted to buy.

We gorged on the cheap souvenirs, the official portraits, the Day of the National People's Army greetings cards. We went for brand names: cigars called Sprachlos – speechless – presumably because one draw could render you so; Victory Cigarettes, for the authentic Orwellian smoke; aftershave called Shudder. One day we all decided to buy toasters and stepped into an electrical goods shop off the Frankfurter Allee. The pop-up variety was of course out of stock but they did have two other models. Mark bought one made out of dull, tinny metal, where you slotted the slices into hinged compartments on either side of one central heating mechanism, and then either burnt or nearly electrocuted yourself trying to turn them over. Trevor and I bought the next model up. The bread went into a wire basket that fitted inside between two heating elements. Glass windows enabled you to see when it was ready. Then you lifted the basket back out again with a movable handle that either locked up or folded down out of the way. Although they had the toasters, the shop didn't stock the cables to power them. For those we had to go to a lighting shop several blocks away.

I was proud of my East German toaster and connected it all up when I got home that night. The next morning my neighbour Ellen used it at breakfast. The comforting aroma of toast filled my small flat as she lifted out the perfectly browned slices. Then the handle abruptly unlocked itself, the basket-thing jack-knifed, the toast tumbled back into the innards and promptly caught fire. Ellen flicked through her options and decided to panic. She threw a cup of water over the blaze, the glass shattered, the electrics shorted. Goodbye toaster.

Another time Torsten produced a tantalising object. It was a fake hand grenade – actually a real grenade casing, painted pillar-box red and stuffed with grey rubber. In East German schools you had to throw one a certain distance as part of your sports exam. An ample stock was soon uncovered in the big 'sport and free-time' shop at Frankfurter Tor, a snip at 5 East marks 45 pfennigs apiece. One of our favourite shops was the 'Organizationsladen' on Grünberger Strasse. This stocked all accoutrements for official occasions and routine boy scoutery: blank diplomas and certificates; simulated leather binders and menu holders stamped in gold with the Party device; portraits and busts of Marx, Engels, Lenin and Ernst Thälmann; pointy things to put on top of flagpoles; holders to slot the flagpoles into; flags of fraternal socialist countries, sold both individually and in sets, to be hung out from buildings everywhere on state visits and the appropriate Days of Friendship. Soon my wall back West was decorated with a huge Mongolian flag: bright red and blue with a symbol that combined yin-yang and the communist five-pointed star.

From the Organizationsladen we would usually proceed to the nearby Karl Marx Buchhandlung. Here were maps of the moon and Mars – destinations about as accessible for DDR citizens as most of the other places for which maps were produced – and Romanian guide books called, somewhat threateningly, '*Komm Mit*', and full of lurid adverts for Transylvanian oscilloscopes and vitamin-enriched fish paste. Soon, opposite the Mongolian flag, my wall acquired a giant school relief map of the 'Socialist States of Central Europe'.

Upstairs at the Karl Marx Buchhandlung was a record department. Here Mark spent East marks like he was on trial for the Olympic Classical Record Buying Event. An East German LP cost 15 marks 60 pfennigs, a Russian import 12 marks 10 pfennigs. Mark bought them by the dozen, lugging home huge boxes every time. One day he found a 12-inch single of the Russian national anthem, complete, like a Western pop single, with two different instrumental versions on the b-side. Cassettes were a little more expensive – 20 marks 10 pfennigs for normal tapes, 23 marks 60 pfennigs for East German digital recordings on chrome – but still cheap enough, at about 3 marks in Western cash, to buy unheard and in bulk and then investigate at leisure. For the first time in my life I began working systematically through various composers and had soon built up an extensive collection at a cost of virtually nothing.

Cafés sold ersatz coffee and dry cakes topped with some kind of rubbery fruit jelly substitute or iced in suspiciously gaudy hues. Restaurants offered passable food if you liked great slabs of pork or beef, usually served with some kind of herb butter or heavy sauce, but if you didn't eat meat it was difficult. Very occasionally there was a mushroom soup or omelette. The main course vegetarian plate was always the same thing: a selection of unappetising sterilised peas, diced carrots, cabbage, beetroot and some over-boiled potatoes topped off with a perfectly circular but imperfectly fried egg. Desserts were usually salads of tinned fruit, dressed up with ice cream, liqueurs and glutinous chocolate sauce.

In vain would you try to order alternative fare, restaurants being especially diligent in refusing to prepare any combination that wasn't listed and squarely priced on the menu. We were excited to find any restaurant that offered something different, eagerly comparing notes and exchanging intelligence. Several trips were made to the Ratskeller in Pankow, simply because they offered *Kartoffelpuffer* – a spherical potato croquette – as a side order. We once all trooped miles to a fish restaurant that someone had declared sold the best French fries he had ever tasted in his entire life. The fare was the usual muck. Our informant shamefacedly confessed that perhaps it had not been the chips that were good, but the biscuits he had eaten beforehand.

Hash biscuits were an invaluable aid to our enjoyment of East Berlin. These were simply produced by crumbling a quantity of the finest hashish – softened by a brief spell in the oven, wrapped in silver foil – into your mother's favourite biscuit mix. Roll, press out shapes, bake carefully. The crumbling was the crucial part. Do it ineptly and your regular shapes would produce wildly irregular results. From time to time, especially after being washed down with quantities of East German beer or Bulgarian Cabernet, a rogue biscuit could reduce one to a state of stoned gibbering idiocy. In lighter measure, biscuits would sharpen your sense of humour, intensify curiosity and generally enhance your appreciation of crap. Everything would acquire an illogical air that suited the absurdities of a Stalinist system. It was easier, say, to cope with slow, surly waiters who couldn't get an order right; instead of getting annoyed, you just found the phenomenon interesting – as indeed it was. Sometimes East Berlin was less like Wonderland than a day-trip to Fawlty Towers. No, you can't have seven people on that table for six, even though it only means adding one more chair from the twelve empty tables that we've marked with reserved signs because we can't be bothered to work them. Oh, you ordered the slimy fried egg and sterilised veg special, did you? In that case I'll grudgingly take back this plate of raw steak tartar. Here you are, your vegetarian omelette with bits of ham in it. But what can possibly be your objection? Ham is not meat. Here is the bill. Please notice the 20 per cent surcharge I have added for lining my own pocket, as well as that of the head waiter. I know you will not complain because it's all Monopoly money as far as you're concerned. Many thanks for your visit.

The GIs, wary of piss-tests, left the biscuits alone. But we took over loads when we were with them, leaving bags behind for friends to sample and us to dip into on our next trip East. We'd also leave East marks, and thus have something to spend even when we were over as normal civilians. Anything we purchased on those trips, we'd leave with a friend like Torsten until we returned with the GIs to cart it all Westwards. We had become expert at crap smuggling.

After driving up and down Torsten's street a couple of times, looking for a parking space, we finally pulled up on the pavement opposite his house. Buttle unlocked the boot and we began pulling out boxes, making a lot of noise as we did so.

'Where's the bag with the avocados?'

'Hey, who brought the Herb Alpert & His Tijuana Brass cassette?'

'I did. I've always been a big fan of Herb Alpert.'

I started whistling 'Tijuana Taxi'. Buttle surprised me by joining in. Mark hissed us all quiet. 'Shut up for Christ's sake. We pull up here in broad daylight in an American car and then start making enough noise to interest the whole neighbourhood. Be sensible, will you?'

I looked around. The street was deserted but there were any number of windows from which we could be observed. Coming over in Buttle's car was so easy that you could forget that you were deep in East Berlin. This was Pankow, a district favoured by diplomats and East German officials. Now it sank in how conspicuous we must be.

We carried our load upstairs, silent and quick. As well as smuggling crap out, we were always smuggling it in. For Eastern friends we brought magazines and books, tapes and records, food and drink, cosmetics and toiletries, odd items of clothing, anything that had taken their fancy or we thought they might like. Today was Torsten's birthday and Mark and I had decided to cook a big meal, some kind of food they'd never tasted before. Thai? Greek? Indian? We deliberated long and settled on Mexican. It was easy to prepare in bulk, suitably exotic and offered various 'theme' possibilities. Buttle purchased special necessities at the American PX: taco chips, jalapeno bean dip, sour cream, chilli sauce, José Cuervo tequila and Corona beer. We even managed to find a tape of 'Hot Mexican Hits'.

Mark and I spent all afternoon preparing a vast pot of chilli without carne, rice, tortillas, guacamole and various kinds of dip. The main dish we spiced lightly, in deference to local fears of hot food. One sour cream dip, however, we gradually laced with Encona West Indian Hot Pepper sauce to a point where even we, keen aficionados of the piquant, were barely able to take it. At first deceptively cool on the tongue, it scorched an aftertaste that detonated sweat glands and sent you reeling in search of cold liquid.

'We should call this,' Mark gasped, mangling a couple of Mediterranean languages, 'Salsa Diavola Sorpresa.'

By the time all was ready, there were maybe twenty people gathered to eat it. I taught them a tequila toast and they all joined in and downed the liquid, bemused by the business with salt and lemon. Mark announced the special dip with a proud, chef-like gesture: 'Salsa Diavola . . . Sorpresa!' They cheerfully dunked taco chips, smiled at the first taste and then all roared and screamed as if they had just ingested napalm. Nothing in a bland East German diet had prepared them for this. Torsten and Tina had organised a game to follow the meal in which the first to identify each of a series of taped musical excerpts won a prize. I was by this time drunk and slumped in a chair, but managed to raise my head and slur a few correct answers. I went home with a packet of 'roulade needles', a tin of fish paste and a bottle of 'Skin' aftershave. Torsten, too, had an eye for crap.

A couple of weeks later, Mark and I trooped over with another gang of Westies for the birthday of Geier from Die

Vision. Geier, who had announced he would cook vegetarian, was startled to find we had actually turned up. He showed us around the small flat. On the bathroom wall was a large map of the USA. Reading matter by the toilet included old copies of *Ich und Mein Staubsauger*, *Newsweek*, *American Studies Newsletter* and a town plan of both East and West Berlin. On the balcony outside the living room were stacked about a hundred empty Coca-Cola cans, gradually fading to pink in the daylight. Thinking of my room with its Mongolian flag, schoolroom map of socialist countries, bottle of Skin aftershave sitting on a shelf next to a red dummy hand grenade, I smiled as I recognised its looking-glass image.

In the kitchen were laid out all the ingredients Geier had assembled: spaghetti, some pale kind of cheese, lots of misshapen tomatoes, nothing else.

'What are you going to cook with that?' I asked.

'I, um, well, I'm not really so sure,' admitted Geier.

So I ended up cooking again. Torsten went out and found some onions. In the fridge there was milk in bags; in the cupboard, cooking oil of indeterminate origin in an industrial-looking yellow plastic container. To use either you had to snip a corner with scissors, then place the receptacle in some supporting container. Every Eastern household had a special plastic jug for bags of milk. The trick was to remember to put bag in jug, then cut the corner. If you snipped the bag first, you could never get it in without squirting milk everywhere. There seemed to be no special jug for the oil, so I left it propped upright against a jar of pickled beetroot.

Presently there was a tomato and onion salad in vinaigrette, spaghetti in cheese sauce. Edible, at least. The Westerners wolfed it down, but the Easties sniffed at it with suspicion. Spaghetti in cheese sauce? Who ever heard of such a thing?

'You're so special to them, you know,' Ellen said, a little chidingly, the night after Geier's birthday. She'd been along for both meals, the only times she'd been East in half a decade as a Berliner, and kept herself well in the background. 'You should see the way they look at you, the way they watch these big guys from the West, these special English and American guys. It means so much to them that you go there, to do these things for them.'

I thought about this. It made me feel a little guilty. Recognising the attention, I also had to recognise that I enjoyed it immensely. In the West I had no role at all. In the East I played the local hero. It was fun to be able to give someone a taste of a different life, to participate in their enjoyment as you passed on some small experience they were normally denied. But I realised I was also taking advantage of this captive audience. Cynical man of the world among people who couldn't even visit the other half of a city that was much more theirs than mine, I needed the strength I drew from their ability to cling to a certain innocence. Along with the classical cassettes, it was something I took back home.

They needed us, too. More than mere bearers of small gifts or presenters of eccentric cuisine, we were their only tangible contact with another world – a world that otherwise existed only in aspiration or propaganda. To have friends from the West was the next best thing to going there: it made them feel part of the broader current of civilisation. And that we could be different, more carefree and reckless, in our individual demeanour at a party or restaurant just as in the whole of our crazy Western lives, made some sense of their estrangement from the tight-lipped society they could not leave.

Normally they didn't meet too many from outside. Most West Germans were too busy not noticing the Wall ever to think of actually going over it. Others could tell you stories of contact with Easties that had ended in blackmail attempts by Stasi agents. But there were also Westerners who would come up to Mark or me a little shyly, wonder if they could come over with us sometime, because they didn't know any East Germans, and would maybe like to meet some. At the birthdays of Torsten and Geier, many West Germans were meeting people from the other half of their city for the very first time in their lives. As the contacts multiplied, our little game was getting bigger and bigger.

But the West Germans, who came and went without ever

really getting involved, were strangely incidental to the plot. The key was the unlikely three-cornered relationship between expatriate English, American soldiers and dissident Eastern youth. What we all had in common was that we all viewed the Wall as a challenge to be met. We broke rules and regulations, ran silly risks, partly for the sheer merry hell of it, partly just to keep up human contact in a situation contrived and maintained to limit such contact as much as possible. It was important. They were our friends. And if your friends are in a bad way, then you help them if you can.

There were times in the East when you looked around and wondered just how any landscape could get so grey. A cliché perhaps, but no less true for that. There were grey concrete tower blocks and leaden grey clouds, grey smoke from grey smoke-stacks, cars in any colour you liked as long as it was grey. The greyness seemed to fall from the air, seep up from the ground, work its chilly way into the whole urban fabric. It stifled any stray splash of colour. Against it the sooty orange trams, the peeling paint on residential balconies, the occasional limp red flag, could offer no cheer at all.

Such was the area around the junction of Leninallee and Ho Chi Minh Strasse, where tower blocks lined up against the sky in grim rank and file. The district was called Hohenschönhausen – 'High Beautiful Houses' – an old name transformed by the Five Year Plans of the 1970s into two-thirds truism and one-third rank misnomer. The buildings, their monotony broken here and there by the inevitable smoking chimneys, were certainly high. As one of East Berlin's biggest post-war housing projects, they provided homes for around 50,000 people. But not even proud party officials, itemising the achievements of their social welfare programmes, could ever have considered them beautiful.

One of the tenants of this great, grey ant-heap, housed halfway up one block among many, was our friend Norman. His had been one of the faces in the crowd at Torsten's birthday party – a face with hamster cheeks, pale

99

like all the others. In his early twenties and a graduate of
the same extended school as Torsten, Norman was supposedly studying one day a week at a church. 'It's my alibi,' he
would shrug. It seemed he rarely turned up there and it
was hard to tell exactly how he passed his days. Judging by
the contents of his small room in the flat he shared with his
mother and an aged lodger who rented a camp bed on the
living room floor, he spent much of them collecting rubbish. The room was stuffed with old tools, broken radios,
bits of clothing, scraps of material and lengths of wood he
judged might come in handy somehow. On the desk was
evidence of a little private enterprise: assorted paints and
cardboard stencils Norman had used to make smudgy
Coca-Cola t-shirts. Between casual trade in this sort of
stuff, odd jobs and presumably some help from his mother,
Norman managed to keep a bit of money in his pocket as he
mooned around town and wondered how to dodge the
draft.

There was gathered about Norman a cloak of awkward-
ness and uncertainty that made him hard to get to know.
He had sad, anxious eyes and a fringe he would toss back
nervously whenever it fell down over them. In groups he
was uneasy, dithering self-consciously around the edges of
a conversation, speaking only either when spoken to, or
when he could insert an aside to a single individual. His
voice was so quiet you had to lean close. Mark was always
looking up from a parley with him to call out: 'Hey, listen to
what Norman just told me.'

We saw a lot of Norman in the months following Torsten's birthday. The main reason was that his mother had a
telephone. To get a phone in East Berlin you practically
had to put your name down at birth. Torsten didn't have
one, so you had to wait until he rang you. Norman we could
call up any time, suggest a meeting the next day. We usually
met in the same place: a gay café off the Schönhauser Allee,
where the underground line to Pankow clattered up into
the open air. Intriguing in itself − gay venues of any sort
were rare in East Berlin − it was also an excellent meeting
place. The café was comfortable and quiet, served a passable cup of coffee and, as an all-day rendezvous for an

assortment of single young men, it served to make our meetings with Norman more discreet.

Norman also liked the café because, as he shyly admitted one lunchtime, he was attracted to one of the waitresses. A tall, supremely self-possessed black woman, she came back and forth to our table without ever giving us a second glance. It was clear Norman's seduction kit was inadequately equipped. He could offer none of the more obvious inducements, being poor and without a car, his wardrobe stretching no further than the standard issue East German marbled denims (brand-name 'Golden Rifles') he wore all the time. Above all he hadn't the slightest idea how to strike up a flirtation. We egged him on, of course, and Norman would shift about in embarrassment whenever we dwelled upon the subject. Mark made him a cassette he could give to her, pretending he'd recorded it himself. This giving of cassettes was a standard part of Mark's seduction routine, but it didn't work for Norman. After weeks of nail-biting deliberation, he finally plucked up the courage to go and present the gift. It was her day off. Norman never dared to go back.

'But I like the cassette,' he muttered. 'I wanted to keep it myself.'

'Norman,' I told him, 'you're hopeless.'

In the plainest of senses, hopeless – without hope – was exactly how Norman appeared. This was another reason we saw a lot of him. Norman had none of Torsten's resolution, was bereft of schemes or contingency plans. He paced his cage, wishfully thinking of going West and, well, studying something probably, he wasn't really sure, without ever making the smallest effort to get out. This hopelessness attracted Mark, who was one of those people who always needs someone to look after, lost souls to take under his wing. I – on arriving from London – had been one such soul. Mark had spent the summer doing anything he could think of to coax me out of my dark mood, his method a barrage of small, straightforward kindnesses that added up to a lot of heartfelt support. Norman was clearly a suitable case for treatment and Mark was always worrying about him.

As another kind of exile, Norman stirred my sympathies too. On a walk around the Müggelsee one Sunday afternoon, he argued with me about Brecht ('Nobody could like him if they heard how they talked about him here') and asked what I thought of Thomas Mann. We ended up discussing Mann's old argument about the German *Innerlichkeit* – literally, 'inwardness' – the tendency of classic German culture to suppose a separation between inner, spiritual freedom and outer, political freedom. Here, argued Mann in 1945, was some clue as to how concentration camp commandants could listen to Bach while bundling people off to the gas chambers. The shadow of this separation fell on East Germany too, as people lived outwardly conformist lives, did what was required of them at work, hung out the right flags on all official occasions, and sought their true selves in art or sport or the private universe of family life. Unable to emigrate in the ordinary sense, neither was Norman capable of such 'inner emigration'. The small stands he made – not working, not eating meat, spending what time he did at the Christian library pursuing an interest, as far as it was possible, in the religions of the Far East – simply left him all the more dislocated. East Berlin was no place for an unemployed, vegetarian Buddhist.

Fellow non-meat eaters, Mark and I took him the occasional slab of tofu, head of broccoli or jar of peanut butter. We looked at the drab foodstuffs in the Eastern supermarkets, the small selection of deformed and anaemic vegetables on offer, and suggested some recipes he might try. I asked around among friends involved in the esoteric, hunted him out a couple of suitable books on Buddhism. Mark sized him up with a tape measure one day, then brought him over a grey Luftwaffe jacket like his, which Norman had always admired. In small things like these, we did what we could to smooth his way.

He in turn gradually began to appreciate both our sense of humour and our sense of crap. He'd dig around for us, come up with odd items he knew we'd find funny. His little room at home began to fill up with bits of Russian and East German uniform, old maps and atlases, communist badges and an assortment of dodgy memorabilia. For Mark he made a cassette of 'Golden Easties' – a selection of dreadful socialist anthems, sung with solemnity by choirs of soldiers and secret police and painstakingly compiled after many trips to the record library. Me he presented with a green *Volkspolizei* pennant, the device of the Vopos on one side ('For the protection of the might of workers and farmers'), on the other several sketches depicting life in the force: happy people's policemen buzzing round in little cars, boats and helicopters, against the usual iconographic back-drop of factories and combine harvesters.

'Yes,' I told him, holding it appreciatively to the light. 'That is indeed the sort of thing we crap smugglers are after.'

Norman liked that phrase. 'The crap smugglers.'

For some stuff we would pay him. Mark was always willing to fork out for a Soviet infantry cape or East German tank driver's helmet. Seeing a chance both to please his friends and supplement his income, Norman began to range further afield. He took to hanging around corners in Karlhorst, asking Russian soldiers if they had anything to sell. Unofficial commerce with the Soviets was nothing unusual. It was notoriously well-known that East German farmers would pay impoverished conscripts a pittance for help bringing in the harvest, or could purchase army petrol on the sly. Soon Norman was coming up with beautiful enamelled badges and elaborate Soviet military insignia.

In a Prenzlauerberg shop we found a coffee table edition of *Military Decorations of the USSR*. It was filled with glossy colour prints of everything from badges worn by the low-liest foot soldier up to the medals that encrusted Soviet generals like shiny barnacles. We pored over this volume, admiring the tinny images of tanks and submarines, bombs and parachutes, quaintly fashioned and picked out in rich dark reds, blues and golds. This was where Eastern design excelled.

'It's great,' said Mark. 'We can pick out the ones we want and get Norman to, like, order them for us.'

'Yeah,' I said. 'We've got the catalogue.'

Norman shook his head and smiled: 'The crap smugglers.'

There came a day at the gay café, as I watched a pair of ragged winos out of the window, surprised to see them and wondering what life could be like for a tramp in the East, when Mark jerked me back into the conversation with a sharp nudge in the ribs.

'Did you hear what Norman just said? He can get Kalashnikovs!'

The going rate was 600 West marks, with a hundred rounds of ammunition thrown in. It seemed incredible. Kalashnikovs. They were available. We could afford them. We might even have got one of the damn things back over the border in Spud's car. While most West Berliners stepped but rarely into the East, content to leave that side of the city a vast and unexplored blank spot, after a couple of months in Berlin here was I, deep enough into the game to get hold of bargain Kalashnikovs and possessed of the means to smuggle them out.

'You know something, Mark,' I was filled with euphoria. 'We have really cracked this town.'

The sights of East Berlin were tightly coralled into the Mitte district. Tourists rarely strayed beyond it. Up and down Unter den Linden they flowed, dutifully taking in those exhibits catalogued by the guide books, once round Alexanderplatz and back to their Western hotels. Normally I was oblivious to their meanderings, but one July morning as I stomped across the Marx-Engels Bridge, a pair of young Americans detached themselves from the crowd to solicit my attention.

'Excuse me, do you speak English?' the male of the species enquired. He spoke slowly, his pronunciation exaggerated: a talking-to-foreigners voice.

'I *am* English.'

'Oh,' he was disappointed. 'Well perhaps you can help us. We'd really like to talk to some local people, but we can't find anyone that speaks English.'

'No one,' said the girl, 'wants to talk to us at all.'

'How have you been looking?'

'Just, you know, stopping people in the street here.'

I was amused. Like many Americans abroad in that slightly dangerous Disneyland they take the rest of the world to be, these two were dressed like children. It was a dull day but both wore baggy shorts, sports socks and running shoes. He was tall and thin, with thick glasses, baseball cap, Nikon hanging over the name of some college on his bright orange t-shirt. She was dumpy and mousy, mouth hanging open, map in hand, with a Charlie Brown shirt and some kind of sun visor. Each carried a knapsack, bulging with all they judged necessary to survive their day out. They couldn't have looked more like naive tourists if a costume company had fitted them for the part.

'Oh, I wouldn't ask people round here. Just about anyone on this street who isn't a tourist is going to be a secret policeman.'

'Re-e-eally?' the girl was worried. 'Secret policeman?'

'Really,' I lowered my voice. 'You have to be careful, you know.'

They looked around anxiously. I'd said it to spook them but it wasn't so far from the truth. Across the vast car park full of little Trabants that was Marx-Engels Platz stood the Palast der Republik. Among the many uninspiring ingredients in this dry sandwich of smoked glass in concrete was the *Volkskammer* – People's Chamber – where undemocratically elected representatives sat a few days each year to rubber stamp Party decisions. Those decisions were made in other buildings on the square: those housing the Central Committee of the SED, the Politbüro, the Council of State and the Foreign Ministry. Stasis were indeed the only East Germans likely to be hanging round street corners in this part of town. In the interests of international understanding, my American friends had probably been tugging the sleeves of secret policemen all morning.

'Listen,' I said. 'The only advice I can give you is to get on a bus or a train, get out of the centre of town, find a bar or a café somewhere, have a beer and see if you can get into a conversation.'

At Alexanderplatz I caught a U-Bahn in the direction of Frankfurter Tor. It was strange to step from a platform full of socialist-realist billboards on to a train that had obviously been freshly imported from the West. Like the border posts, it was green and fake wood veneer, but strong Western shades instead of pale Eastern colours: a deep green, a dark brown. It was exactly the same as trains which ran through my local West Berlin station. If you'd just sort of landed there, it might have been hard immediately to tell which half of the city you were travelling under. Of course there was no advertising but only a schooling in the nuances of fashion told you that the profusion of marbled denim was East Berlin this year rather than the West a year or two before. Other clues would have been the preponderance of moustaches on young men, the jeans usually tucked into short white boots on women. A boy opposite me wore a white 'fashion' sweatshirt – an imitation of an imitation of something French that was only clinched as Eastern by the tell-tale streak of rust running from one of its cheap metal rivets.

In the secondhand department of the Karl Marx Buchhandlung, on one of their two shelves of English-language books, I found that morning a 1940s guide to Calcutta, the city where, in the last decades of British imperialism, my father had been born and my grandfather had died. Norman sneered when I showed it to him later.

'A lot of use that is to people in the DDR.'

We were sitting under trees in the tiny railed-in beer garden of Zur Letzen Instanz – a 450-year-old pub next to a sole surviving chunk of the original Berlin Wall, the medieval one. A waiter in a leather apron pulled beers from a keg as those around us tucked into *Eisbein*, a traditional German dish consisting of half a pig's leg on a plate with a bit of cabbage and potato.

'Well, rest assured that 99.9 per cent of the people in Britain will never go to Calcutta either.'

'But they could travel there if they liked.'

'If they had enough money they could travel there.'

'At least they have the choice.'

'That's the point. They don't really. Here your movements are limited by the political system, there they are limited by your access to money. Sure, you can theoretically choose to save all your cash and blow it on a trip to Calcutta, but it's simply not an option for most people. The furthest most of them get is to package holiday destinations in Spain, which are cheap because loads of people go and scarcely resemble travelling at all because everything is set up for them the way they like it.'

Norman was unimpressed, of course.

'But I can't even go as far as West Berlin.'

He spoke of the other half of his own city as I might speak of Samarkhand. All through Norman's life, West Berlin had seemed a glittering 'miracle city' of barely imaginable possibilities. Just to move a couple of miles in a Westerly direction would for him have been more exciting than a hundred trips to the Costa del Sol for anyone in my home town. From the converse perspective of Mark and I, East Berlin was not as grey as it was painted. This was only partly because a communist capital was as exotic to us as the fantasy island of West Berlin was for Norman. In the back of our minds the comparison was not with West Germany, but with our home towns in the North of England. Manchester's Arndale Centre was uglier than Alexanderplatz and I had seen no East Berlin housing as bad as the post-war slums along Newcastle's Scotswood Road. Statistics, tweaked a little, could even be made to show that East Germany's average standard of living was actually higher than that of the UK. Though we didn't really believe that one, we nevertheless had limited sympathy for anyone who wanted to leave just to get themselves a big Mercedes and a West German lifestyle modelled on American excess.

But, of course, we had left our home towns. It was hardly my place to discourage Norman from emigrating, as I knew that his problems stemmed from trying to live, in his different context, a life not too different from mine. I too would have hated not being able to live where I liked, read what I liked. I too would have dreaded the prospect of three years in the East German army. On the other hand, I was determined not to foster any illusions about how green the grass actually was on our side. The West, Mark and I were always trying to impress upon Norman, was not all it was cracked up to be. Hard currency meant hard work, something for which Norman was obviously ill-suited. Not everyone in the West lived in a Martini advert. Some people even lived in flats as horrible as Mark's, which was described to Norman in such sickening detail that it seemed to make him even more eager to emigrate, just to see this crazy room for himself.

Later we walked over to meet Mark by the World Time Clock in Alexanderplatz. This official meeting place at the heart of the 'new socialist city centre' was a classic of communist design. A cylinder of tarnished aluminium rotated on a column etched with a map of the world and told the times in a selection of cities people of the DDR could never visit. It was topped off by a crazy black and silver atom-thing, evidently an attempt to represent the solar system, though whoever designed it had clearly never heard of the plane of the ecliptic. Over on the other side of the square was an equally unsightly Fountain of International Friendship. These chunks of municipal furniture, plonked down in this draughty pedestrian-only expanse, were meant to make East Berlin feel like a great international capital. Actually they just reinforced the impression of a puffed-up provincial shopping centre.

When Mark arrived we caught a tram up to Weissensee. That night, at the cycling stadium, Bruce Springsteen was playing a concert billed as the opener for an FDJ-organised Nicaragua Solidarity Festival. Big concerts were rare on this side of town and, though none of us were exactly Springsteen fans, we had been looking forward to it. Munching a biscuit on the walk up Rennbahnstrasse, however, we wondered if we were making a mistake. Huge crowds flowed in the opposite direction. Once inside the stadium, we began to understand why. Springsteen was somewhere miles away across a dense, impenetrable crowd of blue: powder-blue marbled denims on its outskirts, the royal blue of massed FDJ shirts in the best places around the stage. The sound was muffled and indistinct, the ground seemed to slope away from the stage in a manner that made it impossible to catch even a glimpse of the performance from anywhere in the neck-craning crowd. Springsteen might as well not have been there. The contrast with the Toten Hosen concert was absolute: a mood notably lacking in any joy or excitement, a muted aggression in the air. Norman's Golden Rifles denims blended into the background but Mark and I were both wearing suits and ties. This provided a focus for people's resentment. Anger flashed at us from eyes in the crowd, every last male member of which seemed to wear a moustache.

'They complain about lack of freedom of choice,' I muttered. 'But when they see someone different, they hate it.'

Mark shuddered. 'Let's get out of here.'

At the edge of the crowd a gang of maybe a dozen men, all in grey-green anoraks with red trimmings, were herding people from a terrace.

'Look,' Norman muttered, barely moving his lips. 'Stasis. You see the jackets. It's like a uniform that's not a uniform, so people know what they are.'

'And if there are so many obvious ones,' I said, 'think how many there must be that aren't so easy to spot.'

Norman nodded impatiently. For him that was just a fact of life. From a side street near the stadium, a lone taxi appeared, its light shining slightly against the gathering dusk. Several groups converged straight upon it, but we clinched the vehicle by addressing the driver in English. He got his fare in West marks when he dropped us off. We walked through the Nikolai Quarter, an old district roughly reconstructed in prefabricated concrete, looking for somewhere to have a drink. Nowhere had room for us. The tables are all full. The tables are all reserved. Standing in the bar is forbidden. On nights like these, East Berlin could seem the most miserable place in Europe.

We ended up in the Palast der Republik, wandering through the vast foyer festooned with thousands of spherical lamps that made it look like a giant lighting shop, past empty cloakrooms with space for thousands of coats. In the basement was a ten-pin bowling alley, its eight lanes always booked up for weeks in advance. There we found three empty stools at the bar. A barman mixed East German-style cocktails: yellow fizzes and pink flips and things with blue curaçao and tinned fruit in them. Screening us off from the bowling lanes were several tall, thick columns of primary-coloured perspex. These made me feel happy somehow and I looked at them a long while before I traced the emotion. They reminded me of an image in a science fiction movie my father had taken me to as a child, an image of giant bubbling test tubes below the surface of the moon.

'Norman,' Mark was saying between sips of sweet pink flip, 'what if you didn't like the West? We're all right, we can go both ways, but remember that unless you left by getting married, you wouldn't be able to come back. It would be difficult to see your family, you would be cut off from everything in your life up to this point. I bet, if you went over and had the chance to come back here, you'd be back in East Berlin again in a matter of months.'

Norman shrugged and toyed with his untouched cocktail. Our discussions of East and West often ended up at this point, and it was clear he was worried Mark might be right. He was always asking us, did we maybe know any girls he could marry? This was his only hope. Please could we look for one? Please? Some family of his in Hamburg would maybe pay her some money. It shouldn't be a German woman. That would be complicated. They'd be unlikely to let him out if he married a West German. Some other nationality was better.

'The best of all would be a black woman,' he'd murmur. 'Then you can claim they're being racist if they don't let you out.'

'Yeah, yeah,' we'd tease. 'We know all about you and black women.'

And Norman would blush and look away.

We tried, how we tried, but he was difficult to match. First there was a Japanese woman, then an American we knew. Either could have used the West German residence permit which was the main thing they'd get from the deal. Norman, however, bungled both encounters. Even more nervy than usual when addressing a member of the female sex, it was as if he had a neon sign flashing the word 'loser' on and off above his head. To any hard-headed seeker after a marriage of convenience, Norman seemed like a bad risk. The clincher was that, to set it up properly as far as the DDR were concerned, they'd have to come over often, fake a romance with this jittery young man. If the worst came to the worst, the women seemed to feel, they could always find themselves a nice, uncomplicated West German boy.

'Good place, this,' I said watching the barman cracking eggs into hammered metal cocktail shakers, holding bottles by the neck and tipping them to pour with little finger extended cheekily outwards. All East German barmen poured this way – they obviously learnt it in barman school – but this one mixed my next brandy fizz with a panache and pride in his work that was unusual in the East.

'I can't understand,' said Norman, 'why you like East Berlin so much.'

It was a hard one to answer. When I was a child, someone told me that if you worked in a sweet factory you could eat all the sweets that you wanted. I thought it must be a brilliant job. But of course, they only let you eat them because they knew you'd soon get tired of them. If it was forbidden, you'd carry on wanting. There was the difference between East and West. On our side we gorged on sweets until we were sick of the sight of them. Nothing mattered. You could travel where you wanted but most people just went to the same few places. You could read what you wanted but most people just chose to read rubbish. You could say what you wanted but couldn't expect anyone to listen or care. In the East the sweets were still forbidden. There was so little happening that it made whatever actually did go on seem precious and special. Even a crap Springsteen concert or a bar in a bowling alley could entertain and amuse. Over here, for Mark and me, the sweets tasted good again, but there was no way I could explain that to Norman.

'I like it because no one wears black leather trousers,' I said, fumbling in my pocket for the last shreds of *Schwarzgeld*. Soon Mark and I would have to break for the border, but there was time for one more brandy fizz.

7.
THE EASTIE BOYS

'We gotta get Norman out,' said Spud. 'We could *do* it.'
The 'do' was underlined with a slap on the steering
wheel. Spud was nothing if not a positive thinker.

'What about Torsten?' asked Salman.

'And that means Tina too,' said Mark.

I sighed. 'All three of them? How the hell are we going to
do that?'

Spud overtook a Lada with Soviet diplomatic plates
and turned the corner into Mühlenstrasse on the Eastern
bank of the Spree. We were just on the other side of the
Oberbaumbrücke checkpoint but the river – like
Kreuzberg beyond it, the Turkish fishermen on the opposite bank and the red and black flags that fluttered from the
roofs of Western anarchist houses – was invisible beyond
a Wall unblemished, on this side, by any spraycanned
expressions of unofficial opinion.

'We could take them uniforms and then they could just
walk through Checkpoint Charlie,' said Spud. Easiest thing
in the world, his tone conveyed.

'You could get complete uniforms for all three of them?'

'I guess so. Sure.'

'It would take a little time,' cautioned Salman.

'And the East Germans just let anyone in a uniform walk
straight through?'

'Sure,' said Salman. 'I've walked through before. They

just let you stroll straight on by.'

'After giving you a good, hard look,' said Mark.

'They must keep some kind of record of how many go over, what rank they are and so forth,' I pointed out. 'Maybe they even take pictures of you all. If they can't control the traffic they can at least keep an eye on it. So say Norman and Torsten walked out as two sergeants, and there'd only been one sergeant going in that day, they'd be fucked.'

'Then we'd just have to plan it,' said Spud. 'Arrange it for a holiday when lots of soldiers are going over. Maybe a Saturday before Christmas or something. Have them come back early enough so there are still plenty over here.'

'If the uniforms we got them were the same rank as ours,' said Salman, 'then we could go over and wait until they've gone through before coming back. If the worst came to the worst, then we'd be the extra ones they'd try to stop.'

'And they'd have to let us go,' said Spud. 'We're obviously not East Germans trying to escape.'

'Yeah, but in the same way they're obviously not Americans,' Mark protested. 'Can you imagine Norman or Torsten in an American uniform? Everything about them's just *wrong*. Their haircuts, their complexion, their build, their posture . . . '

'We could get their hair cut right,' said Spud.

'If Norman got one stern look from a border guard,' I said, 'he'd go straight to pieces.'

'Someone would just have to ask them a question in English. They'd go: "Vot?" and that would be the end of it. Prison. For years.'

'And can you see Tina as a female GI?'

Tina was small and even more shy than Norman. There might have been the vaguest possibility that the boys could learn to simulate a military bearing, carry themselves with something of that self-assurance which comes only after resolute months of square-bashing and unarmed combat training. But Tina? It was impossible to imagine her ever having run around chanting 'bodies, bodies, bodies'.

'Never,' said Mark. 'And what about the dog?' She and Torsten had recently acquired some slavishly affectionate

113

brand of puppy. Torsten viewed the animal with reserve but Tina just loved it to bits. Mark and I had regarded it as a bad sign. Tina was putting down roots, had sort of given up hope.

'It might work,' said Spud, resolutely ignoring all problems. 'We could ask them if they want to try it.'

'What about the next stage?' Mark wanted to know. 'Even if by some miracle they manage to get past the East German guards, they're not going to fool your MPs for one second.'

'And then they're going to get held and questioned about where and how they got their obviously authentic uniforms, and you two are going to have to trust them not to break down and say where they'd got them. Smuggling people out is against all the agreements, right? If the MPs caught you it would be court martial and dishonourable discharge and maybe a couple of years in prison.'

'And goodbye to your college money,' added Mark.

'And probably they would just get handed over to the Russians, who would hand them over to the DDR, who would of course lock them up too.'

'Oh, I don't think they would hand them back,' said Salman doubtfully.

'Do you know that for sure?'

'No.'

We all went silent for a moment. On one side of the road was a sprawling chemical works: dirty towers and chimneys and great, grimy metal tanks. On the other was a railway line paced by a series of ducts which looped up at intervals into the air.

'Maybe we could get Norman in the trunk,' said Spud.

'But the MPs often look in the trunk,' Salman pointed out.

'Not every time.'

'Most times.'

'Maybe 50 per cent of the time,' Spud conceded.

'Great,' I said. 'So then there'd be a fifty–fifty chance of everyone getting into deep, deep shit and achieving absolutely nothing at all except jail sentences all round. Sure we should try and help Norman and Torsten, but our responsibility doesn't extend to messing our own lives up because of it.'

'You could also,' said Mark, 'get them into even worse shit than they're in already.'

The sun peeped out and decided to stick around for a while as we parked on the edge of Köpenick old town and strolled by the river in the gardens of the palace. Two ragged old derelicts were playing chess on a jumbo-sized board that had been painted on the ground. On a bench nearby, we continued our argument.

'But just think if we could *do* it,' Spud thundered with an enthusiasm that made us all motion to quiet him. 'Just think what a great book it would make.'

'Book?'

'Yeah. How we smuggled Norman out of East Berlin. It would make a really great book.' Spud went a little starry-eyed. Book signings. Lecture tours. The admiring surrender of the girl next door.

Before driving out here we had spent all morning in the service of Spud's latest obsession: postage stamps. His father collected them and Spud, sensing a need to butter up the old man, had decided to collect some for him. Quantity was the thing. Spud had no idea about quality. In the West he demanded all the stamps from letters I received, a one-man Blue Peter appeal. In the East he had been dragging us around philately shops full of cheap commemorative sets featuring things rarely found in their country of issue: hot air balloons from Angola, vintage cars from North Korea, fresh vegetables from Poland. That morning I had found an East German stamp commemorating the twenty-fifth anniversary of the 'Anti-Fascist Protection Barrier'. It pictured a pretty blonde girl in FDJ uniform handing flowers to border guards in gratitude for their vigilance against the forces of imperialist aggression. Banned in the West – the Bundespost simply refused to deliver any letters that bore it – the thing clearly also wasn't too popular in the East. A first day cover went for a mere 80 East pfennigs.

But stamps were one thing. Escapes were another.

Spud's motives were as exasperating as his schemes were ridiculous. Last week he'd been talking about firing a signal flare at an East German watchtower. Why? Because he thought it would be funny. Now he was thinking about springing Norman because he wanted to be a hero and sell the film rights. Any last doubts I had that these plans would ever work evaporated clean away in the afternoon sun. I knew that I didn't want to be involved in anything that serious with a blundering Spud on the team. From the look in Mark's eye I could tell he thought the same.

'Listen,' I said, trying to calm everything down. 'We've got to think about this very, very carefully before we say anything to Norman or Torsten. Absolutely the cruellest thing we could do would be to raise their hopes and then tell them it wasn't going to happen.'

Mark nodded slow and serious. 'That's right. Don't mention it when we see them tonight, eh?'

Spud was silent for a long moment, scratched his head and looked at the chess players.

'I'm gonna see if I can play the winner,' he muttered and went off to talk to the old men.

The rest of us walked into the old town to purchase the makings of a picnic. I glanced back to see Spud in uniform, crouched in concentration by the chess board, pitting his wits against an old wino with a woolly hat.

'Look at him,' I said. 'He probably imagines he's up against some dissident grand master. You know, expelled from the state chess organisation for his political unreliability, a broken man but still a demon with a queen swop.'

'At least,' said Salman, 'it'll make him feel like a man.'

Later we met Norman, Torsten and Tina in a Weissensee restaurant called Rebecca's. We'd been meaning to try it for ages. It was a private place, one of a handful in the East, which was supposed to mean the staff tried harder and the food was more nearly edible. It was pretty much the same old story. Despite assurances to the contrary, the tomato soup came with pieces of ham in it although the fried egg special was, in all fairness, a little less slimy than usual.

We had been talking about names for groups. Spud and

Buttle both played in one back West that was three-fifths American GI and two-fifths East German *émigré* – the latter two old friends of Torsten's. The group was called The Nimrods, but they wanted a change. Mark proffered The Stealth Bombers. Salman came up with The Stars And Stripes. I suggested The Crap Smugglers. Spud preferred The Screaming Weasels and was trying to think of ways to be both shocking and original.

'Hey, I could drink a load of beer and stuff and throw up on stage. That would really be something. Imagine, throwing up on stage!'

'Spud,' said Mark, 'I don't know whether you noticed, but about ten years ago there was this thing called punk . . .'

'The name should definitely be something military,' I said. 'Let's face it, the fact that you're mostly GIs is about the only thing you've got going for you. You should, like, paint all your gear in camouflage colours.'

'It's been done,' smiled Mark, who had done it.

'What if Torsten and I had a group,' asked Norman. 'What should we call that?'

'I know,' I was suddenly inspired. 'You should call yourselves The Eastie Boys. Instead of wearing Mercedes or Volkswagen symbols around your necks like all those bands in the West, you could wear the Trabant emblem.'

The chrome insignia of West German motor manufacturers, prised from bonnets and slung round the neck like trophies, had long been part of the hip hop street uniform. That summer it had only been a year since a white group called The Beastie Boys, often thus attired, had turned a mix of heavy metal, rap and relentlessly obnoxious behaviour into a hit with a song called 'Fight For Your Right (To Party)'.

'The Eastie Boys could play "Fight For Your Right" too,' said Mark.

'It makes sense but it's too obvious,' I mused. 'How about "Born In The DDR"?'

'Yeah,' said Mark. 'In the publicity they could claim, in a sarcastic sort of way, that they were inspired by that Bruce Springsteen concert.'

Already the idea was running away with us, but Torsten was smiling uncertainly and Norman looked distinctly unimpressed. The Eastie Boys? Trabant emblems?

'Whoever would be interested in that?' he asked.

'Maybe no one over here,' I told him. 'But in the West, you'd be surprised.'

Norman shook his head. He didn't believe a word of it.

I thought about it all the way home that night: sweeping past the flat blocks on the way to the border, holding my passport up to Spud's car window, waiting while the MP at Charlie opened up a boot in which, had Norman or Torsten been hiding there, they would surely have been discovered. Over the next few days in West Berlin, the idea would not leave me alone. Not only was the name a solid, satisfying pun, it was also the beautiful coincidence of international street style adopting the icons of West German capitalism. Trabant emblems would be an especially good piece of satire. As a concept for a group from the other side, it was perfect. The pity of it was that even though we'd spent the rest of the evening in Rebecca's chewing it over with them, Norman and Torsten still couldn't quite see the joke.

Sitting in my kitchen one afternoon, with some black leather trouser music reverberating from Olga's flat upstairs, I found I could resist the temptation no longer. I picked up the phone, dialled the London number of *The Face* magazine and prepared to do something I had never, ever done before: fashion a story from a complete and utter pack of lies.

'Hi, it's Dave Rimmer . . . Yeah, well I've been out of town. In fact I'm ringing from West Berlin, I've been here for the last few months . . . Well, I've come across one unusual story – this group in East Berlin. They call themselves The Eastie Boys . . .'

The music editor was intrigued, as I knew I would have been if I'd been sitting around in a magazine office with pages to fill. As long as there was a good picture it would make a good story.

'The thing about the photo,' she said, 'is that it's got to be obvious that it's in East Berlin. It can't look like it's been faked in someone's bedroom.'

I promised to find an authentically Eastern-looking location. There was a statue of Lenin, I told her, various other monumental examples of communist iconography. Two minutes later I was ringing Mark. Up to this point I had been considering the thing nothing but a small media prank. Mark, however, on learning what I had just set in motion, immediately raised the stakes.

'We should make the record,' he said.

'And you thought no one would be interested.'

I grinned at Norman and Torsten over a table outside the Opera Café. On the other side of Unter den Linden, tourists were snapping the guards in Russian-style helmets who stood watch outside the Neue Wache. We had worked our way through the idiosyncrasies of the café's system – coffee and lurid cakes at one self-service window, soft drinks and cheap alcohol at another, runny ice cream from a waitress who would serve nothing else – and were now settling down to discuss The Eastie Boys.

'The thing about *The Face*,' I told them, 'is that it's the kind of magazine that other magazines copy. It's fashionable, gets on to new things quickly and editors all over the place read it to see if there's anything they should cover. If we put this story in there, we're bound to get interest from some other magazines. A couple of West German magazines are definitely going to pick up on it, if only because they feel they've been "scooped" by an English magazine.'

'And then,' said Mark, 'we release the record.'

'The best thing,' I continued, 'is that we control it completely. We're not going to use your real names, you're in East Berlin somewhere, so no one can contact you except through us. We can invent any story we like. And even if they suspect it's a load of bullshit they're still going to use it as long as it's funny and interesting.'

Torsten and Norman were bemused. Our little game was turning into a lesson in the corrupt workings of the capitalist media. Things worked very differently in the East. Pop music was something the population wanted, maybe even something that a modern society ought to have – like toasters or television towers – but the power structure neither liked nor trusted it. If they had to have pop music they would keep it trussed up with bureaucratic controls. To release records you had to be accepted as an official group. Several years at music school were necessary just to 'qualify' as a musician. It was possible, if you curried enough favour with the local FDJ, to form a group and get an amateur gig at a youth club somewhere. Geier and Die Vision, for example, had got that far by the summer of 1988 and were angling for a shot at the next step: an audition before a panel of Party and FDJ stalwarts, academics and officially approved music critics, all sitting there sternly with notebooks and spectacles.

Every musician, group or DJ would have to go through this and your entire career would depend on the results. At worst this dry bunch would immediately show you the door and you'd end up manning the production line of the local plastic cruet factory. Scarcely preferable was to get out of music school and be condemned for life to the house band of some awful restaurant, sitting in the corner in a dicky suit playing frilly cover versions of 'Isn't She Lovely' and 'If I Was A Rich Man' on a cheesy electric organ. If you were lucky – if your music caused some old Party hack to tap his feet, if your lyrics were bland, wholesome and innocent of anything that could be construed as political commentary, if you generally corresponded to what members of this Stalinist Juke Box Jury perceived to be suitable for socialist youth – then you would be graded according to one of several official categories.

The grade awarded would determine what kind of venues you could play, how many copies of your single the state record label would press, how much you would get paid. You'd start out as an official amateur or semi-professional. As long as you didn't put a foot wrong – start singing politically suspect lyrics or disporting yourself in an unwholesome manner – subsequent auditions (you had to return for them regularly) might see you ascending to higher grades and thus playing bigger venues, having more records pressed, generally being more 'famous'.

Official pop magazines would write about you because there was no one else to write about; shops would stock your records just as they stocked whatever else the state distribution system sent them.

Success as measured by sales undoubtedly had some small influence on the relevant cultural committees and time-servers at the Ministry of Records. Sometimes, testing out a new group, they'd allow the radio to make and broadcast a tape. Listeners' response to this, if there was any, might be taken into consideration. Further up the ladder, if they pressed up to 10,000 copies of your single and sold only ten, they'd undoubtedly reconsider your status. But otherwise Eastern popular music had little to do with popularity. People would go to concerts and purchase albums simply because they were there. No matter how many records you sold, you would remain on the salary designated for an artist of your category. As a mechanism for the manufacture and maintenance of abject mediocrity, this system was peerless.

The contrast with the strategy outlined by Mark and me fascinated both Norman and Torsten. We spent the rest of that afternoon discussing ideas for their outfits, sketching out roughs of an Eastie Boys logo, deciding on locations for the photographs. Arrangements were made for Mark and me to come and do a styling session, once Norman and Torsten had obtained all the relevant bits and pieces.

It was in a bit of a dream that I pottered about the kitchen a few nights later. I'd had a relaxing smoke and was now slicing tofu, adding lemon juice to the peanut sauce, chopping up vegetables to be gently stewed in coconut gravy. The phone startled me when it rang.

'Hallo?'

'Could I speak to Mr David Rimmer?'

It was a North American voice.

'Speaking.'

'This is Special Agent Davis of the US Military Police Criminal Investigations Department.'

'Come off it, who is this?'

'Special Agent Davis of the –'

'Yeah, yeah. Who is it really?'

I racked my brains. The GIs were big on 'jigs', as they called practical jokes. It couldn't be Buttle; there wasn't the smallest trace of his Southern twang. It didn't sound in the least like Spud. Could it be Salman? His accent was the least distinctive: sort of generically American, like this one was, though nowhere near as cold and chilling.

'This is not a joke, Mr Rimmer. Your name has repeatedly come up in connection with certain, ah, irregularities involving members of the US Forces. We'd like you to come in and talk to us.'

I felt a little rush of fear. My name was on all the forms Spud or Buttle filled out every time we went East together. A background anxiety I had been feeling about our activities now pushed its way to the fore. We had been pushing our luck. What if it was indeed Special Agent Davis? Had they found out about the GIs' contact with East German civilians? Oh God, maybe Spud had been mouthing off about his crazy plans to help Norman escape!

'Why, uh . . . Talk to you about what?'

'Just some routine questions, Mr Rimmer.' He invested the word 'routine' with a particular menace. 'Could you report to me at US Army Headquarters, Building Three, on Clayallee at nine o'clock on Thursday morning?'

'Um, ah, what will happen if I don't come in?'

'We could always send the local police around to see you, but of course we would like to avoid any unpleasantness.'

'Um, well, OK then. Your name is Special Agent Davis?'

'That's correct. Building Three, US Army Headquarters, Clayallee, nine on Thursday. There is a telephone in the entrance to the building. Just pick it up and ask for me.'

I was still in a state of turmoil when Mark turned up an hour later. He watched and listened with a worried eye as I babbled out the story, so jittery I spilled the beansprouts on the floor. He didn't seem to know what to say. Yes, he supposed it could have something to do with Spud's escape plans. He had no idea what the military could do – just about anything, probably. As far as he could see the trouble was . . . and then he laughed.

'I can't keep it up any longer. You look so worried. It was Salman.'

A gush of relief.

'How do you know?'

'Because he tried it on me first.'

'Did he fool you?'

'Sort of. But when he asked if I'd go in to answer some questions I just said no and put the phone down.'

I felt like a fool and a coward for not having done the same. A few minutes later the doorbell rang. I opened it to the two GIs. Salman could tell I had twigged it from the look in my eye.

'Sorry,' he grinned.

'You bastard. I only knew it was you because Mark just told me. What were you going to do if I hadn't sussed it? Just let me stew all night?'

'I don't know. I was just going to play it by ear.'

'And on a night when I was cooking you a meal. You rotten bastard. It was particularly underhand because the main reason I would have gone down there was to try and keep you fuckers out of trouble.'

They both stood there grinning, like a pair of Mormon evangelists.

The Trabant symbol was a little circle with a flattened 'S' shape across the middle. Norman and Torsten liberated a couple from parked cars – a delicate task because, unlike sturdy metal Mercedes emblems, they were brittle plastic and tended to snap instead of coming loose. Buttle brought the things back West. Mark deployed skills honed by a lifetime's model-making to paint them silver, attach a small metal ring to the top and string them on a couple of heavy metal chains. They looked really good but hung a little oddly: the cheap plastic was too light to exert any tension on the chain.

Come the day of the photo session – a day on which all the GIs were off on field exercises somewhere in West Germany – the only problem was how to get them through Friedrichstrasse.

'These are going to be a little hard to explain,' I mused. 'I mean, it's obvious where they've come from and difficult to account for where they're going.'

Mark shrugged. 'We'll just have to wear them under our jackets and, if they still find them, say we bought them at the flea market.'

The camera I had borrowed was easier. I just hung it around my neck as a tourist would and trusted that the half dozen rolls of film in my bag would plausibly fall within the bounds of a day's holiday-snapping. In the event, no guard so much as glanced at us. We emerged from an easy crossing at Friedrichstrasse and caught the tram for Pankow in ebullient spirits. The sun was out, the light was good and an unusual day lay ahead of us.

At Torsten's flat we inspected the preparations. They had designed an Eastie Boys logo which placed the Trabant S-in-a-circle inside a five-pointed communist star. Torsten had drawn this on a little blue cap as well as on the back of a black denim waistcoat jacket. He wore a red *Staubsauger* t-shirt, a present from Trevor, which featured a hammer and vacuum cleaner in a take-off of the Soviet flag. His trousers were held up by a Russian army belt. Norman had obtained a rust-red track suit jacket of the Stasi-sponsored Dynamo sports club. The logo had gone on the back of this too. On the front, along with a Russian badge bearing an enigmatic number 2, he had phonetically rendered a cyrillic version of the group's name. Down one arm were also sewn FDJ, Young Pioneers and Free German Trade Union patches. His t-shirt was a silk-screen 'Trabant Turbo' one he'd found in the little street market outside the Centrum store at Ostbahnhof.

A few final touches were needed. Torsten had a box full of enamelled communist badges that lauded Marx and Lenin, commemorated state occasions and proclaimed membership of various Party organisations. We pinned the brightest and best all down one side of his jacket, the way generals wear their medals. As Torsten had the Eastie Boys hat and a pair of mirror shades, I lent Norman my Def Jam baseball cap and Cutler & Gross sunglasses. Once they were togged up, we stepped back to review the results. It hit just the right note, mocking both Western street style and

Eastern iconography. It was also mostly their own work. They covered the whole mess with big coats, I loaded the first film into the camera and we all left the house to journey to the first of our two locations: the huge statue of Ernst Thälmann, dungareed and clenching a communist fist, that stood in the park named after him.

Turning the corner out of Torsten's street, the first thing we ran into, barely fifty metres from the house, was a whole truckload of uniformed militiamen, hefting Kalashnikovs, spilling out of their vehicle to block the entire pavement. We had to walk right through the middle of them, tensely affecting unconcern. The militiamen just kept on chatting – they appeared to be waiting for something to happen – but gave us a long, slow look up and down.

'Saxons,' muttered Torsten, once we were safely past. 'Really stupid people. They come from the south of the DDR where you can't pick up Western television so they believe everything the Party tells them.'

'But what the fuck are they doing here?'

'I don't know. They must have been specially bussed in for something.'

It was even heavier on the main road. Uniformed police stood at ten yard intervals all along the pavements in both directions. One by one, heads turned as we passed. Suddenly we were aware of how suspicious we looked. Norman and Torsten's coats, far too heavy for the warm afternoon, were buttoned right up to the top and contrasted oddly with the sunglasses they both wore.

'Stasi,' Torsten muttered as we passed a pedestrian, lips barely moving. 'And another one. Look, there's more.'

A crowd of men in leather jackets were occupying all the tables outside a café. Apart from us four, every last man on the street seemed to be some kind of policeman. With a measured stride, looking straight ahead, we proceeded to the station. There we finally worked out just what was going on. The Hungarian president and Party leader, Károly Grósz, was on an official state visit to East Berlin. The day we had chosen for the taking of highly dodgy photographs in two very public places was one in which every last secret policeman in town was out and on the streets.

The area around Ernst Thälmann Park station was well off the route of the official motorcade, but about two hundred metres short of our destination, Norman and Torsten gasped in surprise and frustration and skidded to a halt.

'There's another one,' Norman nodded ahead.

Too far ahead for me even to have noticed him, let alone suss him as a secret policeman, a guy in blazer and grey flannels hovered around by a parked black Tatra – right at the spot where we wanted to take photos. We paused for a quick conference and decided to carry on. If he didn't go away we would continue to the next intersection and catch a tram to our second location. The Stasi was obviously waiting for something, not just watching the street. As we passed him, we saw what. Three guys in suits, Party officials, returned from some mission in the flat blocks beyond the park. The Stasi opened the car door for them and they all drove away. With a sigh of relief – it had begun to seem feasible he might be waiting for us – we doubled back and set to work.

Mark stood lookout. Norman and Torsten removed coats and took up position in front of the statue. I directed them quickly through various poses, cursing the unfamiliar camera's lack of a motor-drive. Stand like this, stand like that. One roll of black and white, one of colour. At one point Mark cried out and we had to pause as some people went by. We stood around the statue, feigning nonchalant conversation, until the coast was clear again. At the next location – the statue of Vladimir Illich at Leninplatz, a busy traffic intersection – we were getting the hang of it and things went even quicker. Towards the end of the last roll, Norman and Torsten started smiling and waving to someone behind me. I turned to see a whole coachload of goggle-eyed tourists at the traffic lights on Leninallee, many of them also snapping the unfamiliar scene, apparently persuaded that they were in the presence of some genuine celebrities. The Eastie Boys were beginning to enjoy themselves.

On the tram back to Torsten's flat, Mark and Norman talked about songs the Eastie Boys might record. Mark suggested 'All Along The Watchtower', Norman thought they should do 'No Milk Today'. I said the video should be like East Side Story. As we neared Pankow station, Norman pointed to a group of leather-jacketed young men, leaning against the wall and chatting outside a pub. In the West this might have indicated a gay bar. Here in the East it was obviously a bunch of Stasis, their job of guarding Grósz's route over for the afternoon, waiting to be collected and returned to HQ. We laughed at them standing there, pleased with our afternoon's work. We had run their damn gauntlet and they hadn't caught us.

That evening we went to an FDJ club somewhere in Lichtenberg. Some bloke in an ersatz cowboy outfit was mangling Johnny Cash's 'Ring Of Fire' in a commando comic German accent. Our numbers had been swelled by Torsten's sister Kerstin and a boy in black leather called Ulli. Five minutes later an official was making Norman and Mark stand up so he could remove the extra chair we'd added to our table and replace it at another where no one was sitting. In the DDR such petty rules were enthusiastically enforced: no, I'm not going to serve you until you take your bag from the floor under the chair and put it in the cloakroom, kissing at the tables is forbidden. There were times I thought that if I lived in the DDR I'd find this relentless pettiness, this urge to regiment even a Friday night teenage disco, more depressing than restrictions on free speech or travel.

After the country singer, the dancing got going. We found two adjacent tables by the dance floor and watched girls dancing round handbags to last year's Western hits. On the DJ console, a sign: 'Discoteque Kontakt' and a cartoon of the male and female halves of an electric plug rushing towards each other with open arms. The sound and lighting effects were poor but the crowd on the dance floor was undeniably pretty.

'Have you got any chocolate in your bag? For the little girls?' jeered Ulli, watching me watching.

An old man all of twenty-eight years, Ulli had a car and

we trooped out to find it in a parking area full of identical, off-white Trabants.

'How can you tell which one's yours?' grinned Mark.

The irony was lost on Ulli. 'From the number, of course.'

Somehow all six of us managed to cram into his tiny vehicle. Legs, arms and torsos all got tangled up and crushed but it seemed an achievement to be proud of.

'I don't believe it,' said Mark. 'Six in a Trabi!'

'Six in a Trabi,' I echoed. It was obviously another Eastie Boys song.

As the overloaded car puffed and strained up Ho Chi Minh Allee, we experimentally chanted a refrain: 'Six in a Trabi, six in a Trabi – No (beat) sleep (beat) till Pankow!'

Our destination was known only by the name of the long, dreary street on which, if you knew what to look for, it could be found: Buschallee. Lurking behind a supermarket and flanked on three sides by the inevitable flat blocks was a long, low building, unmarked and unremarkable. By day it was used as a school dinner hall. By night, from Wednesday through Saturday, it became a gay and lesbian disco. Getting into Buschallee was harder than penetrating the VIP room of the trendiest New York City club. The doormen would always insist the place was full. It was possible to bribe him, but only when his colleague wasn't watching. You'd kick your heels for ages in the gloomy yard outside, waiting for the chance to palm a twenty West-mark note. Patience usually won the day. After half an hour or so someone would unlock the door, lift back the curtain and usher you discreetly in.

The wait was worth it. Buschallee was one of the best discos I ever found anywhere in the Eastern bloc. The bar was a shambles of course. No ice and a long queue. Every permutation of the few things they sold was solemnly listed above the bar – vodka cola, vodka tonic, vodka kirsch, brandy cola, brandy tonic etc – just as English snack bars list every possible combination of eggs, bacon, sausage, beans and chips. But the atmosphere, for East Berlin, was remarkably loose. The mixed crowd looked much the same as such crowds did any place in the world. The dance floor was always full as the DJ, working with two cassette decks, mixed gay disco classics like Sylvester's 'Menergy' or Gloria Gaynor's 'I Am What I Am' with compatible pop from Marc Almond, Pet Shop Boys or Erasure.

On our last visit we'd been impressed by the DJ – the only one I'd ever seen working with cassettes – and this time brought him a present: a pre-release copy of the forth-coming Pet Shop Boys album. We had wound it to the beginning of the new single, 'Domino Dancing', and Mark went over to give it to him. The DJ was suspicious. At first he didn't get the idea – 'What's that? I'm not going to play that. No I don't want it.' – but the penny finally dropped. Here was someone offering him a free cassette of an album that wasn't yet even released in the West. Most DJs, work-ing with turntables, couldn't have used it, but for this guy with his tape decks, it was perfect.

We ended up with the best seats in the house and a free bottle of sweet East German *sekt* and sat back to watch the dancing. The DJ presently picked up his microphone and went into a long, rambling introduction to the Pet Shop Boys tape, announcing a special preview of their fabulous new single. This was in fact, here at this school dinner hall among the flat blocks of a blighted East Berlin suburb, the world dancefloor premiere of a song that would soon be a top-ten hit all over Europe and North America. The DJ pressed the 'play' button, the music began . . .

And within seconds the dance floor had cleared.

October 7 was the thirty-ninth anniversary of the founding of the DDR. Mark and I had been looking forward to it for ages. Also in town was our friend Nick – an English drummer who passed through Berlin from time to time playing with The Gun Club. He was a nervous Northern boy, a chain smoker with a dry sense of humour, and another East Berlin enthusiast. Late on the evening of 6 October, after Nick had finished playing the Loft, the three of us set off for Friedrichstrasse. The plan was to cross the border just after midnight, say we were going to sleep at the Palast Hotel (Nick had enough traveller's cheques to make this plausible) and then spend the night at Norman's. In the morning we would be up early enough to find a good place for the grand anniversary parade.

Friedrichstrasse was always eerie: a point of limbo, not West nor yet quite East, a lone white spot in the dark area of the yin-yang city. On the eve of this sensitive occasion it felt even stranger than usual. There were double the number of guards on duty, hardly anyone trying to cross. Only one lane was open and the handful of people passing through were all in transit: on their way to catch trains to points further East. We knew we were trying it on. As the guy at the visa desk perused our documents, I felt Nick's habitual nervousness feeding me a little contact paranoia. We shot each other anxious glances. The guard took our money, stamped our day visas – a moment of euphoria: it seemed he was letting us through – then picked up a phone and summoned a superior officer.

We were told to wait on a bench in the grim, tiled hall. One by one we were taken off and searched. Mark went first. When he came back I was taken off without us having any time to talk. The guard went through my things slowly and carefully. He asked where I was going, and I told him our story about the Palast Hotel, the truth that we just wanted to watch the parade. He asked how I was going to pay for my hotel room, there being barely enough in my pockets to cover the obligatory currency exchange, and I told him that Nick had all the money. He X-rayed my cigarette packet, placing it in a primitive device and peering through an eye-piece that looked as if it belonged on a World War Two U-boat periscope. A sweatshirt in my bag occasioned especial attention. It was black with a turtle neck. The designer label was affixed to two buttons on the lower left arm, a gimmick of the Italian company. He fingered this with suspicion, examining a logo that resembled a rifle sight, and my heart jumped as I realised it must look to him like a fascist black shirt, complete with some kind of armband.

I whispered this to the others when we were all back on the bench. Nick chuckled softly:

'When I emptied my pockets, I realised my keys were on this ring with a picture of General Franco.'

'A Franco key-ring? What the hell were you doing with that?'

He shrugged. 'I bought it in Spain.'

'Why did you bring it with you?'

'I just never thought about it.'

I shook my head.

'They'll never let us in now. A Franco key-ring and black shirt with an armband and Mark looking like, well, like Mark. We're obviously a bunch of total fascists.'

We were kept sitting there for another hour or so. East Germans in civilian clothing – clearly Stasis, as they seemed immune to border controls – appeared from here and there and walked across the hall. Some of them seemed to be coming back from West Berlin, most I would never normally have spotted as secret police. They looked very ordinary. An officer eventually appeared from a door opposite, our passports in his hand.

'So you are going to stay at the Palast Hotel and watch the parade tomorrow?'

'Yes!' we cried. Another moment of exultation. We were in.

'Your application to enter the DDR has been refused.'

Early next morning, me with a different sweatshirt, Nick without Franco key-ring, we tried our luck at Checkpoint Charlie. Again we were given visas but stopped at the customs desk where the worst of all the officers was on duty. A tense, ugly man with nostrils that flared in anger, he alone was sufficient reason to avoid this checkpoint. He had long hated Mark. Just the look of this funny little Englishman, obviously up to no good, was enough to send him into a bubbling fury. He sent him to be strip-searched every time. One day – please God, let it be one day soon – he would nab him for something.

As Mark was hauled off to remove his clothes, the guard shouted at Nick and me to empty our pockets, shouted at us to show him the contents of our bags, shouted questions about what we were doing and where we were going. I pretended not to understand a word, which infuriated him further. He boiled and seethed and shouted some more.

'There's really no need to raise your voice,' I told him calmly and quietly. 'We just want to go and watch the parade.'

Half an hour later we were back in the West, our passage denied a second time. Nick was pissed off because it had ruined his day off. Mark and I were fearful for the many days to come. Our names had presumably arrived on some shit-list and the ban might be a permanent one. Life in Berlin without the East? It was a gloomy prospect. Maybe we were living in fairyland, but the experience of constant crossing, the luxury of being able to pick and choose what we liked from either situation, run away from whatever we didn't, was something unique, the one thing that made this city truly special. Fairyland was not something it pleased me to consider giving up. There would at least still be the possibility of going over with the GIs, but it was depressing to think of access to the East always being restricted by Buttle's schedule or Spud's cartoon enthusiasms. Anyway, Mark couldn't go over with them and neither could I, once there was a residence permit in my passport.

I went home in a bad mood and crawled back into bed. An hour or two later, I was woken by the phone. It was Mark, his voice quivering. He had arranged to meet two Japanese girls at Alexanderplatz. They had just called him from an East Berlin phone box.

'Norman and Torsten have been arrested by the Stasis.'

Details were hard to come by that dreadful afternoon. Much later, I got the full story from Torsten. While we were being refused entry at Checkpoint Charlie, everyone else had turned up. The Japanese girls arrived, then Buttle breezed up and said hello, warmly shook Torsten's hand. Large crowds were flurrying about the square, and looking among them trying to see if Mark and I were coming, Torsten spotted a man with a camera, focusing on their group through a big zoom lens. Torsten got his own camera out, tried to take a picture of him taking a picture. The man hurried away. They continued chatting under the clock until, glancing around once more, Torsten saw the mystery photographer had returned. Again he got his own camera out, again the man melted into the crowd.

Norman and Torsten became aware of two guys nearby, apparently listening to their conversation, but as all the talking was in English, they weren't too worried. Buttle went off on his own to watch the parade. The others hung around a little longer to see if Mark and I would appear, then gave up and walked off too. The Stasis had obviously been waiting to see who else would turn up. Now that it was clear no others were coming, they moved straight in.

'*Fahndungskontrolle*,' they said, flashing *Kriminalpolizei* badges and positioning themselves to block off Norman and Torsten from the Japanese girls. '*Kommen sie bitte mit.* This will only take ten or fifteen minutes.'

A *Fahndungskontrolle* was a routine check for missing or wanted persons. Torsten knew that normally they just checked names and addresses against a list they all carried. If that's all it really was, there was no need to haul them in. This was bigger trouble. Torsten quickly told the Japanese girls his address and asked them to go round and tell Tina what had happened, then the Stasis were pulling them away.

'No talking,' they said, as they led Norman and Torsten off. Soon the photographer joined the procession and the five of them marched on. Torsten considered legging it, but apart from the fact that they had overheard his address, it was pointless running in Alexanderplatz. Even on a normal day there were Stasis everywhere. He remembered how a friend of his had once sprinted down the road here, just for the hell of it. The guy was tackled by a Stasi at the very next corner. 'What are you running away from?' Torsten and Norman allowed themselves to be led up the road, round the corner and into the main East Berlin police station at Keibelstrasse. This was a big, square building, as ugly as its reputation. You heard rumours of people disappearing in here and then 'accidentally' falling down the stairs. As the doors closed behind them, a dreadful question struck Torsten, as it must have struck many before him: now he was in here, was he ever going to get out again?

They were taken up to the third floor and told to empty their pockets. A Stasi disappeared with Torsten's camera and he gave silent thanks that he didn't have his address book. In a cold, grubby room two cops sat watch, making sure they didn't talk to each other. The walls were the usual institutional shade of DDR mildew; the window was covered with wire mesh; the two men opposite, Torsten reflected, really did look like pigs. Norman asked if he could go to the toilet. A cop told him to shut his mouth. The silence stretched out, no clue as to how long it would last, only dread as to what might follow.

Norman was taken away and Torsten left alone for a while. He looked out of the wire mesh window, could see only similar windows across an inner courtyard. Presently he too was removed to another room, identical to the first save for a table in the middle. Behind this sat a Stasi, a new one, who gave an icy smile and lost no time fingering, as he doubtless did every day of his working life, the fear that everyone on the other side of his table must feel. Over there, he said, gesturing out of the window at the rooms across the courtyard, over there sat the unlucky ones. Those people could not leave this place. Torsten should know that it was possible he could join them.

Torsten knew all right. He knew you could be sent down for a three-year stretch for any contact with 'organisations working against the aims of socialism' – the US Army, for example. What he didn't know was how much the Stasis knew. Or how much they knew he knew. Torsten had been thinking that a spell in prison, which should lead to being either kicked over the border or else bought out by Bonn, might provide his only route West. In moments of particular frustration, he even found himself experiencing a crazy yearning to be caught and locked up. At least then he'd know that something was happening. But now that incarceration stared him coldly in the face, he instinctively began manoeuvring to avoid it.

What followed was the hardest interrogation Torsten ever had. The cop who came round to see him when he was controlled for being a punk, the people at Pankow Town Hall who processed his application to emigrate – they had been stupid and easy to handle. This guy was a professional. His questions stalked Torsten in ever-tightening circles, pinning him down to positions he couldn't retract later. Torsten struggled to come up with a consistent story, always fearful Norman might have contradicted him in advance.

What was the soldier called?

Tricky one already. He couldn't say 'Buttle' but he had to know him as something. Torsten made up a nickname: 'Stiff'. This was enough like Buttle's first name, Steve, to cover himself if Norman had told the truth.

What did the nickname mean?

For some reason Torsten had been thinking of Stiff Records, or the group Stiff Little Fingers, which right at that moment – his mind was skittering all over the place – he was confusing with the album 'Sticky Fingers'. It was something to do with The Rolling Stones, he said.

Family name?

He didn't know his second name, hadn't wanted to know.

His rank? His job in the army?

Torsten hadn't wanted to know that either. He had asked 'Stiff' not to tell him.

What about the two Japanese?

He had never met them before.

So how had he met 'Stiff'?

A moment of panic. They must have asked Norman that question too. What if he'd answered that he met Buttle at Torsten's birthday party? No time to worry about that right now. Torsten named the old friend who had left East Berlin and now played in a group with Buttle. That was safe. The friend was already forbidden to visit the DDR.

What was the name of the group?

Which of course made Torsten remember the conversation at Rebecca's. The Crap Smugglers, he said, and in the middle of this horrible situation found himself drawing strength from the act of repressing the faintest of grins. Helpfully, he spelt it out: C-R-A-P.

What about his photography?

Oh, just a hobby.

Did he take pictures of . . . buildings?

Not usually.

Sometimes he did, then?

No . . . No, not really. He took pictures of friends, of things he found funny or interesting, the same as anybody did.

Was he aware that it was forbidden to take any pictures of trains or stations?

No he wasn't, but anyway he hadn't done so.

Had this 'Stiff' shown any interest in his photography? None at all.

What did he and 'Stiff' talk about, then?

Oh . . . God and the world. All sorts of things . . . nothing concrete.

Did Torsten want to leave the DDR?

Yes, he replied. This was already a matter on record.

Had he discussed this with 'Stiff'?

Torsten thought fast. What might Norman have said? Yes, they had talked about that, but he didn't know discussing it was forbidden.

Did 'Stiff' want to help him leave? Quickly now. Don't keep thinking so long before answering.

Torsten protested: But he must pay attention to what he was saying.

Come on. A direct answer. Did 'Stiff' want to help him?

Yes . . . Yes of course they had talked about the fact that 'Stiff' could help. But Torsten didn't want him to. The wish to leave was his problem alone. He knew he'd get out officially some day and in the meantime didn't want anyone to go to prison on his behalf.

Around they circled, but Torsten had already established a foundation of reasonably solid half-truths. As the interrogation plodded on, doubled back and plodded on some more, he kept his footing without mentioning any names, without admitting much more than what the Stasis had witnessed that afternoon. But although he knew he was handling himself well, Torsten could never forget that the pictures being developed somewhere else in the building – pictures of a citizen of the DDR clasping hands with a serving member of the US Army under the World Time Clock, Alexanderplatz, East Berlin – were already sufficient evidence to send him away. Hours of question and answer proceeded inexorably to the completion of a seven-page statement, four copies of which were at last laid out on the table in front of him. Torsten sighed and signed his name to them, twenty-eight times.

A mile or two south and West, I was prowling my grey box in agitation. Over at his place, Mark was in much the same state. We felt responsible. On the phone we had chewed over all the problems and possibilities. The uncertainty was the worst thing. Beyond the stark fact of their arrest, we knew only that there was nothing we could do, no way even to find out more. We were banned from going over and it was obviously the wrong time to call anyone on a monitored East–West phone line. The other half of the city suddenly seemed as remote and inaccessible as the West must have done to our friends over there.

After months of mocking the division of Berlin, here was an overdue lesson in uncomfortable realities. Wonderland was more than a pack of cards; our playground was their police state, our games their crimes against socialism. We had known it to be so without ever really considering the consequences of our actions. Now I sat chain-smoking in the kitchen, my mind showing sequences from a new Eastie Boys video: beatings and torture in a gloomy cell, a bright splash of blood on a grimy tiled wall.

Buttle rang. He was back in West Berlin, in a call box, it being as foolish to discuss this on the lines out of Andrews Barracks as it would be on a cross-border connection. When he left for the parade he'd arranged to meet Torsten later at the flat in Pankow. He'd been sitting there, talking to Tina, when the two Japanese girls arrived. They hadn't quite grasped the situation. The main reason they'd rung Mark was to check Torsten's address, not having had time to catch it when he was being led off. Now they told Tina that Norman and Torsten would be along a bit later. They were having some problem with the police but it was probably OK: the men who had taken them away said it wouldn't be more than fifteen minutes. Tina had under-stood straight away. So, after a second, had Buttle. Though Tina was in a state, there was no way he could stay and keep her company. For the Stasis to find him in the flat was absolutely the worst thing that could happen. He got the hell out and took the Japanese girls with him.

Tina was still alone in the flat and paralysed with anxiety when Norman arrived around four o'clock. His story was similar to Torsten's, except Norman claimed he didn't know the soldier, had never seen him before, was merely acquainted with the Japanese girls. He had made a statement and they let him go. Whatever was happening to Torsten, the most important thing was to clear anything dodgy out of the flat. The Stasis might be round any minute. He and Tina quickly packed up all the incriminating snapshots, address books, copies of the *Staubsauger*, bits of Russian and East German uniforms Torsten had collected for Mark. It had to go somewhere, Norman warned, that the Stasis wouldn't know about – not to her parents' place, for example. Tina left a coded note on the door, directions only Torsten would understand, and they carried everything off to the home of a colleague from her work.

Tina spent the next couple of hours wondering whether she'd ever see her husband again. Everyone started when there came a knock at the door. Tina's colleague opened it a crack and peered out to see Torsten standing there, face creased into a rueful smile. Tina threw herself into his arms. It had been like the 1930s, she said, with the Gestapo, just like they had learnt at school. You never knew if people would come back from the Gestapo. Torsten, who to his surprise had been released right after signing his statement, was filled with a strange euphoria. Never would they get a better chance to nail him and jail him. They'd had him there, had him in their ugly building for more than six hours, had him in their hands with all the evidence they needed to put him away. They'd had all that, and instead they had let him go.

I'd already decided to junk the Eastie Boys. The last thing these two needed right then was to appear in a Western magazine as part of a highly satirical jab at the DDR.

Torsten didn't seem to care much one way or the other. Norman was emphatic that it was a bad idea.

'It's OK for Torsten. He's applied to leave. But I've got nothing to gain from this situation. Nothing.'

'Don't worry, Norman,' I told him. 'The Eastie Boys are history.'

Norman and I, with an American journalist I had brought over for the day, were walking through tatty backstreets between Schönhauser Allee and the Planetarium. It was about a week after the interrogation and I'd had no idea whether they would let me over the border. Whatever the guard at Friedrichstrasse found in my passport had caused him to pick up the phone and confer at length with some superior. I expected then to be turned back but they had let me in. Now I was looking back over my shoulder down the long, empty street we were taking. It seemed likely that either Norman or I were being followed, but if there was anyone on our tail, then I couldn't spot them.

Although his interrogation seemed to have gone even better than Torsten's, the experience had reduced Norman to a jabbering bundle of nerves. He shot anxious glances left and right, jumped at sudden noises. He became especially agitated whenever we neared a uniformed officer of the law. As the American journalist, whose name was Ed, put it to me later: 'That guy was walking around with a "kick me" sticker on his back.' It was true. If I'd been a people's policeman I would have picked him up as soon as look at him. Norman was a mess, every syllable of his body language screaming confusion and guilt.

'It's safer on the streets,' he said. 'I get up every morning and go straight out of the house. Yes, it's better to stay out on the streets.'

'Not if you don't calm down a bit.'

'How can I calm down?' He was angry.

'Norman,' said Ed the American. 'I don't know much about your situation, I don't know you at all, but one thing I do know is this: the only dog that ever bit me was the one I was scared of.'

He was right of course, but in a way Ed just made things

139

worse. It was his first time in the East and he kept loudly comparing what he saw with New York City or Paris, France. I could feel Norman's irritation mounting. Later, as we looked for a beer in the Nikolaiviertel, I ushered Ed to the window of a Delikat shop, hoping to amuse him with Ronhill cigarettes and the East German 'Scotch' with the cowboy on the label. Instead we'd been surprised to see a pyramid of canned Nopalitos – cactus in brine – a Mexican delicacy. Ed had been struck by the sight, a little piece of life back home in Texas. It set him off talking about the difference between Mexican food in Texas and Mexican food in Mexico.

'Big chance I have to go to Mexico,' Norman spat in a please-change-the-subject tone of voice.

That night, to the standard experience of finding no place with any room was added a double dose of brute paranoia. Every time we looked in a bar, Norman would glance around and mutter: 'Stasis'. We would then hastily withdraw to the street. Soon I too was seeing them everywhere. When you looked closely, the only people you could be sure weren't secret policemen were the ones wearing normal police uniforms. That night every bar seemed full of those too. Ed the American couldn't take it. After the fifth bar he suddenly started remembering previous engagements. Normally I stayed in East Berlin until the bitter end but this night I was glad of the excuse to head home early. Norman accompanied us all the way to Fried-richstrasse, where the usual long queue for the border controls undulated out into the station courtyard. He waited with us until we were almost inside.

'You've got to find someone to marry me,' he implored. 'It's my only chance. A black woman would be best, or a Jewish one. Then you could say they were being anti-semitic.'

'Norman,' I said. 'Get out of here. It's not good for you to be hanging around at the border.'

As Ed and I filed into the entrance of the route back West, Norman's last desperate words were still ringing in my ears.

'Please look for me. Best of all would be a black Jewish woman. It really is my only chance now.'

Some chance, I thought, as I reached for my passport and showed it to the first of the waiting guards.

8.
'IN THE MOUNTAINS, THERE YOU FEEL FREE'

If Charlie was a fortified filling station, then the check-point at Drewitz, controlling 75 per cent of the traffic in and out of West Berlin, was a motorway service complex among border posts. The route out of town went past sleepy Western controls at what the Allies called Check-point Bravo – though unlike alliterative Charlie, this name hadn't passed into common borderspeak – and down a long stretch of no man's motorway. On a tall concrete plinth stood a Russian tank, supposedly the first to have entered Berlin in 1945. Angled on an incline, its cannon pointed as if about to rain shells on the West Berlin suburb of Wansee, this served as a brusque reminder of just whose Zone was now being entered. A couple of kilometres later, the road split into a dozen or more lanes that filtered traffic through a row of control points maybe 300 metres wide, the tarmac forecourts covering an area several times the size of Alexanderplatz. At a peak period like Friday after-noon, when weekenders began streaming across the transit routes back West, the whole place would clog up with cars. Other times, traffic was more sparse. At 2 a.m. on a dark and drizzling Monday morning, for example, the only vehicle weaving its way across the asphalt expanse, driver evidently vacillating about which lane to follow, was the secondhand Mercedes containing Trevor, Mark and me.

We were off on our holidays. Trevor, relaxed at the

wheel in green corduroy jacket, orange paisley shirt, psychedelic kipper tie and brown flat cap, looking like a
vintage car enthusiast on acid, was motoring away from a
cruel summer of waiting tables and marital strife. Mark,
hunched down in the back with his Luftwaffe jacket zipped
right up to the neck and lately so dejected he had made
himself ill, was seeking distraction after his relationship of
four years' standing had finally broken up for good. And
me, I certainly needed to stretch after seven months of
carefully husbanding resources both financial and emotional, struggling not to slip back into depression. The
recent episode with Norman and Torsten had done
nothing to improve our spirits. We were wound up tight.
We were looking for release. And we were heading straight
for a Czechoslovakia that was still, in the month of
November 1988, one of the sternest police states in Europe.

As DDR border guards went, the one whose job it was to
search us that night was a decent sort. He poked around a
car that was littered with crap. The toys for the children of
friends in Prague failed to arouse his curiosity. The couple
of dozen cans of beer, each and every one a different brand
because a friend had told us he could sell exotic empties
down the flea market, excited no interest at all. He paid
scant attention to the boxes of food – ingredients of meals
to be cooked in Prague as well as provisions for the road
that were chiefly the non-meat components of US Army
MRE field rations – and thus completely missed the
hundred or so hash biscuits camouflaged among them in a
plausible-looking tin. He actually seemed to like us, asking
Trevor about his family, smiling faintly at the Soviet Army
fake fur hat (dark spot in front where the badge had been
removed) he found in Mark's battered suitcase. Finally,
polite and friendly, he invited us all into his little hut to
empty our pockets.

It was the usual sort of place: ugly metal furniture,
grubby curtains with fading pattern, tepid green walls, fake
wood veneer covering every surface. On a shelf, next to a
tired potted plant, stood a metal stand supporting a glass
funnel-thing inside which rested what appeared to be a
small wooden truncheon. The recesses of Trevor's horrid

jacket proved to contain nothing illicit. Nor was anything in the least suspicious located among the assortment of objects in Mark's miniature knapsack. I think I was actually smiling as I watched Mark empty the pockets of his jacket – and then I remembered. My scalp crawled and my heart pounded and a little knot of dread drew itself tight in the pit of my stomach. In the breast pocket of my leather jacket – I could feel the weight shifting as I moved my left arm – was the pack of secret playing cards.

The lights in the small room suddenly seemed very bright as I tipped out my other belongings: a bunch of keys, cigarettes and disposable lighter, the inadequate roll of currency which was all that I had in the world. I tried to pass over the incriminating pocket, patting the general area as if there was nothing within. The guard leaned over and parted my jacket. Just what – he jabbed a finger – was in there? I reached in with a sigh and dropped the thing on the table. Mark was bent over fussing with the buckles on his bag. As the pack thudded down by his nose, he jerked straight upright, eyes bugging in fright and recognition, a reaction that scotched any last chance the guard might overlook the dodgy nature of the item.

'US Army,' the pack was labelled loud and clear. 'Restricted Issue Only'.

The guard picked it up, tipped out the cards and began shuffling slowly through. Each card, as well as the usual configuration of hearts or spades, bore a Russian word, a phonetic description of that word and an English translation. Some bright spark in the Pentagon had figured that the only way to teach their GIs a little of the enemy tongue was to sneak it up on them as they dealt a few hands of poker. Salman had given them to me at the Pinguin before we left. I'd smiled at the time – imagine having these on you at the border, ha, ha, ha – and then forgotten to leave them in the flat when I picked up my bag. It could have been worse, I calculated. Some of these packs were to do with armaments or aircraft recognition. This one had only words concerning transportation. But even so, as the guard dealt them out, I could see the Russian for 'military' and 'nuclear reactor' face up next to 'truck' and 'fork lift'.

'You stupid bastard,' cursed Mark as I got back into the car. 'Now you've thrown a great cloud of suspicion over all of us.'

Cards in hand, the guard was disappearing into an office behind us. Trevor had his elbow on the steering wheel and his hand over his eyes. Normally nothing that happened at a border could faze him, but this was too much.

'Are they letting us go now?' he asked, pushing back his flat cap.

'No. He told me to wait.'

They might hold us here for hours, I thought. They might let the others go and keep me behind. They might keep us all behind. They might go back through the car and analyse the hash biscuits and put us all in prison for a very long time. They might, oh God, they might . . .

'Hell,' I realised, 'I'm really stoned.'

'What are you going to tell them about the cards?' demanded Mark, shifting nervously in the back.

'I don't know,' I shrugged. It was already too late to think about it. The guard was coming back with an officer in a fancy uniform who strode magisterially as if he owned the whole checkpoint.

'Where did you get these?' he asked. We were back in the little room.

'I was, ah, given them.'

'But they are from the American army. Restricted issue. Secret.'

'Yeah, well, ah, these American soldiers sometimes come in my local bar and, er, I told them I was going on holiday to Czechoslovakia and they said, uh, that I ought to take these. It was, like, a joke.'

My words sounded unconvincing even to me – and I knew it to be the truth, more or less. I'd been imploring Salman to give me a pack for ages. Behind the officer's shoulder I could see the truncheon in the glass funnel-thing. My brain lurched into paranoid imaginings as to its likely use. I was, at that moment, quite light-headed with fear. But at the same time, deep down, I knew nothing serious was going to happen. I was, after all, just a tourist. A stupid English tourist, not a CIA spy. Honest.

145

The officers looked at each other, trying to decide whether to believe me. A moment's silence, then an almost imperceptible nod passed between them. The officer handed the cards back and formally announced that I was free to go. In the flush of surprise and relief, I almost handed them back: Here, keep them, a present for your Stasi. But maybe that would be pushing things just a little too far. I went outside and climbed back into the car.

'It's all right. Come on, let's get out of here before they change their minds.'

The pair stood and watched as we accelerated on to the Berliner Ring. You could see what they thought by the look on their faces: What a bunch of nutcases.

'You better get rid of those things,' urged Mark, 'otherwise we're going to have the same trouble at the Czech border.'

I passed the pack from hand to hand, wondering what to do with them. A few kilometres further on, I chose a moment when there were no cars visible on our tail, then flung them out of the window as hard as I could. The pack flew open in the wind and a small snowstorm of secret playing cards flurried out in the darkness to settle on the road behind.

'Now,' said Trevor, 'they'll probably get us for littering.'

We drove through the night, stopping once to eat bread, cheese and lurid cakes at a dimly lit service station near a place called Finsterwalde – 'Gloomy Forest'. It was dawn by the time the transit road led us around the outskirts of Dresden. Domes and spires stood in silhouette across the Elbe, the skyline of the rebuilt Old Town. Here and there on our route stood pieces of mutilated baroque statuary, oddly juxtaposed with the inevitable blocks of flats. These figures had survived the 1945 fire-bombing of the city only to be blackened with the soot of lignite-burning power stations, their features eaten away by acid rain. We were driving into the most polluted area of Europe, where the fires of heavy industry in southern East Germany, Polish Upper Silesia and the northern Czech lands pumped out poisons to ravage earth, air and water.

The transit road, reduced to two lanes, meandered up through snowy woods into the hills Germans call the Sächsische Schweiz – the Saxon Switzerland. On top of the ridge was the Czech–DDR border post at Zinnwald, where our crossing was cold but uneventful. It was coming down the other side that the horror began. The woods to either side were completely lifeless. For mile upon mile, hundreds of thousands of trees that were once tall and green now tilted at unnatural angles on the hillsides, their stiffened roots no longer able to clutch the earth, their branches a sickly grey as if some pale deposit had settled on them from the sky. We stared at the dead forest in silence. There were no jokes to crack.

'You've got to see this guy. You'll love him.' Mark rubbed his hands in enthusiasm. He'd been here before.

It was late morning in Prague and we were walking into a low, square building occupied by that branch of the police with whom foreigners wishing to stay in private Czech homes had to register. In the entrance hall we filled out forms in quadruplicate and then Mark led us into one of a row of small offices. The room had flowery curtains and a tank of tropical fish; the man at the desk, in tweed sports jacket and spectacles, radiated a keen and wholesome intelligence. He laid out our paperwork in front of him, opened the lid of an ink pad, flexed his fingers like a concert pianist and set briskly to work. Spinning a carousel of rubber stamps, he plucked one from among them and sent it pattering between the ink pad and various points on our documents. The second stamp was in his hand almost before he'd replaced the first. Patter, patter, patter. Everything on the desk was meticulously arranged. No motion was wasted. With the other hand he scribbled initials here and there. A third stamp appeared as if from nowhere. Patter, patter, patter. A fourth, a fifth. His arms a blur.

Trevor and I were grinning in astonishment. Mark watched our reactions, proud of his discovery. The man was a magician, an artist. A virtuoso of the rubber stamp. However many years he'd been practising this routine – day in, day out, processing the same set of documents – he still infused his performance with a sense of discovery, an air of the precious and unique. The pattering rose to a crescendo and then stilled. No space on our papers had been left unstamped. The ink pad snapped smartly shut, the last rubber stamp rocked gently in its cradle. The man's arms were already folded as he leant back in a sudden silence which cried out to be filled with applause.

Trevor and I were each on our second trip to Prague, though my last visit lay seven years in the past, his only seven months. Mark was there for the thirtieth time. We were staying with old friends of his, a couple called David and Andrea, a Czech and East Berliner respectively. They lived in a small but cosy ground-floor flat on a leafy residential street of the Smíchov district.

Andrea was in when we arrived, feeding breakfast to the younger of their two children. She was a wry, tough but sweet-tempered woman who worked for ADN, the East German news agency, brought up their kids and sometimes wondered whether marrying David and moving to Prague had been the right road to take in her life. David was a good-hearted, coarse-humoured hooligan who socialised on the 'dissident' margins, had bug eyes and an evil laugh. His job at a paper recycling plant seemed to involve nothing more strenuous than sifting out the valuable books from the crap and bringing them home at the end of the day. The library in their living room was impressive. Any books David didn't want to keep, he sold at the monthly flea market to raise some extra income.

That morning we took turns in the bathroom, washed down biscuits with hot coffee and headed straight back out the door. Tired as we were after the overnight drive, the only thing to do was to press on with the day. Across a dilapidated park we strolled, down some old stone steps below a building supported by a tangle of wooden scaffolding, over a lumpy street scored with tram lines, down more steps into Moskevská underground. The Prague Metro was clean and quiet, free of advertising, grand and mysterious in a 1960s science fiction style. Machines bleeped as they belched out tickets, electronic chimes presaged routine announcements that sounded vaguely ominous in calmly voiced Czech. Moskevská station looked, felt and sounded like a set from *2001: A Space Odyssey*.

'Of course, they had to put it underground,' smirked Trevor as we waited for the train. 'If they put it on top it would show everything else up.'

The contrast with the surface was indeed absolute. While the clean lines, marbled floors and subtle lighting of the underground expressed the modernist dream of an efficient, rational future, the medieval and baroque city overground had a feeling of prodigious age enhanced by the tattiness accumulated over four decades of inefficient communist reality. But winding through the maze of the Old Town, crossing the Vltava by the Charles Bridge, flanked by baroque statues and with the castle of Kafka's inspiration looming high above, reality was never the first thing to strike me about Prague. Even without biscuits to bolster it up, the atmosphere was dream-like. On initial explorations, back in 1981, I was constantly turning corners to be startled by some ornately macabre building, emerging from claustrophobic alleys into the jarring contrast of great, gaping squares. Even as I developed an acquaintance with the city, I never quite lost the sense of having to expect the unexpected.

Sometimes you were drawn into gazing up at the castle or trying to spot secret policemen in the crowds on the street and felt as if you heard all around the tickings and shufflings of a sinister, barely comprehensible bureaucracy. Maybe a teenage fascination with Kafka was responsible for that perception. But if the fantasies of the young clerk Franz had arguably been prompted by a combination of Prague's medieval gloom, baroque intricacy and an experience of the administrative machinery left over from the Austro-Hungarian empire, then why should the city evoke anything different now? Prague was physically still the same and the operations of the post-1968 state apparatus had, if anything, far outstripped even Kafka's imaginings. In a country like Czechoslovakia in 1988, just because you were paranoid it didn't mean they weren't after you.

But sometimes all the elaborate architectural detail, the

dated cars, the smartly old-fashioned army uniforms worn
by many on the street, the naively decorative design of shop
windows and posters, the funny central European pork-pie
hats, the way all the Czechs looked so wonderfully, well . . .
Czech – sometimes all this made it feel like you were
walking around in the clean-lined cartoon realism of Tintin, in the imaginary Slav nation of Syldavia, for example,
and its capital city of Splodj.

Mark and I lunched on pea omelettes, Trevor on a schnitzel, sitting at one of the long wooden tables in U Medvidkû.
Later we ducked into a model shop off Národní. Mark
looked for model aeroplanes while I investigated the Lego
department. It was painted in Lego colours, decked out
with Lego flags, Lego banners, Lego posters, Lego stickers,
dedicated Lego display stands – but there was not one
solitary brick of the stuff on sale. Trevor bought a balsa
wood aeroplane kit: the kind that comes in about three
pieces and flies powered by a wound-up elastic band.
Sometime later, having drifted back to the modernist
future at the Hlavní central station, we put it together and
wound it up and sent it puttering around the capacious
main concourse. Dodging through crowds of purposeful
citizens, we chased it and caught it and sent it flying off
again. We were still playing this game, running around like
children, when the train we were waiting for at last arrived
and Norman stepped into the scene.

It had been Mark's idea. Why not take Norman with us?
He badly needed cheering up, could obviously use a break
from what had, since his arrest, become an excessively
anxious routine. Czechoslovakia was the one country in the
world to which he could travel without a visa, and with our
Western cash to purchase black market money we could
afford to pay his way. Norman had agreed to come, but
from the look on his face as he saw us scampering anarchi-
cally about the station, it was clear the idea of this holiday
filled him with trepidation. Justly so, it must be conceded.

That night, we took the bus with David to the Klamovka
district, walked into the Klamovka park and there drank
beer in the Klamovka bar. It was a foul place. The gents was

a filthy bare room, brown-tiled up to waist height, with a gutter running round the edges and a drain in one corner. People just pissed anywhere. The rest of the establishment wasn't much smarter and neither was the mostly male clientele. In matters of dress and personal appearance, Czechoslovakian men seemed, on the whole, complete and utter slobs: shapeless anoraks, dirty jeans, straggly hair, drab t-shirts peeling back over beer bellies.

Klamovka was a hangout for artists and malcontents, musicians and layabouts. One or two of the people we'd expected to meet were absent that night. This was the twentieth anniversary of the Prague Spring and Soviet invasion. On 28 October there had been a demonstration in Wenceslaus Square. Eighty-seven had been arrested. While Poland and Hungary were then experiencing the first flickerings of reform, in this corner of Europe it was still a dark time, a time of knocks on the door in the night, a time when Klamovka regulars might not turn up because they'd just been thrown in prison. Still, the mood in the bar was boisterous and good-humoured – even though no one would have dared to predict that in little more than a year, many of the slobs in the place would be putting on suits and ties and getting involved in the government of their country, that this current darkness was actually that which comes before the dawn.

A couple of hours later, we were walking back from the bus stop to David and Andrea's. Above the front door of every house, as above front doors all over Eastern Europe, were screwed pairs of flagpole holders – short lengths of metal tubing, angled up at about forty-five degrees. This being an official day of Czech–Soviet Friendship, above each door hung the Czechoslovak tricolour and Soviet red flag. As in Václav Havel's famous example of the green-grocer who puts the sign 'Workers of the world unite' among the vegetables in his window, the real meaning of these flags was distinct from the apparent one. They didn't say: 'I think Czech–Soviet friendship is so great a cause for celebration that I will put out the flags.' The message was more like: 'I am afraid and therefore unquestioningly obedient.'

We were eyeing these flags. Quite nice, some of them. Suddenly David was cupping his hands and Trevor was getting a leg up to rip a red flag off the pole. Seconds later he was helping Mark do the same. Then Mark grabbed a Czech flag. I cupped hands so Trevor could follow suit. On up the street we went, a Hansel and Gretel trail of bare poles in our wake. I was biding my time, looking for a really fine red flag. Just around the corner from David's, I found the one I wanted: a satisfyingly deep shade of red, the hammer and sickle sewn on rather than printed. Difficult though. Higher than the others. Even with a leg up, I couldn't quite reach it. I clambered to a ledge at the side and, with a steadying hand from Trevor, stretched out towards it from there. It was tricky to work the thing free . . .

This was taking far too long for David, who abruptly disappeared. When we finally crossed the road, me with my prize stuffed under my jacket, we found him hovering behind a hedge.

The Czech authorities were always keen to relieve you of as much hard currency as possible. To us, this was a challenge. There was no way out of the hefty charge for a visa, nor of avoiding the obligatory exchange of currency at the absurd official rate. We'd done this at the border – twenty-five marks for each day of our visa's validity – and then fattened our wallets further in a transaction with David. If motoring, you were also supposed to purchase petrol coupons with hard currency, which made fuel several times more expensive for us than it was for the locals. Up in the Zinnwald, Trevor had bought the absolute minimum.

'I'm not paying through the nose for their fucking coupons. We must be able to get it on the black market.'

The Mercedes ran on diesel. In case this proved hard to find on our travels, packed in the boot were a couple of fuel cans. The morning after Klamovka we were due to set off from Prague. First, though, we had to fill those cans. Having downed a breakfast of boiled eggs and yoghurt which appeared, from the graphic on the carton, to be red-striped-triangle flavour, we set off with David, who had ducked out of work to help us, in search of a black market diesel coupon dealer. We stopped at several places before he found someone willing and able to accept hard currency in exchange for some of the necessary yellow vouchers. Now the problem was exchanging these for fuel. The morning wore on as we drove from garage to garage, trying to locate one that had some diesel. The coupons weren't valid for Western tourists, so each time we had to park the Mercedes out of sight and wait while David checked things out.

At the fourth or fifth place, in a shabby area near the river, we at last struck lucky. Trevor parked behind a block of flats while David and Norman – assigned as helper because of his authentic Eastern look – disappeared round the corner with empty cans, struggled back again with full ones. Without David the coupons were useless, so we had to fill the tank straight away and top up the cans while we could, hurrying to complete the business before anyone in authority chanced upon us. Trevor swore and cursed as he tried to direct the flow of diesel, Norman helping steady the can. The foul liquid splashed everywhere, over Trevor's hands and down his trousers, collecting in a noxious puddle on the tarmac below.

'Next time it's your turn,' Trevor warned me and Mark. 'I'm not doing this again. We're going to have to try and find some rubber gloves and a funnel.'

We finally dropped David back at work about two hours after we'd started. His excuse for being gone so long was that he'd had to get something photocopied. That this was plausible was the crowning absurdity: in the Prague of 1988, the simple act of photocopying was as complicated and time-consuming as any Byzantine black market transaction.

We were heading East, though quite how far East was as yet unclear. Mark was keen on motoring right to the Soviet frontier. Trevor and I wanted to go up into the Tatra mountains on the Polish–Slovakian border and then see what we felt like doing. Norman kept his own counsel. We passed around the biscuit tin, only Trevor the driver abstaining, and dreamed away an afternoon of motorway and dreary forest. At one point we were stuck behind a bus belching out a cloud of smoke so black and dense we could barely see where we were going. The bus windows, we noted as we passed, were so thickly sooted it would have been impossible to see out of them.

'A fine example of Czech technology,' I said.

'You mean a fine example,' said Mark, 'of Czechnology.'

The weak winter sun was dipping down as we skirted the city of Brno. An endless vista of identical flat blocks swept by to our left and managed to look almost pretty in the sunset. We paused to eat at a grimy motorway café. Mark leafed through his phrase book. Instead of asking, say, if they had anything without meat in it, he said to the waiter:

'We three are vegetarians.'

It came out like a challenge. The waiter just stood there, this statement as far beyond his powers of understanding as if Mark had said: 'We three are Zillons from the planet Tharg.'

'We three are vegetarians,' Mark persisted, gesturing towards Norman and me.

'Omelette,' grunted the waiter.

'What kind of omelette?'

'Pea omelette.'

So it was three more of those and another schnitzel for Trevor, everything cold and greasy and discoloured. The bill, when it came, was enormous. Czech waiters were as keen as the authorities to relieve you of your money. The simplest of the many strategies adopted was to spend a long time over the bill, pretending to add it up, while writing down illegible squiggles and inventing large figures to put against them. Calculations were made as to your likely gullibility. Numbers first thought of were doubled. Surcharges were slapped on top. And if you tried to argue about it, well of course they then spoke only Czech.

Ultimately they relied on the fact that their money meant nothing to you. They knew you'd change on the black market. Frequently they'd offer to change it for you. Cheating tourists was the rule, not the exception, and arguing every single time over what were indeed small sums never seemed worth the bother. We just paid what they asked for, but made sure that they knew that we knew, salvaging some dignity with a sneer.

Our route steered north off the motorway. The intention was to spend the night in the town of Olomouc. Mark had suggested the place, interested because back in the Third Reich (under its German name Olmütz), it had been the capital of Nazi Sudetenland. Until three hundred years before that, it had been the capital of Moravia. These days it had a huge Soviet airbase in the vicinity. Mark was fascinated by military bases, insisting on trying to take pictures from the car every time we passed one.

'Give me two biscuits,' demanded Trevor, as we drew up in the cobbled town square. It was about five o'clock and dark already.

'Two? You pig.'

'You've all been munching them. I've got some catching up to do. Come on, two biscuits. I'm not driving any more tonight.'

There was a hotel off the square, an old woman behind the counter. She smiled malevolently and shook her head. No rooms. *Alles besetzt.* Were there any other hotels? Yes, but they would have no rooms either. How could she be sure? She shrugged and picked up the phone, called a number, her body language underlining the futility of the attempt. No, nothing. Her smile now said: 'I told you so.' She dialled a second number. Ah, maybe here was something. Her hand held out the phone but her smile held little hope. The woman on the other end spoke no English or German and I ended up struggling in schoolboy French. Four people? It seemed she might condescend to rent us two holiday bungalows at an exorbitant weekly rate. For one night only? No, that was not possible. I replaced the receiver. The crone at the counter was pleased as Punch, whom, it now struck me, she resembled.

'What the hell are we going to do now?'

'Try another town?'

'And I've just eaten two biscuits,' said Trevor, the only one of us who could drive.

'*Gute Reise,*' cackled the old woman as we trudged out the door, somehow transforming the ritual wish for a good journey into something chilling and sinister. It was the way Transylvanian villagers in Dracula movies always bid farewell to travellers bound for the dread castle, knowing they would never come back.

'*Gu-u-u-ute re-e-e-ise!*'

It was a hundred kilometres to Ostrava, the nearest big town and the only place we could be sure of finding somewhere to stay – a hundred kilometres of poorly lit single-lane highway, of nearly invisible road markings, of signs that didn't reflect, of oncoming headlights looming crazily from the darkness. This was not a road to be driving on with two hash biscuits slowly sanding the edges of your concentration. Trevor battled to keep control, his tension infecting everyone else in the car. We lurched with fright at every apparent near miss. Now and then I found myself frantically pressing an imaginary brake pedal. Mark tried to soothe things by slotting a John Barry cassette in the machine. Gentle violin music filled the car like sweet, soporific smoke.

'Turn that off,' Trevor shouted. 'Do you want to fucking send me to sleep?'

I pulled something from his bag of cassettes. The rest of our ride was accompanied by Pop Will Eat Itself, which just made things even scarier. When finally we pulled up in Ostrava city centre, right opposite a giant Interhotel, Trevor slumped in relief across the steering wheel.

'Hotel Imperial. Looks expensive,' I observed.

'I don't care how much it costs,' Trevor snarled. 'I'm not driving another inch.'

It turned out to be two hotels in one: an expensive 'A' hotel and a cheaper 'B' hotel. We took a single room with bath in the expensive part so Trevor the driver could rest in comfort, a triple room for the rest of us in the spartan 'B' accommodations. Most of our floor was occupied by a troupe of Russian dancers. The door of our room was hanging open as we readied ourselves to go out and explore. A tall, stony-faced Russian appeared in the corridor, stood there and stared into our quarters.

I went over to him. 'Can I help you, mate?'

He acknowledged my presence only by a slight craning of the neck necessary to continue looking over my shoulder. I opened the door a little wider, sarcastically beckoning him in.

'Perhaps you'd like to step inside, get a better look?'

Still he ignored me, peering into the room. I slammed the door in his face.

'Who was that?' called Mark.

'I don't know. Fucking KGB man or something.'

He was probably guarding the dance troupe, we decided. All through that night, there were one or two Russians sitting at a table in the corridor, apparently working in shifts. We waved a cheery greeting every time we walked past. They answered us only with cold, suspicious eyes.

Down-town Ostrava, the centre of a large industrial city, was like a ghost town. Nine o'clock at night and the only sign of activity in the old town square was a few scraps of litter, wheeling in a sudden gust. We trooped through the scene, scouting for food, drink or any kind of entertainment. A glimmer of light down a side street drew us like a beacon. It was a restaurant, deserted but for a couple of workers in the corner, watching the fuzzy image of a black and white TV. The only decoration on the bare walls inside was a sign advertising Pilsener Urquell, but that was just a sign. Whatever beer they brought us tasted like dregs from the tray below the tap. Encrusted matter on the pale brown tablecloth seemed to indicate that at some point in the establishment's history, food had been served here. We decided we were hungry.

'Omelette?' we asked.

'Is not there,' said the waiter.

'Schnitzel?'

'Not there.'

This had us stumped. Mark leafed through food questions from the phrase book. Nothing was 'there' but still the waiter hung around. It was as if they actually had something, somewhere, yet he was magically restrained from telling us what it was until we came up with the right question.

'Give that here,' said Trevor. He grabbed the book,

ruffled through, held it up and pointed something out. The waiter took it from him, examined it carefully, lips moving as he read, then scuttled to the kitchen, muttering in Czech.

'What did you ask him?'

It had been a reaction at least.

'I was just winding him up,' grinned Trevor. 'I pointed to where it said, "Have you got any salmon?"'

Five minutes later a woman appeared, her face lit with a happy smile, waving our phrase book around.

'Fisch?' she asked us.

We all nodded. Salmon is a fish.

'Fisch?' she repeated.

That's right. All nodding and smiling. She started nodding too.

'Fisch?'

Yes indeed, we roared. Fish. Everyone was now beaming and laughing and slapping each other on the back in a mood of jubilant affirmation.

'Fisch nicht,' she snapped and dropped the phrase book on the table with perfect comic timing.

Back across the deserted square and down another side street we found a place much nicer than the first. There were people in it, for a start. There was low lighting, old beams in the ceiling, a kindly waiter who spoke English.

'Do you have anything without meat in it?'

'I can offer you . . . a pea omelette.'

'Better make it a schnitzel for me,' said Trevor.

'How many pea omelettes have we had?' I wondered as the waiter walked off. It was obviously the Czech answer to East Germany's fried egg and sterilised vegetable special.

Mark considered. 'Two in U Medvidků before Norman got here, three this afternoon . . . eight so far.'

An idea struck me. I pulled out a tiny blue notebook I'd bought in Prague and under the heading 'Pea Omelette' made eight small marks.

'I'm going to keep a tally, like a statistical record of this holiday. What other categories can we have?'

Soon there were entries for schnitzels, times we had been controlled, times we'd been ripped off, times we'd ripped them off, portions of chips, beers and biscuits. I pondered this last total.

'Is that how many we've eaten already? At this rate we're going to run out in a couple of days. Maybe we need some system for the biscuits. You have to earn them.'

'Like play a game,' said Mark.

'Exactly. Say the first person to get back to the hotel tomorrow with rubber gloves and a funnel wins a biscuit.'

'Nah,' said Trevor. 'This is Czechoslovakia. We'd end up with four funnels and no gloves.'

'Or else eight left-hand gloves in size 106.'

The waiter apologised when we asked if there was any dessert.

'I'm sorry, there is nothing and now we must close. But the food was good, no?'

We stared in astonishment. A Czechoslovakian waiter who took pride in his work – it was like sighting a giant panda on Oxford Street. The food had in fact been much better than usual: the chips dry and crisp, the omelette light and firm, everything hot and cooked in fat that had actually been changed some time in recent memory. The sum on the bill even fell within the bounds of plausibility. We tipped him in West marks.

'New category,' suggested Mark. 'Times we were not ripped off.'

The only nightlife in town turned out to be the 'Video Disco' in our hotel. On a table by the entrance sat an old guy with a cashbox. When we tried to buy a ticket he sighed and shook his head.

'What's the problem? We're staying here.'

He hauled himself to his feet, looked us carefully up and down.

'You are not dressed properly.'

He pointed to Mark's leather jacket, Norman's pullover, my sweatshirt, his movements slow and melancholy. Everything about him radiated a sense of great tragedy.

'What are we supposed to wear then?'

'A shirt. A tie perhaps.' His manner was grave. This duty appeared to pain him. 'You are from England? I was once in England.'

'Yeah? Where?'

'In Blackpool.'

Blackpool? All but Norman burst out laughing. I leapt to the attack.

'And when you were in Blackpool, did they make you change your clothes just to have a drink in the hotel where you were staying?'

The old man's shrug was eloquent.

'Ah,' he pronounced with regret, 'but you are in Czechoslovakia now.'

There was no disputing that. We ran upstairs and changed the offending articles.

'Actually,' I said, as we scurried back down past the watching Russians, 'the last time I was in Blackpool they wouldn't let me in a club for precisely the same reason.'

Later, in the disco, as we settled to sip Crimean champagne so sweet you could practically hold it up to the light and see the sugar crystallising, watched couples in polyester suits and crimplene party dresses dancing timidly to old Bee Gees hits, like they were gently nudging pennies, foot to foot, I realised that I felt at home in such places. Yes, we were in Czechoslovakia now, but Blackpool wasn't too far off the mark. In its pettiness and provincialism, its grubby industry and its terrible food, the place reminded me of nothing so much as an English northern town.

Over breakfast the next morning, I read out excerpts from a leaflet about the Tatra mountains I had found at reception.

'"The High Tatras, sometimes dubbed 'the smallest big mountains in the world' rank among the leading European mountains . . ." I love that. "The leading European mountains." Like all the other mountains are trying to catch up.'

'Or,' said Mark, 'they're *rank* among the leading European mountains.'

'"The streams are rich in salmonoid fish . . . "'

'Salmon*oid* fish?'

'Exactly the sort of fish you would find in rank mountains. It goes on: "The tall peaks and large black shadows of the valleys conjure up a panoramic image dominating the whole area . . . The new buildings have altered the appearance of the area and represent a foil to the beauties of nature." I love that too. "A foil to the beauties of nature" – i.e. they're just dead ugly.'

We examined the pictures of hotels on the leaflet. One was triangular, an attempt to resemble a mountain. Mark put his finger on another: a building of an apparently impossible shape, like some hypothetical polygon from a maths lesson. It flared from the base, wider at the top than at the bottom. On one side it was stepped back, on the other gradually bulged in an implausible overhang. The Hotel Panorama.

I read out the last sentence: ' "This, then, are the High Tatras, 'the small big' mountains of Czechoslovakia. Welcome!" '

'I'm glad,' said Trevor, 'that even the mountains are third-rate.'

Mark and I went off to look for the gloves and funnel. Far from proving a task worthy of any reward, this took about five minutes. One quick scout around a Prior department store and there they were. Rubber gloves and plastic funnels, we realised, were exactly the kind of crap this system would manufacture in abundance.

The town centre actually bustled in the daytime and in the pale winter sun the square could have passed for picturesque. The outskirts, though, were grim. We drove out past giant filthy factories, the powerhouses of Czechnology, loosing enough smoke to turn the blue sky powder grey. An Orwellian touch was added by the angular loudspeakers, hung in pairs on lampposts, ready to make pronouncements about successes in the Five Year Plan. At traffic intersections stood rusting watchtowers from which agents of Big Brother might scrutinise the goings-on.

It wasn't long before we crossed the border into Slovakia. This was nothing, just a sign at the roadside, like passing from England into Scotland. Our route ran through broad valleys fringed with pine-forested hills. It would have been wonderful countryside if every single valley hadn't contained at least one factory to act as a foil to the beauties of

161

nature. The works were usually surrounded by ranks of grimy flat blocks and shrouded in an industrial haze fuelled also by the smoky clouds which wheezed from every vehicle on the road.

We stopped for lunch in a town called Žilina. It was the usual modernist nightmare on the outskirts but felt like a Wild East filmset in the middle: rococo buildings and statues of Lenin, ominous in the long shadows. At one point I paused on a corner to gaze at a rounded pink building that looked as if it had been baked from gingerbread, then glanced around to find I was being watched by two not-very-secret policemen – from Tintin to Josef K. in a turn of the head. As we translated the menu of the Restaurácie Zilina our spirits perked: asparagus, spinach, potatoes cooked in their jackets, mushroom omelettes and curry rice were all on mouthwatering offer. The waitress, when she came, curtly dashed all hopes.

'Is not there, not there . . . no, not there.'

We ended up with a kind of cold omelette, wrapped in a stale bun and washed down with warm Pepsi, in a self-service café off the square.

'"Not there",' I said, 'is like the national motto of Czechoslovakia.'

'That or "change money, change money",' said Trevor.

There was an elongated hammer and sickle statue on a curve of the road out of town. As it caught our attention, the police hiding behind the corner caught us. It was just a speeding fine, but Trevor had to spend twenty minutes filling out forms on the bonnet of their car before forking out a hundred crowns.

It was dark before we reached the mountains. Trevor pulled up at a dimly lit filling station in a small, dimly lit village. It was hard to tell whether the place was open or not.

'I suppose we'd better use up some of these coupons,' he said.

The woman inside displayed not the slightest scrap of interest in our sheaf of yellow vouchers. Trevor flashed a twenty West mark note and that was enough to fill the tank.

This raised a laugh: all our running around in Prague, all the fuss with the gloves and the funnel – for nothing.

It was getting late but we were just on the edge of the Tatras. Studying the map, I announced that we seemed to be only a few kilometres from the mountain village of Štrbské Pleso. Trevor was pleased by the news.

'Give me a biscuit then.'

'No, Trevor,' Mark pleaded. 'Remember last night.'

Trevor laid out his case like a lawyer. 'Look: we're nearly there, it's late, everything will be closing down shortly after we arrive. I want to relax and have a good time after this long day's driving. A biscuit takes about an hour to get working and if I take one after we get there I probably won't feel the effects until everything's shut and it's time to go to bed. This way, I'll just be getting nicely stoned when we arrive.'

Mark caved in before this barrage of apparently sound logic. Round went the biscuits, Trevor stuffing one into his mouth as we turned off the main highway and on to the road for the mountains. Although it had looked a short distance on the map, the road twisted and turned in its efforts to gain altitude. Deepening snow, as we hair-pinned up the hill, further impeded progress. Time wore on, dense forest closed in on either side, biscuits metabolised. There was no other traffic. The cassette machine was playing an Ennio Morricone soundtrack and a gently foreboding trumpet rose up high as we watched the patterns of light and shade cast by headlights on the snow. At one bend, we caught an unexpected glimpse up the mountain, gone in a flash but imprinting an after-image on the mind's eye. Lit like a spectral Christmas tree in the darkness high above, had stood a tall unearthly structure, apparently some kind of upended ziggurat.

'Hey,' murmured Trevor, his voice shaded with a wonder which, at that moment, we all shared. 'The Hotel Panorama.'

Two red deer suddenly sprang into our dream, leaping from the trees to prance crazily into our path. Trevor yelped and swerved. The rest of us lurched to grab hold of something as the car skidded in the snow. Tree trunks loomed in the headlights, white snow, dense green foliage, more trees. As abruptly as they'd first appeared, the deer hopped back into the forest, leaving Trevor to spin the wheel left and right, fighting to regain control of the vehicle on a road now derisively clear.

All pleasant dreams had fled. I concentrated on the road ahead with teeth-grinding intensity, sure that if I looked away for one second then Trevor would prang the thing. I could sense Mark and Norman doing the same. The road now writhed like a high pressure hose-pipe, mere shadows provoked sharp intakes of breath. We proceeded in a tense silence for what seemed like forever, no way to tell how close we were getting, until the agony ended with us bursting from the woods and halting in the car park of the Hotel Panorama. The crunching of the handbrake loosed a gush of sweet release.

Everyone sat quiet for a moment.

'Two nights in a row,' said Mark. 'How many times do we have to go through that scene?'

My giggle was edged with hysteria. 'Until we get it right, I suppose.'

'Come on, boys,' said Trevor. 'Let's go and get drunk.'

The colours surprised me. After days in the monochrome haze, it was startling to look out the next morning at a sky unambiguously blue, a sun shining confident and yellow, unfiltered by industrial fallout. The valley below was a murky pool of mist, lapping at the healthy green of the forest which plunged down to meet it. We had risen above the pollution. Trevor and I stared for a moment, then pushed open the window of our fuggy room to gulp from the cold, clear air.

Strbske Pleso wasn't much of a village – two Interhotels, one bar, a few houses, bus and train stations, all new and purpose-built – but the altitude was exhilarating. We took a stroll around the frozen lake behind the hotel, on the other side of which stood the triangular Hotel Patria, wrinkling eyes against the glare. Despite our high spirits there was yet something strange about the scene. It wasn't just that we were the only Westerners around, our hungover lethargy and scruffy coats a jarring contrast to the wealthy Russians and rich Czechs jogging along diligently in Eastern bloc versions of designer sportswear. I struggled to put my finger on it, this nagging unfamiliarity, until looking up at the mountains, it struck me what it was: the feeling of being on a proper holiday.

The mountains might have been the smallest big ones in the world, but they were still mountains. Tall, pointed things with snow on top. Getting further up one seemed the obvious thing to do, but needless to say the cable car from Štrbské Pleso was closed. According to a map in the hotel lobby, there was an even bigger one, running right up to one of the highest peaks in the range, at a place called Tatranská Lomnica. This was twenty kilometres distant but connected to our village by rail, and as none of us had ever been in a cable car up a mountain before, we were sufficiently excited by the notion to go and catch a train.

The line was a single track, tracing a contour around the edge of the range. We had to change trains and wait an hour at the station of Starý Smokovec. In a kiosk on the platform, my eye was caught by a small bottle of Czech brandy, brand-name Fragopolis. A warming tot seemed a capital idea, so I reached for some crowns and bought it. An exploratory sniff revealed a bouquet like something from a biology lesson and one small sip sent me gasping and retching. This piqued the others' curiosity. Surely I was overacting. The stuff couldn't be *that* bad. I passed the small bottle around. One by one they too all gasped and retched.

Tatranská Lomnica was bigger than Štrbské Pleso and the walk to the cable car was a long one. By the time we reached the terminal the sun was already dropping. It didn't matter. This cable car was also closed. Examining the sign at the entrance, we noted that the only few days in the year when it was out of operation coincided precisely with the dates of our trip. This impressed us as merely typical. A cable-car ride would have been too good, really. Fragopolis brandy was more our speed. The sense of a proper holiday was already beginning to recede as we backed down the road and, drawn by the idea of finding something edible, turned into the door of the Grand Hotel Praha, smartest establishment in town. The restaurant had comfortable chairs and a high ceiling, was lit from tall picture windows and skirted by a balcony on the other three sides. It felt, in fact, like a proper hotel. The waiter was able to offer us fried cheese and chips, which was at least a change, washed down with the first Budweiser beer we'd seen since arriving in the country.

Around us the room filled up with men in jackets and ties, women in smart suits. One minute we were alone, the next surrounded by people clutching agendas and gathering in knots to discuss whatever business had just concluded. Soon every seat was taken. A man and a woman perched at our table, clearly both East Europeans from different countries. While we were cackling our way through some stoned sequence of jokes, they were having an intense conversation in English. Presently the man went off to the toilet and left his companion alone.

'Excuse me,' I leaned over and asked her, struggling to be polite and appear normal. 'Can you tell me what is going on here?'

'Oh,' she was surprised to be addressed. 'It's an international conference of mining trade unions.'

'Really?' I was genuinely interested. 'Are there any people here from England, from the NUM?'

'The NUM,' she echoed. 'You are very well informed.'

'Yes,' chirped Trevor. 'That's because we're spies.'

There was a sudden, shocked silence. This was not the kind of joke that went down well in Stalinist Czechoslovakia. I thought of those signs you saw in American customs: 'We take everything you say very seriously.' The woman just gaped. At the other end of the table, Norman stiffened and turned white. Mark doubled up in silent hysterics. I was left leaning over, frozen in attentive posture, caught between fantastic embarrassment and the urge to erupt into laughter. Trevor was just sitting there, his features formed into a cocky grin that told the rest of the world he was very pleased with himself indeed.

The woman was the first to break the tableau, springing from her seat and hurrying away. She intercepted her companion on his way back and steered him in a different direction, whispering as they walked. Both turned back warily to glance in our direction.

At some point in the afternoon we calculated that we didn't have enough money left to pay the hotel bill. It was uncanny. Not only had we spent all the crowns purchased officially at the border, but also the even larger roll we had acquired from David at the black market rate. We started joking about self-spending money: notes that fade and go blank after a spend-by period, homing coins that hop out of your pocket and jingle their way back to the bank. But when we all woke after a recuperative early evening nap and assembled in Mark and Norman's room to review the situation, it was clear there was cause for worry.

The problem wasn't simply the prospect of having to change more West money at the official rate for a hotel that was expensive enough already in black market Czech crowns, it was also that if we did, then we probably wouldn't have enough left to continue the holiday in the style to which we had become, if not exactly accustomed, then at least inured. Norman looked on in concern as the rest of us emptied wallets on the table and pondered the resulting small pile of notes. Only one course of action suggested itself. We would take what we had and go and get drunk with it.

Mark wasn't feeling up to it and crawled straight back into bed. Norman and Trevor and I set off to trudge around the frozen lake and sample the triangular delights of the Hotel Patria. It was a clear night. Snow squeaked underfoot, mountains loomed ahead in the light of a thin, sickle moon. I wasn't used to this kind of landscape, this kind of air, the special way it makes you feel good. With the exception of one quick hitchhike across the Brenner Pass, I'd never before got much higher than about halfway up Ben Nevis. A voice from Eliot's *Waste Land* popped into my head: 'In the mountains, there you feel free.'

I looked back at Norman, traipsing a few paces behind me, eyes fixed upon his feet. He was always traipsing behind somehow, reacting to the rest of us, carried along

helpless in our wake. Sometimes he was struggling to follow
our foreign sense of humour through a fog of hashish and
alcohol. Other times, he was plunged into a state of mute
terror. Often, when Trevor started acting up, he clearly
didn't know whether to laugh like a drain or else wish that
one would swallow him up. Although he'd already had a
taste back in Berlin, this sustained lunacy was something
else. Also different was that everyone here, save the hotel
receptionists who handled his passport, just assumed he
must be English or West German. That never happened in
East Berlin. There it was obvious, to other locals, that he
was a local too. For the first time in his life, Norman was
experiencing how it was to be treated as a Westerner.

And while Norman's was a passive role in the unfolding
drama of our holiday, it was, in its way, still a central one.
His was the silent figure on stage around whom all action
revolved. We had brought him along to give him a break,
now we were keenly watching his reactions. At one point I
had said to Mark: 'You know, this is Norman's story, really.'
He had nodded in immediate agreement: 'I know what you
mean. Norman's Progress.' It had seemed to me this day
that, apart from the 'that's because we're spies' episode,
when he had very nearly crapped in his pants, Norman was
loosening up a bit, relaxing into the experience of just how
much it was possible to get away with when one was classed
as a Westerner. There in the mountains, Norman too was
beginning to feel free.

The Horizont Club, up at the apex of the triangle, was
the place to be seen in Štrbské Pleso. While the Panorama
was classified, according to the official system, as a hotel of
the second category plus 30 per cent, here at the Patria it
was top of the line: first category plus 40 per cent. The
prices were heftier, the crowd more rakish. There were
men with perms, women in designer-style clothes, a menu
listing dishes that were meant to sound sophisticated:
Minced Poultry Meat in the Tartar Style; Trout of the Hut
at the Zabie Pliesko Mountain Lake, Garnished; Mixed
Sterilised Salad; Steak in the Rebel Style; Cheeses on a
Wooden Plate.

Norman was at his ease, the calmest I had seen him since

before his arrest. Usually a cautious drinker, tonight he happily paced Trevor and me, beer for beer. When, with a blush and a stammer, he confessed lustful thoughts about a girl on the next table, Trevor and I exchanged a grin. Perhaps we should try and get Norman laid.

I had already noted the young blonde woman, object of his attentions. The obvious manoeuvre would have been to send a bottle of champagne to her table, which she shared with another ski-resort woman and a man with lots of gold chains, but counting our remaining funds we found barely enough to cover the last round of beers. This also ruled out other pretexts to join their conversation. It would hardly get Norman off to a flying start if we had to sit there without drinks in front of us, as if hoping to be bought some ourselves. No, there was nothing left to do but pay up with our last few crowns, go to bed and somehow deal with the hotel bill in the morning.

Trevor was motioning to the waiter when the man with the gold chains leaned over and muttered a refrain that was sweet to the ears.

'Change money, change money?'

Minutes later, Trevor's wallet newly stuffed with Czech crowns, we were all on our way down to continue festivities at the hotel disco. In the control on the door, Norman and I were instructed to shed coats but Trevor was denied entrance altogether. His big, heavy walking boots were deemed unsuitable. Determined to continue the evening by any means necessary, he hurried off to the Panorama to change them. By the time he reappeared, maybe half an hour later, I was alone at the bar, relieved to see him because he had all the money. I had plied the woman with alcohol, talked to her long enough to learn that her name was Katarina and that she worked at our hotel. I'd then made Norman sit down next to her and retreated to leave them alone. While I watched the band playing covers of old Beatles songs, they appeared to be managing some kind of conversation.

When Trevor and I joined them, Katarina refused another drink.

'I have to get up early tomorrow. I'm travelling to Brno for the weekend.'

'We're going to Brno too,' Trevor announced. 'Why don't we give you a lift.'

Norman and I stared in surprise. In truth we had finalised no travel plans for the morrow. As far as Mark was concerned, we were still on our way to the Russian border.

'We've got a big Mercedes,' he blustered, waving his arms around. 'Very good music, very loud.'

She looked at the three of us – Norman suddenly a little scared, me trying to suppress a laugh, Trevor blown up in mock pride about his big bad automobile – and considered the offer that was hanging in the air. Her answer was a powerful argument against the existence of female intuition.

'OK,' she said. 'Thanks.'

On the way out, much later, having been roundly ripped off for the drinks, we were drawn to the souvenirs at the cloakroom counter. There was a relief map of the Tatras, the range pressed out in bumpy plastic, various enamel badges. We requested this and that and the woman laid it all out on the counter: the badges, the relief maps, our coats . . . and three pieces of home-made cake wrapped in cling film. It wasn't until she was totting up the bill that I noticed them sitting there.

'What are these?'

'You don't want?' she affected surprise.

'No, we don't want.'

She removed them with a little sigh, crossed a figure off the bill. It left me with a sad feeling as we trudged back round the lake.

The next day began with Trevor smashing up the hotel room. Breakfast had just been delivered, Mark and Norman had come down to discuss plans and I had slipped into the bathroom to shower. I didn't hear a thing. When I emerged, it was to find broken glass and crockery all over the floor, puddles of milk and orange-style juice spilling off the table and on to the carpet, butter smeared over the mirror, the contents of the stationery folder scattered everywhere, soft-boiled eggs smashed open on the bedside table, slices of cheese adhering to white walls next to long, brown splashes of coffee. Mark was taking a photograph of Trevor, who was lying naked on the bed, pretending to insert a bread roll in his arse.

'Oh dear, Trevor,' I tutted, towelling my hair. 'Do you have to be so rock and roll?'

We concluded it was now wise to exit the resort in a hurry. The hotel bill was settled with a sigh of relief, Katarina met us in the lobby and we rushed out to the car. It wouldn't start. Trevor lifted the bonnet and started messing around. Katarina went back into the hotel. We tried a push-start across the car park, but it was futile in the snow. Sarcastic cracks about getaway cars were ringing in the mountain air when some workmen with a snow plough came to the rescue. They towed us to their depot, wheeled out a fantastic piece of Czechnology and attached a pair of crackling electrodes to our battery. The engine quaked into life. Back to the Panorama. No sign of Katarina. Trevor kept the motor running, afraid it wouldn't start again, while the rest of us fanned out to look for her. Five minutes later Norman bumped into her ambling out of the hotel kitchen. Round to the Hotel Patria because Mark wanted one of the relief maps. I went in with him to buy cigarettes. There was a different woman on the cloakroom. No cakes this time but instead of my change she handed over an obviously worthless disc of goldish-coloured alloy, faintly embossed with a figure in profile. It looked like chocolate money.

'What's this?'

'A lucky crown.'

I shrugged and dropped it in my pocket. Stepping back into the car, I noticed an empty beer bottle on the floor. Don't need that, I thought, and placed it carefully on the kerb outside. From the back seat, where Katarina was sandwiched between Mark and Norman, came a gasping sound.

'What's the matter?' asked Mark.

She said: 'I've never seen anyone do *that* before.'

As we hurtled back downhill, Billy Idol booming from the speakers, a surreptitious hand curled around from behind my headrest. It was Mark's, proffering a biscuit.

'Shall I offer her one?' murmured Mark in my ear.

There was a note of mischief in his voice. I craned around to look him in the eye. Katarina, sandwiched between Mark and Norman, was staring straight ahead, face giving nothing away. She was an employee of the state tourist organisation Čedok. In Stalinist Czechoslovakia, dealing with foreigners was a sensitive business. It was well known that many of these Čedok people doubled as secret police. From stuff she'd told us already, about holidays in Italy and Austria, it was clear she at least enjoyed the trust of the authorities.

I tried to phrase my reply in English she would not understand: 'I am not of the opinion that this thing you are proposing would, ah, fall within the best interests of all concerned.'

The look in my eye put the matter more simply: Don't be so fucking stupid. Even if she wasn't a secret police informer, she was anyway straight enough to be shocked by littering. The last thing we needed was her floating off on some evil biscuit trip and imagining she was going mad.

From the first tribulations with the car, it was clear Katarina had regretted accepting the ride. She had no time to lose, must be in Brno by a certain hour, had to meet friends. When we stopped to take a group photograph, Tatras on the horizon behind us, she'd nagged us to hurry up. Often she referred to her watch, crossly observing the lateness of the hour. This drove Trevor mad. Having gone out of his way to persuade her to come with us, he now started flinging out comments designed to torment the woman.

'Why,' he challenged at one point, 'does everything in Czechoslovakia look like it's closed?'

His tone indicated that he held her personally responsible. Katarina shifted nervously in the back, unsure what the game was here. Seconds later, as we whipped past some political slogan on a billboard in a field, Trevor started chanting:

'Czechoslovakian workers united – against democracy!'

Thus far it was actually funny in a nerve-racking kind of way. But when he suggested putting on some cassette he had brought, a compilation of old Nazi songs, I felt I had to draw the line.

'No, Trevor. No fucking way.'

I could see her relating all this to one of her superiors: Yes, they were all giggling and acting sort of funny, and then they started chanting anti-socialist slogans and playing these fascist anthems. It was a dark brown Mercedes. I didn't get the number but it must be among their registration details at the Hotel Panorama . . . No, it simply didn't bear thinking about.

'OK,' said Trevor, finally seeming to grasp the point. 'I suppose you're right.'

We raced on, back through the pine valleys and smoking factories, making good time until, on the outskirts of Žilina, the very place we'd been stopped last time, a motorcycle cop appeared from nowhere and flagged us down.

'Hallo, John,' chirped Trevor, winding down the window as the cop approached the car. 'What can I do for you then, mate?'

The cop said something in Slovakian. Confronted by this authority figure, Katarina had stiffened into a modified position of attention. Now she made some reply. The cop beckoned Trevor out and then, almost as an afterthought, looked back and beckoned Katarina too. The three stood talking by his bike.

Trevor was beaming when he came back. 'It was nothing. Just another speeding fine. When he looked through my passport, this thing fluttered out.' He held up the receipt from the fine we'd paid last time. 'He laughed when he saw where it was from and then told me I had to pay either ten West marks or a hundred crowns.'

This was a subtle choice. Ten marks was much cheaper at the official rate, but a rip-off at the black market rate. Trevor had immediately flaunted his intimate knowledge of the shadow economy.

'I gave him a hundred crowns and said, "Here, take that,

173

it's cheaper." He looked well pissed off until I told him not to bother about a receipt.'

The cop detained Katarina a little longer. By the time she got back in the car, we were bristling with curiosity and apprehension. What the hell had they been talking about?

'Oh,' she said, 'he wanted to know if he could see me again.'

A round of sour chuckles.

'He came from Bratislava, like I do. I told him,' she announced brightly, 'that my brother there is also a . . . a sort of policeman.'

We all caught the ominous ring in that 'sort of'. For a moment of silence, it vibrated in the air.

'Well then, Trevor,' I said. 'Shall we put your fantastic tape on now?'

It was my job to read the map. Between Žilina and Brno there was no obvious direct route, just a dense tangle of red and yellow lines connecting every single town with every other one. Trevor would scream for instant instructions whenever we hit an unexpected intersection. Katarina was no help at all. She said nothing when we made the right decision, moaned and consulted her watch when she felt we had made the wrong one. It was like someone directing you by calling out: 'Cold . . . warm . . . hot . . . cold . . . very cold.'

After the clear mountain air it was disheartening to be back in the dense toxic soup ladled into the bowl of every valley. I started sketching smoking chimneys, experimenting with ways of drawing thick clouds of pollution. At one factory, the tallest smoke-stack was vertically lettered with the word: 'CHEMICELULOZA'. Around the top of the two giant storage tanks beside it, to make them look 'nice', someone had stuck rows of happy red and blue flower shapes, a giant version of the kind of thing that used to cover 1960s kitchen surfaces. The river by the road was an unsettling greenish-brown, flecked with evil yellow scum: where the salmonoid fish came from, presumably.

For miles we sat in silence, too saddened even to think about playing music. Mark tapped me on the arm. I turned around to see Katarina asleep, her head on Norman's shoulder. He was tensed in the corner, hands folded across his chest, too terrified to move. We had been instructed to pretend, in Katarina's presence, that Norman was a Westerner. This was supposed to make her more receptive to his charms. But what hope had that strategy? We had chatted Katarina up, bought her drinks, diverted the whole route of our holiday simply to offer her a lift and thus supply Norman with the pretext for developing their relationship. This endeavour had at last, with the minimum of work on Norman's part, thrown up a golden opportunity to nudge their acquaintanceship from the platonic towards the physical. And there was Norman, stiff as an ironing board propped up in a cupboard, no more capable of sliding a gentle arm around her shoulder than he was of emigrating to Australia.

Trevor pulled into the car park of a roadside restaurant. Inside it was deserted save for about four waiters in black suits and bow ties. A smell of burnt fat hung in the air and the whole place – walls, ceiling, furniture, tablecloths, net curtains – was stained a deep nicotine brown. We settled in a booth by a window. Ten minutes later a waiter swaggered to our table. He offered no menu, so as later to be able to invent some fancy prices. Mark asked Katarina to ask him for something without meat in it. His reply surprised no one.

'Omelette.'

'What kind of omelette?'

'Omelette with ham.'

'Ham is meat.'

He shrugged.

'Can you make us an omelette without the ham in it?'

The waiter shook his head. Trevor completely lost it.

'Can't your fucking cook even make an omelette? Anyone can make an omelette. I can make a bloody omelette.' He turned to Katarina. 'Translate for me, will you? I'm going to tell this ignorant fucker how you make an omelette and he can go and tell the fucking cook. It's easy. You take a couple of eggs, right? Crack them into a bowl,' he was acting this out over the table, 'add a bit of milk, a little pepper, stir it all up. Tell him,' he shouted at Katarina. 'Tell him to go and tell the cook. Just tell him, will you?'

It was a violent performance, filling the whole room with a powerful tension. Katarina quivered in mute confusion, mouth opening and closing. The other waiters were gathering round, staring with impassive eyes. It was too much for me. I got up from the table and walked outside, Trevor still raging behind me.

'Tell him in order to make an omelette without ham, you simply do not add the fucking ham. Do you think the cook can understand this? Perhaps I should just go in the bloody kitchen and do it myself . . . '

I settled on the steps outside, flushed out the stench of burnt fat with a deep breath of smoggy air. After days on a diet of tepid crap saturated in enough rancid animal fat to leave a greasy puddle on the plate, sluiced down and churned up in a foaming torrent of beer, the normally robust mechanism of my stomach was beginning to rebel. It bubbled and seethed, erupting now and then with a sharp, acidic belch. The thought of another omelette, with or without ham, simply made me feel sick. If the head chef from Maxim's had walked up at that moment and personally offered to prepare his celebrated *Omelette de Petits Pois aux Fines Herbes Magnifique*, I would have told him to take a hike.

There was no way Trevor's outburst was going to result in the delivery of anything edible, but I shared the frustration which powered it. It wasn't funny any more. I had even begun to understand why all the dissidents liked Thatcher. Their enthusiasm for the woman usually made me feel uncomfortable. It wasn't that I couldn't agree that Western society was freer and more prosperous than the East, the goods less shoddy, the factories less filthy, a better quality of life provided for most, if by no means all. It was that there was still a moral price to pay. The London I'd left had been a cold and unscrupulous place, a place where conformity was called style, indifference was called rational self-interest and greed was called greed. Only two things distinguished the Western yuppie from the Czech catering

176

worker: his pickings were richer, his uniform suit of a higher quality.

But at least a Western cook could usually manage an omelette. To get a job as a cook in the Czechoslovak Socialist Republic, you had to attend catering school for three long years. None seemed to have emerged from the experience capable even of boiling a kettle. The waiters, for their part, cared for nothing but the chance to cheat you, the only aspect of their job that gave them any incentive. Sitting there on the steps, I could feel the last shreds of my youthful leftism being blown clean away. Maybe competition and market forces were indeed the only way to shake some quality of life into a system with results like these. Damn it, maybe greed, in this sense, was good. And yet, and yet.

One of the waiters had followed me out. He stood to my left, lit a cigarette, pretended to watch the traffic which wisely continued on its way. From the side of his mouth, he muttered:

'Change money, change money?'

'Fuck off.'

We reached Brno in early evening. By the time we'd dropped Katarina off at the swanky Hotel International and located a cheaper place for ourselves, everyone was dazed and exhausted. The receptionist, a bitter, middle-aged woman in a Čedok uniform, didn't like the look of us and started firing questions.

'How much money have you changed?'

'The prescribed minimum,' we told her. The details were all in the paperwork in front of her.

'That is all?'

She examined our faces, pinning us one after the other with a hard, suspicious gaze.

'Then how could you afford all these hotels?'

The sheer bluntness of her attack threw us all out of kilter. Two things were clear. The first was that if Katarina hadn't been a secret policeman, then this woman certainly was. The second, that if this were real trouble, we were far too stoned to handle it. We had, however, allowed for this problem, knowing we could expect such a check at the border. Our sums indicated that one more night in a hotel would not exceed our official amount of money. Even if they suspected us of changing on the black market, as this woman obviously did, no one could prove how much we had spent in restaurants and bars – not even if that appeared to have been nothing at all. But what if we had made a mistake? As she leafed through our visas, examining the hotel stamps and totalling up on a primitive calculator, I found myself gripping the lucky crown in my pocket.

The woman flung all the paperwork back on the counter and shot us a glance that said: You got away with it this time, but you'd better watch your arses around me.

Brno, capital of Moravia, a town whose history stretched all the way back to its location on ancient amber routes, was like a smaller, shabbier Prague. There was a similar mixture of the medieval and baroque, another castle on a hill. We set out for the evening and lost ourselves in the cobbled tangle of the old town. After the trial of our hotel check-in, it felt like we were back in Syldavia again. We stopped at a socialist realist version of a 1950s coffee bar and Mark ordered some chips from their small selection of snacks. On the table stood a bottle of Czech tomato ketchup and, in a spirit of experimentation, Mark upended it over his plate.

'Hey!' His face lit up with the first taste. 'This is brilliant.'

It was the reverse of the Fragopolis brandy. One after another we dipped explorative chips. To palates deadened by the local cuisine, the ketchup did indeed seem very tasty. We burst into an approving chorus.

'This stuff is excellent.'

'Full-bodied and fruity.'

'Just a hint of vinegar. A fine ketchup.'

Our excitement was pathetic. Round after round of chips were ordered, just so we could sample more.

'I wouldn't mind getting a bottle of this tomorrow,' said Trevor, wiping his last plate clean. 'Take some home with me.'

'Don't be stupid. It'll taste horrible when you're back in West Berlin.'

'Maybe I will take some back to East Berlin,' said Norman. 'It will probably taste OK there.'

Mark looked at his watch and elbowed Norman. Their faces acquired a sly, sheepish expression.

'I'm afraid we two are going to have to leave you now.'

I sussed it immediately.

'You've made a date to meet Katarina.'

'Together with her friend,' confessed Mark.

'Right,' said Trevor. 'Fine. You just go on ahead without us. We don't mind, do we, Dave?'

'Not in the slightest. Far be it from us to cramp your style.'

'We're not pissed that we set the whole thing up for you and now you're leaving us in the lurch.'

We accompanied them for a couple of blocks and waved goodbye outside a beer hall. They disappeared in the direction of the International. The beer hall was huge, raucous, Bacchanalian. Along and around several great wooden tables, drunken monsters roared and bellowed, quaffed huge mugs of beer, hurled things at each other. Waiters weaved between, ducking under flying objects, swerving through fistfights, never spilling a drop from the trays of beer they hefted at shoulder height. We grabbed a couple of glasses as one passed. You only had to order once. From then on they'd keep replacing your empties until you asked them to stop. This admirable custom was made simple because apart from beer, the place sold only tonic water and some kind of cola. Hardly anyone was drinking those.

Propped against a wall, we absorbed the local colour. With the latest round of biscuits beginning to come on strong, it was like drinking in a Breughel painting. Grotesque faces leapt out of the crowd. Nearby a strange, slow-motion fight was going on. A misshapen mutant would belt his companion. The second guy would absorb the blow without reacting. He'd just stand there, squinting out from under a brow so low it left his eyes in deep shadow, until finally a dim light winked on and he realised what had happened. He would then roar and slug the first guy back. This one too had a reaction time you could have measured with a sundial. He'd sway in silence for several minutes, wrapped up in what was presumably some sort of inner life, before yelling and hurling a fist at a third guy.

Trevor and I smiled happily. It was the best bar we had found since the beginning of our holiday. We felt immune to the violence simmering around us, even though totally overdressed for the place. The slow-motion fight was slowly gathering momentum. The violence bubbled, the volume rose, the whole place seemed to teeter on the edge of an all-out brawl. I had a vision of blood, broken glass, drunken monsters tearing each other limb from limb. The scene was in danger of slipping from Breughel into Bosch . . .

At which point Mark and Norman walked cheerily in. It was as if a plug had been pulled.

'What are you two doing here. Stood up, perhaps?'

'No,' said Mark. 'Katarina's got three friends with her. We thought you might as well come too.'

'Do we want to?' I asked Trevor.

'Might as well have a change of scene.'

The drinks at the video disco of the Hotel International were about five times as expensive as the beer hall. So were the people. Waiters in tail coats proudly purveyed chinking cocktails and sparkling wines to a crowd in leisure suits and costume jewellery. Now we were underdressed. On stage a band in glittery clothes and page-boy haircuts played a cover version of an Abba song. The female singer had cleavage, long blonde hair and a forced smile. In a small corner of the large floor, Friday-night couples did their penny-kicking dance. On a table at the side, stiffly sipping glasses of white wine, were Katarina and her friends.

Norman sat down next to Katarina. The other girls resisted all attempts at even the most innocent chatter. Indeed, so manifest was their distaste for us that it encouraged a couple of smooth Italians to approach with the classic 'Are these men bothering you?' opening. I tapped the nearest on the shoulder and told him to 'Vaffanculo.' The Italians took a good look at us, Trevor leering back, the lights of the disco casting his scar in sharp relief, and hurried off to try their luck elsewhere. After that the girls clammed up completely. We didn't care, hadn't really been interested in the first place, and when the band struck up a pathetic cover of Modern Talking's 'You're My Heart, You're My Soul', got up and decided to dance.

Trevor, Mark and I began jumping around in a wild and unabashedly ridiculous parody of 1970s disco routines, twirling around and rotating our hands in the air. The crowd parted nervously, clearing a space around us. When the song ended, there was a polite ripple of applause. We joined in, calling 'Bravo' and 'Encore'. Long after everyone else had stopped clapping, the three of us kept on going – looking around encouragingly as if trying to get the others to resume. A faint aura of embarrassment began to rise from the crowd. The keyboard player put up a hand to shield his eyes from the lights, tried to see what was going on, then counted the band down into a version of Europe's 'The Final Countdown'. We redoubled our idiotic dancing, pretended this was the most exciting thing we had ever heard. This time we sustained our clapping and cheering for an agonisingly long time. Others on the dance floor were getting annoyed. Now the bassist joined the keyboard player in scanning for the source of this irritation, but the singer took it dead seriously. Obviously, we were clapping for her. She bowed in silent gratitude and dedicated the next song to us, her wonderful, wonderful fans.

Said Katarina, when we finally sat down: 'You lot are worse than the Russians.'

'When we're back,' Norman said as we went shopping the next morning, 'the next time you come to East Berlin, maybe you could bring a Western postcard over with you.'

'Yes, if you want,' said Mark. 'But why?'

'I want to write to Katarina.' He was shy about this. 'You could maybe post it for me in West Berlin.'

'It would do you a lot of good marrying a Czech,' I said. 'Then you'd be able to emigrate to the one country you're allowed to go to anyway.'

'Norman's not thinking about marriage,' said Trevor.

'He's still hoping Katarina will suck his penis because she thinks he's a Westerner and wants to marry *him*.'

Norman blushed. The previous night he had said good-bye to Katarina without their relationship having progressed beyond the pleasant conversation stage. Now it looked as though it never would.

I stopped in front of a department store. There, in the window, was a display of plastic Christmas trees. 'Just look at that. Judging from our journey, this whole damn country is covered with real Christmas trees. And yet somewhere, perhaps in one of those places we drove by yesterday, they are making plastic Christmas trees – with the very industrial processes that are destroying all the real ones.'

It was still with us, the shock of yesterday's descent from mountain air into industrial smog. We all stood and stared in the window for a moment, lost in the sad, stupid irony of the sight.

We had heard there were catacombs in Brno and stopped an old man to ask if he knew where they were. He told us that the catacombs were closed. Perhaps we would like him to show us the castle? He was about five feet tall, thick spectacles perched on a perfect button nose, raincoat and pork-pie hat – another Tintin character. With a solemn and regular tread he led us down alleys, across parks, over bridges, up a long flight of steps. By the time we reached the top, all of us were puffing and blowing, but on the man trod, never flagging or varying his pace, back always perfectly straight. As we marched around the castle walls he spoke of battles and conquests, of a dizzying number of empires: the Carolingian Empire, the Great Moravian Empire, the Holy Roman Empire, the Habsburg Empire, the Austro-Hungarian Empire, the Third Reich. The steadiness of his tread was hypnotic, tapping out a meas-ured counterpoint to the confusion of history. Brno had been conquered by everyone, borders had swept over it like waves, yet the old man just plodded on, staunch as a Brecht character, waiting for the end of the last empire, the Soviet one.

On the run back to Prague, I sucked on a bottle of beer and watched the motorway pass tediously by. The first biscuit of the day said, let me take you away from all this, and led me by the hand into a daydream. A guard had found my little notebook at the border, examined the pictures of smoking factories. I see you have been sketching our industrial installations, Meester Reemer. Very interesting. And what are all these little marks in the back? You have been counting something. The number of beers you have been drinking on your holiday? A likely story. But allow me to take you at your word . . . at so much per bottle of beer, this comes out as costing, hmm . . . yes, precisely five times the amount of crowns you would have left from your minimum currency exchange after paying the bills for these hotels which are stamped on your visa. And what means this 'biscuits'? There are many marks here. Why do you hesitate? Surely there must be a simple explanation . . .

Trevor snapped me out of it with his cassette of old Nazi songs. On the first strident notes of 'Tomorrow Belongs To Me', Norman gritted his teeth. For as long as he could remember, he'd had it drummed in about the evils of Nazism. He'd grown up in a country still run by members of the communist resistance to Hitler, where opposition to 'Hitlerfascismus' was still used not only as justification for Walls and travel restrictions, but also as the very basis of legitimacy for the state itself. In the DDR, more than in England, even more than in West Germany, this was the ultimate taboo. Just to listen to these songs in a car far from home was enough to frighten him rigid. Mark and I didn't like it much either. Only Trevor enjoyed the tape, whistling like a bastard along with the hateful music.

'Thank God for that,' breathed Norman as the last chord died down.

There was a long, awkward silence. I stared at the label on my beer bottle and meditated on the nature of perversity. If you hang around with someone because you enjoy the way they shock others, you can hardly complain when they overstep some line of your own.

Torsten was waiting for us at David and Andrea's. Having

driven the hospital van all week, he'd come down by train for this Saturday night in Prague. While Mark and I cooked a curry with the remaining ingredients from Berlin, Norman briefed him on the trip so far, grateful for the chance to gush out his horror stories to a fellow East German. From the tone of the breathless German drifting over the room divider, it was hard to tell whether Norman was sad or relieved that these holidays were almost at an end.

Trevor sawed himself a slice of bread, lathered it thick from a jar of peanut butter we'd brought David and Andrea.

'Hadn't you better leave some for them?'

'Nah,' he said, mouth full. 'Serves them right for not having eaten it themselves yet. They're stupid, the Czechs. You bring them something and they don't dare eat it because they're scared they'll never get it again.'

Five minutes later, I found an open sachet of MRE fortified cheese spread in the back of the fridge. The residue adhering to the inside of the olive wrapper had hardened and discoloured.

'God,' said Mark, 'that must have been there since Trevor and I were here in April.'

The next day I noticed one more detail. In the corner where their daughter Jula slept, most of her toys were shoved rudely into a box. But the doll we had brought was still in its packaging, sitting on a shelf in pride of place next to other dolls from Mark's previous visits. She didn't play with these special Western dolls, she exhibited them. Even a seven-year-old child had already grown into this sad, clinging attitude to all things Western.

We lingered over the meal, our first decent one since the last time in this kitchen, and it was getting late by the time we'd finished. David and Andrea went straight to bed. I could quite happily have followed but Torsten had come all this way for just one night and we had to do something. Mark broke out the biscuits, a new batch, for we had crunched our way down to the reserve supply.

'Here we go again,' I said. 'But where exactly?'

'Let's be tourists,' Mark suggested, 'and go to U Fleců.'

U Fleců was a famous old beer hall, larger and more distinguished than the one in Brno, though still venue for the occasional brawl. It served its own justly celebrated dark brew and was usually full of East German tourists. A dip back down into the bright science fiction underground, a meander through the gloomy old streets of the Old Town and we were there. But before the first mugs of fine black beer had been placed before us, even before we had taken our seats at a long wooden table, I could tell that this latest batch of biscuits was much stronger than the last ones.

We sat in a daze. The background noise swelled and receded. U Fleců seemed to fade away, its half-timbered walls repositioning themselves at some great distance. Our conversation was fragmented, words falling out in jagged pieces that wouldn't fit together. I didn't try to pay attention, just looked at the little sparks of light twinkling off the bubbles on my beer. The waiter would only serve us that one round. It was drinking-up time already. After seven days in the country we had learnt to depend on Czech beer. To have our supply of the stuff cut off so abruptly at this subjectively early stage on a Saturday night was like someone turning off the television and putting up the lights in the middle of some engrossing movie. Confused and disappointed, we stepped out on to the street. Spread out on the pavement before us, reflecting the light from the ancient clock above the entrance, was a large pool of beery vomit.

'I wish I'd had that much to drink,' I said.

The medieval street patterns of the Old Town could have been specially designed to thwart any sense of direction. We drifted off into the labyrinth, once more savouring the experience of being fried out of our faces in the dead, dark centre of a stern totalitarian metropolis, searching for anything at all to do and primed to appreciate whatever it might turn out to be. Bowed figures plodded by in the shadows. The streets closed in ominously around, wide squares opened alarmingly out. Torsten cried:

'We are walking round in circles!'

'No we're not.'

'That's the second time we've passed that car!'

'It's a Skoda, Torsten. Practically every car in the country is a Skoda.'

'We are going in circles!'

A woman in a closing café let us drink sweet white wine while she cleared up. Our big Saturday night continued in an alley off Na Příkopě, where a man was selling beer from a hole in the wall. We bought a bottle each and hung about near a knot of old alkies. The minute we were ready for another beer, the man banged down his hatch. Every possibility for enjoyment seemed to be hedged by strict deadlines. Over the road was the red and yellow sign of Arbat, a sort of McStalin's purveying some kind of vile meatburger. Upstairs the restaurant Moskva was still open, so there we drifted. It was full of tourists. You couldn't drink unless you had something to eat, so we ordered a schnitzel for Trevor and some cheeses on a wooden plate along with beers and colas. The bill was legible for once, having unfurled from the maw of a modern computer till. Mark entertained us with extracts: some steaks, four packets of Sparta cigarettes, five double brandies. A new idea occurred to us. A fun idea. Why didn't we complain? The waiter was summoned. Mark gripped the bill with thumb and forefinger, held it away from his body with great distaste.

'This is false,' he said, wrinkling his nose as he waved it around.

The waiter snatched the bill back without even glancing at it. There was no apology, not even a hint of the old 'I'm sorry, there has been a terrible mistake'. He simply marched off to bring us a new one, openly angry that the rip-off hadn't worked.

While the other three slept at the nearby flat of David's father, an avant-garde composer in uncertain favour with the regime, Trevor and I were on the living-room floor. We were woken early the next morning by David moving around, packing up books, readying himself for the monthly flea market. We hadn't known this was on and struggled out of sleeping bags, eager to tag along.

The flea market was in a hall between Moskevská and the

river. There were indeed a few empty Western beer cans for sale, along with old copies of Western magazines, bootleg cassette compilations of Western pop hits, fake Lacoste shirts, loose crocodile labels, cheap Walkmen and digital watches. Standing around in the corridors were people without stalls, offering one or two Western items in open hands: an LCD game and a plastic lorry; a calculator and a tube of Pepsodent; ten floppy disks and some eye shadow. Near the top of one flight of stairs stood a gang of boys in US Army camouflage gear, maybe twenty or thirty of them, all bartering over belts and knapsacks, boots and jackets. For a while I stood and watched this odd Czech subculture. I couldn't imagine how they got hold of all the stuff, but it struck me that if they hadn't gone out the car window, I could have walked up with the secret playing cards and solemnly named my price.

Apart from secondhand books and sheet music, the main trade was in enamel badges. Different vendors catered to different specialities but three kinds of badge predominated: Czech and Soviet military, football clubs, motor cars. The military stuff was nothing special now that Norman could turn it up in East Berlin. Football didn't excite me much and neither, as a rule, did cars. But here I had acquired an interest. Since the Eastie Boys, we'd all been on the lookout for Trabant stuff. The toy shops and department stores of East Berlin and various Czechoslovakian cities had been combed for Trabant key-rings, model Trabis, anything. To date we had turned up precisely bugger-all.

Trevor and I started hunting. There were badges for every Western kind of car: Mercedes and Audi and Nissan and Opel and Uncle Brit Leyland and all. There were badges for every Eastern kind of car: Lada and Tatra and Skoda and Dacia and Uncle Polski Fiat and all . . . except Trabant. Even here in what seemed to be the car-badge collecting centre of the East, there was frustratingly no trace of the vehicle. Dealers stared in amazement when we mentioned the word. We were clearly fools. They tried to fob us off with Wartburg or Rolls-Royce. It seemed we were the world's only collectors of Trabibilia until at last one dealer conceded a cautious nod. He heaved out an album from the bottom of his pile, flipped almost to the very back, and plucked something from one of the polythene compartments: a small, glittering palmful of Trabant lapel pins.

We got back to find Norman and Torsten had already gone off to catch the train home. Trevor and I decided to send Norman and Torsten their badges by post and sat down to compose an accompanying card. Trevor watched as I scribbled it more than half-full of silly in-jokes.

'I *am* literate,' he remarked.

I handed him the card. Holding pen in fist he scrawled like a five-year-old, half his letters the wrong way round: 'Norman – eat yore knobcheese!' The envelope containing the card and the pins took a whole month to arrive in East Berlin. A lot of people, Norman noted later, must have worked on that letter. Perhaps they imagined it was in code. Somewhere among the Stasi's miles of files – still, as I write, held in secrecy by the unified German government – there must be a report on that postcard.

Around half-past five that afternoon, David turfed us out of the flat. He wanted peace and quiet to help his daughter with her reading. I had just dozed off on the couch and it was in foul humour that I tied my shoes, splashed a little water on my face, stepped out with the others into the shadows of early evening. A pounding in my head was like distant artillery, my digestive system sent up regular caustic reminders of the abuse to which it had been subject, every limb cried out for a cessation of hostilities. As we paced the dim, shabby streets towards our destination, I reached inside to summon a little resolve. Enough, I told myself, pausing on the threshold of the Bar Olympia. Tonight I would abstain from biscuits and beer. It would be mineral water. Early to bed.

And so it came about that by the time our friend Jachym arrived and sat down at our table, I was already on my fifth beer and looking to order more. The Olympia was a sort of combination bar and restaurant, shabby and comfortable, another hangout for the crowd of malcontents Mark knew in Prague. It looked like nothing had changed in it since around 1954. Empty when we arrived, the place had gradually filled with a young but subdued crowd, chatting in twos and fours around wooden tables and large mugs of Staropramen.

Jachym had mournful features, Eastern bloc pale and framed with lank blond hair. He wore American blue jeans and a Czech anorak in characteristic dried mud colour. The editor of a samizdat magazine called *Revolver Revue*, he was about to have a volume of his poetry published in New York and played in a band for whom he hoped we might wangle an invitation to come to West Berlin. He was, in a sense, the classic sort of younger 'dissident'.

A loaded term, 'dissident', conjuring up a travel writer's Prague full of writers in boiler rooms grumbling about the state of things to visiting Western intellectuals. In fact everyone I met in Prague seemed to be some kind of dissident. None were famous, they were just people like ourselves: temperamentally inclined more to the margins than the mainstream, trying to make the best of a situation in which the mainstream was unequivocally repugnant and the margins very marginal indeed. It was hard to think of these scruffy drinking partners as in any way resembling, say, Solzhenitsyn. I, on the other hand, hadn't seen myself as a visiting Western intellectual until, greeting Jachym, I realised I was in the mood for a 'dissident'.

I'd looked at a copy of *Revolver Revue* that afternoon. It was a beautiful object: a fat wad of closely typed carbon copies meticulously interleaved with the occasional monochrome illustration printed separately on heavier paper. According to the English digest of contents which was the only part I could read, the rest comprised fiction, poetry, essays, translations of Burroughs. The cover was a piece of mild porn – a bare-breasted girl with a gun – which in the prevailing puritanical conditions could presumably be considered subversive. The feel of it reminded me of the *Oz* and *IT* magazines I used to buy on the way home from school. In this as in so much else, Czechoslovakia was still trapped in the late 1960s.

I quizzed Jachym about the enormous effort that

obviously went into the magazine's production. He told me that twelve was the maximum number of legible carbons you could squeeze from one typing. Back in Berlin, I told him, I had a computer.

'A computer!' he sighed. 'What I could do with a computer.'

Which was funny, because it always saddened me how little there was to do with mine. What was worth desktop-publishing in a Western world already papered with print media? By the time I left London, after years as a pro-fessional consumer trying to keep up with every latest damn book, film, record, TV show or magazine, in a world where everything was of interest but nothing mattered, I was longing for less, not more – a feeling that certainly underlay my fascination with the East. And here was Jachym, working in an Eastern world that needed any unofficial media it could get, painstakingly typing out translations of Burroughs and distributing them clandes-tinely because that was the only way anyone would get to read them. We all chinked glasses. Between Jachym and us was the distance between Huxley and Orwell, between idle computers and overused sheets of carbon, between one side of the looking-glass and the other.

'So how much,' asked Trevor, bored with our sensible conversation, 'do women cost in this town?'

Jachym was caught off-guard.

'What do you mean?'

'We're rich Western tourists, right? We've got fucking loads of money. How much of it does it take to buy a woman?'

'It depends what you want. Maybe five hundred or seven hundred marks. Or you can get anything, maybe an old woman for about ten crowns.'

Trevor nodded appraisingly.

'Ten crowns sounds about right.'

'There are these old women, they hang around in the streets near factories on a Friday afternoon when the workers get paid, give a blow job for about ten crowns.'

That made us laugh. Jachym looked pleased.

'How about you, Jachym?' Trevor was all smiles and politeness. 'Do you have a girlfriend?'

'I am married. I have a wife.'

'What's she like?'

'She is very beautiful, of course.'

'How much to fuck her then?'

'What?'

'I'll give you three hundred marks to fuck your wife.'

Jachym was half out of his seat.

'What are you saying, you fucking guy?'

'Four hundred?'

He turned to Mark and me, suddenly frantic.

'Should I hit this fucking guy?'

'Dave,' grinned Trevor. 'How about if I give you four hundred marks to fuck my wife?'

'Make it eight hundred,' I said.

Jachym began to calm down.

'Beer for you, Jachym?' asked Mark.

'Oh yes, but I don't have any money until my friends get here.'

'I've heard that one before,' said Trevor darkly.

'No, it is true. They are coming at nine and –'

'I'm sorry, boy, but I'm not having that.' Trevor rapped the tabletop. 'You're not leaving this table until you pay for your beers.'

Jachym was wracked with embarrassment and Trevor pressed his attack. When the waiter brought the next round, scribbling a few more marks on the running tab, Trevor picked it up and affected outrage.

'Hey! That waiter just wrote down five beers when he only brought four! This is always happening. But when we try and complain they only speak Czech.'

'That is very bad,' said honest Jachym. 'I will tell him.'

He picked up the bill and went over to dispute with the waiter. Why, Jachym waved the bill around, had the waiter done this terrible thing? What the fuck, gesticulated the waiter, was Jachym talking about? Jachym looked back towards the table and we all burst out laughing.

'You fucking guy,' snapped Jachym as he sat back down.

Mark turned to Trevor. 'I bet,' he said, 'you don't dare get your penis out.'

It was a masterstroke. For once Trevor was the one made uncomfortable. He wouldn't be Trevor if he turned down a dare like that, but the idea of exposing himself in a crowded Prague bar was not one even he would normally contemplate. He glanced around, lips drawn tight, assessing the situation.

'Come on, Trevor,' said Mark. 'I want to take a picture.'

Trevor breathed deep.

'All right. But give me a minute.'

He scrabbled with his fly buttons under the table. Mark rushed to get his camera ready.

'You'll have to be quick,' said Trevor. 'I'm not standing up like this for any longer than necessary.'

'Necessary!' That made me laugh. 'If ever there was a definition of unnecessary behaviour.'

Trevor shot up like a soldier to attention. His flies were open but his member didn't quite have the strength to part them and push through. A careful observer might just have discerned a tiny glimpse of pink peeping between outer curtains of buttoned brown flannel, inner ones of white boxer short material. Flash! Trevor was back in his seat again.

While Trevor loosed a rueful grin and Mark and I hooted with disdain, Jachym was sitting with his mouth open, totally shocked.

'Tell this fucking guy he must not do that,' Jachym whispered, too scared even to speak out loud. 'He must not. It is two years in prison. Maybe more. Anything could happen.'

Poor Jachym was trembling. It was hard to know how to comfort him. To retort that Trevor only did things like that because they were stupid and dangerous hardly seemed likely to do the job. Of course we all knew how much less dangerous they were for us, as Western tourists, than they were for him, a citizen of the East. That was by now a familiar tune. It was trickier to work through the flip side: that both the content and to some extent the form of our humour were dictated by the way, as Western tourists, we were treated or expected to behave. Trevor's jokes about money came after a week of being dealt with as a walking wallet. The idea of complaining about bills had become ludicrous long before this latest prank. Pretending to expect poor Jachym to pimp for his wife if the price was right was a response to what we had seen of the prevailing cynicism and corruption, of the selling of souls for a West mark or two. And if the humour took, in its English way, a particularly hypocritical, trouble-making form, that seemed only appropriate given the hypocritical, repressive circumstances.

I had been thinking about this since the night when we tore down the flags. In Václav Havel's argument, the pillar of the system was the living of a lie, hypocrisy and repression skipping hand in hand around it. The sign in the greengrocer's shop, the flag above the door, signalled not their overt content but a willingness to conform and obey. More subtly, the greengrocer, displaying the new 'workers of the world' sign because not to do so meant trouble, could still mutter, 'Well, after all, what's so very wrong with the workers of the world uniting?' and so duck the truth of his submission. In each small act of outward conformity, another little lie. As the flags and slogans cluttered every public space in the East, so the lies snarled up every inner life. The system didn't require you to believe, only to behave as if you did: to live within the lie.

The answer: to live within the truth. Say what you think. Organise a punk concert. Write your poem. Try to publish it. Don't put out the flags. The consequences could be grave. In a Stalinist society, any free expression of life, however small or indirect, became a political act. But politics were secondary. The real battle was to lay siege to the lie within, to tear down the Wall in the head, to live in dignity and self-respect, to be yourself. Which is what it meant to be a 'dissident'. Trevor, too, was just trying to be himself, to live within the truth. It's just that the truth boiled down to this: Trevor was a reckless fucking hooligan.

I started telling Jachym stories of our week, the better to put Trevor's savage sense of humour in some context. He was fascinated by our tales of Tatra mountain cloakroom attendants and Slovakian motorcycle cops. In turn, he told us of some Prague punks who had a competition. Dressed at their most extreme, they all started at one end of town and worked their way in towards Wenceslaus Square. The object: to see who could get stopped the most times.

'How many controls did the winner get?'

'Twenty-seven.'

I consulted my notebook. It was more than we'd managed in seven whole days of pushing our luck in a police state.

'It's horrible to put it this way,' I said, 'and it's tough luck on you who have to live here, but to us this whole country just seems like a joke. We come here and everything's simulated or falling apart and we get controlled twice a day and everybody tries to rip us off. Sometimes we get sad and sometimes we get angry but mostly we laugh. What else can we do? If we didn't take the piss out of it, we wouldn't be ourselves.'

Of course Jachym, fellow citizen of Kafka and Čapek, of Hašek and Kundera, understood this perfectly.

'Sure,' he said, 'you either laugh or you make a petition.'

Jachym's friends came in and he joined them at the next table. First Marek and later David turned up to join us at ours. With each new arrival we ordered a new round of beers, and on each of them in turn, Trevor played his that-waiter-wrote-down-too-many trick.

On the next table, Jachym and his friends were sitting stiff and paranoid, heads held unnaturally motionless, eyes darting left and right. Hand to hand, over knees and under table, they passed copies of a document. Some kind of petition? Their furtiveness blared yet no one but me seemed to notice. Perhaps people were carefully looking the other way. Or perhaps it was because our table was making enough noise to attract all the attention. It was curious, though: laughter and petitions now in dramatic juxtaposition.

The waiter took time totting up the bill. David and Marek watched him at work, indifferent to the enormity of the total. There was a strong element of give and take to these East–West friendships. We'd fix things for them in Berlin, they'd sort things out for us in Prague. Currency exchanges were of mutual advantage but it was always understood that we were the rich ones.

'Oh dear,' said Trevor, shaking open his wallet. 'I've got no crowns left.'

'Neither have I,' said Mark. 'I thought you had them all.'

'No, I must have spent all mine at the flea market.'

A look of concern began to creep across David's face. Marek was examining his fingernails.

'It's that self-spending money again,' I said. 'I might have some change, though . . . '

I dumped the contents of a pocket on the table. The lucky crown gleamed brassily among the small heap of coins. I picked it up and tossed it in the air.

There was a long silence. The waiter, who had so little cause to love our table, showed signs of blowing up again. The two Czechs went into a huddle, Eastern wallets inched reluctantly open, notes were counted out. How much did this represent to them? A few days' wages? When we all got up to leave, a shadow stalked us to the door. The mood was as black as the moonless night outside. Never since Chamberlain went to Munich in 1938 can Czechs have felt so betrayed by English.

'Surpri-i-i-ise!'

We pulled out the money. While Marek and David had been in the toilet, we'd all emptied our wallets: one last Western bastard tourist joke about drink bills and currency.

The first thing that came into my head next morning, waking in my sleeping bag on David's couch, was the paper Jachym had given me. Towards the end of the evening in Olympia, Jachym had leant over from his table and palmed me a folded sheet of paper. I'd glanced at it then: a carbon copy of some typed declaration in English.

'No,' Jachym had hissed. 'Don't look at it here.'

'But what is it?'

'A petition, about Ivan Jirous. He is in prison.'

'What can I do with it?' This had flustered me. Ivan who? 'I'm no news journalist.'

'Then for your own information,' Jachym had shrugged, turning back to his discussion.

I'd slid the paper into my pocket and put it from my mind. Now I spread it on the breakfast table. There were two sheets: the first a statement to the effect that one Ivan Jirous, poet and art critic, artistic director of the Plastic People Of The Universe, had been imprisoned for the umpteenth time – on this occasion for a poem about the political prisoners who died in Czech labour camps during the 1950s and 1960s. The dozen or so names at the bottom, Jachym's among them, wished to state the opinion that his renewed incarceration was a bad thing and should be firmly resisted. The second sheet was the poem itself. I wondered aloud what to do with the thing. Trevor was no help at all.

'It's nothing to do with me, I'm on holiday. I'm not having that thing in the car. If you want to take it you can keep it in your pocket. It's your responsibility.'

There was indeed the rub. One minute I'd been skipping happily across the surface and the next I had been handed my slice of responsibility. That I did share some of it was clear to me. Quite what I was to do with that responsibility, in so far as it was represented by this damn petition, seemed far less clear. I agonised over coffee, trying to balance the risks against the likely results.

Even without the petition, things seemed dodgy. On the other side of the breakfast table, Trevor was elaborating shopping plans for the morning. If he got everything done, the car would be packed with several crates of Czech beer, a soda siphon and cocktail shaker set he'd spotted in a shop in the Old Town, all the classical records Mark had bought, various old maps and secondhand books I'd picked up, sundry other crap including a brace of black rubber fake hand grenades. Meanwhile, according to our paperwork, we had stayed in hotels expensive enough to mop up nearly all our currency while travelling the length of the country and back on a tiny handful of diesel coupons.

So there was all that: clear enough evidence, for anyone

who chose to examine it, that several laws of the land had been flung down and danced upon. While this could obviously lead to trouble, we were, in our defence, just a bunch of stupid tourists. But any plea of dumb innocence would instantly be scuppered by discovery of the petition. And if found first, it would certainly lead to a search that would turn up every other detail in the car.

In itself, the petition was an unknown quantity. What kind of trouble might result? Forbidden to come back to Czechoslovakia? And even if I got the thing safely home, then what? For the British media, Czechoslovakia was still a faraway country, of whose people they knew nothing. Few of the magazines I ever worked for were likely to be interested. I could imagine the conversations. Sorry . . . Needs a peg . . . But we did something on Czechoslovakia last year . . . You see, the new editorial format.

I got up and traced a doodle in the condensation on the window. You always tell yourself that in, say, Nazi Germany, you would never have been one of those 'just following orders'; that in some Stalinist situation, you would have resisted the pressure to inform on a friend. But how do you know? Some chap – a writer, one involved in the music of his time – was banged up in a Czech jail precisely for having exhibited moral courage. And I, a writer, involved in the music of my time . . . I realised right then that I really had no clue what it was like to live and work in conditions like his.

Back at the table I toyed with the paper, ardently wishing Jachym had never given me the thing. The possibility of it causing trouble, not just for myself, but for Mark and Trevor too, perhaps also David and Andrea, seemed so much stronger than the chances of being able to use it to better the situation of Jirous, or anyone else in Czechoslovakia, that I decided I couldn't take it. After a week of taking stupid risks for a laugh, to take one serious risk for a petition was beyond me. Here we were, then: fine examples of that 'general unwillingness of consumption-oriented people to sacrifice some material certainties for the sake of their own spiritual and moral integrity'. For the sake of a car full of crap, the petition would have to go. Part of me felt rotten and part of me felt relieved.

From David I scrounged an envelope, addressed it to one of the other names on my letterbox in West Berlin – a Frenchman who collected his mail only rarely, was unlikely ever to travel to Czechoslovakia and with whom, for reasons of romantic complication, I was at that point engaged in a feud. I slid the petition inside and asked David, who was ignorant of the contents, to post it with the letter for Norman and Torsten. Back in Berlin weeks later, when it was clear it would never arrive, I realised I had not only been weak, I had also been stupid. If the Czech secret police hadn't known about the petition in the first place, then they certainly did now.

That evening, on the outskirts of the dead forest, we stopped at a filling station to use up the remaining diesel coupons. A couple were sufficient to top up the tank. Trevor was chuckling as he shredded the remainder.

'Great piece of cheek. We buy the minimum amount of diesel coupons, drive all over the bloody country and then we can't even get the last of them in the tank.'

For all our worry, there was hardly any trouble at the border. A guard asked us to bring our bags into his shed, gave their contents a cursory ruffle, didn't so much as glance at all the other stuff in the car. There could have been a hundred petitions in there, though I couldn't escape a sneaking feeling that if there had been, then he would have searched the car after all.

Once more we skirted Dresden. On the way down, in daylight, this city had looked a mess. Now, in the night, after a week in the serious tattiness of Czechoslovakia, Dresden with its neon advertising Robotron computers and Practika cameras looked like some bright, modern city of the West. It was dark road all the rest of the way, silence in the car. As we turned on to the Berliner Ring, just a few kilometres from home, I pulled out the blue notebook and, in the glimmer from the glove compartment, tallied the final reckoning.

'Well gentlemen, this holiday we have drunk 224 beers,

eaten 106 biscuits, 18 pea omelettes, 8 schnitzels and 48 portions of chips. We were ripped off 23 times, not ripped off 4 times, ripped them off twice and were controlled, if we count customs and passport separately and the DDR–Czech border as two, a grand total of 31 times.'

'Better add a couple more,' said Trevor. 'That's Drewitz coming up.'

9.
THE WALL TOTTERS

The winter of 1988–89 was a mild one by Berlin standards. No snow fell. In my flat the temperature never even dropped so far that I needed to light the old tiled oven in the corner. All the coal my neighbour Ellen had persuaded me we should buy in bulk while it was cheap lay around useless in the cellar. On some days, when money was especially tight, I'd sit in the kitchen and curse this wasted investment, leaning back and looking up at the elaborate patterns of damp and peeling paper on the ceiling where thrice Olga's washing machine had gone AWOL and loosed enough soapy water to drip three storeys down. This is my most persistent memory of that winter: worrying about money and wondering how to stop the rot from seeping back into my life.

Winter anywhere brings with it a certain inertia, but this effect was extreme in West Berlin. As nights drew in and the busy street life of summer retreated behind doors closed tight against the cold, so people drew in upon themselves and nursed their neuroses, not so much dealing with their depressions as coddling and treasuring them. In a city where isolation and enclosure were facts of political geography, this seemed less an affliction of individuals than a characteristic of the culture. The black leather clothes which had looked so ridiculous when the trees were still fragrant and green now looked slightly less so with the branches bare. Even the fact that this black fashion hadn't changed for a decade made some kind of sense in the sullen stasis of a town with too much history and no future at all, iced over not by winter but by the Cold War chill. It took that one winter behind the Wall to teach me that in divided Berlin it was winter all year round. Nothing ever changed. In those dark days before the thaw of 1989, it felt like nothing ever would.

The adventures and explorations of summer and autumn had stilled into cold routine. Since the trouble with the Stasi, most of the carefree thrill had gone out of our activities in the East and our cross-border trips were now conducted with exaggerated caution. West Berlin – all the old women walking their toy dogs, the winos who harangued you in the street, the punks begging money or cigarettes in every café – was beginning to irritate, especially as I recognised that I too was sinking into the city's classic syndrome. I had begun working behind the bar at the Pinguin. This was arduous night work and, given my ignorance of both cocktail shaking and German, a constant challenge to my self-confidence. Still, as bar jobs went, it was a plum. I worked all the shifts that God sent and scraped together enough to cover rent, food and debts in England. Spare cash, though, had I none. Often I'd be in the Pinguin on my off nights too, drinking until the small hours because here at least was one thing I could now do for free. The black of night and the dull grey of those few afternoon hours between my rising and the sun setting became the only colours in my life. As spring approached, I began longing for some warmer shades.

I'd arrived in Berlin intending to visit for a few months and had ended up staying. Having fled London after a breakdown precipitated by complications of romance and housing, there was at least a flat in Berlin. Since my first month there had also been an affair with Ellen upstairs. But over that first winter, both had begun to sour. Although I was paying the rent and bills, the flat still belonged to Elisabeth's boyfriend. He now wanted me out and I lived in constant fear of eviction. From time to time the pair of them would turn up for the weekend, usually without any notice at all, and I'd be turfed out so they could use the flat. It was always unsettling, suddenly being stranded without anywhere to shut the door on the world, forced to interrupt their Saturday morning love-making if I wanted a shave or change of socks and having to suffer, as a final insult, their complaints about the mess. On these occasions, I usually slept up at Ellen's but ours was a volatile and rapidly deteriorating relationship.

When the relationship with Ellen finally fell apart for good, I realised I'd cycled myself right back into the situation that had driven me from London: unable to settle down to anything in unstable accommodations, living with a lover who had turned her head away. It became the sheerest torture, sitting alone in my grey box, trying to focus on reading or writing, listening to the footsteps of Ellen and her new man thudding to and fro across the ceiling overhead. Sometimes I tried to drown the noise with music, more often I simply repaired to the Pinguin bar and tried to drown my sorrows instead. And if further evidence were needed that I still had not learnt my lesson, I ended up running away again.

Easter had rolled around. I looked from the kitchen at the new buds forming on the tree outside and realised a whole damn year had slipped by. There was a possibility of some work in Greece and the idea of going south appealed. In contrast to my life of black and grey, Greece offered colour and light. The chorus of a song by Soul II Soul kept jangling in my head: 'Keep on moving . . . Yellow is the colour of sun rays.' It seemed that if I had to work in a bar then I might as well do so in a place warm and bright, where it was possible to swim every day in the sea. What was the point of sitting round feeling sorry for myself?

I left town both sad and optimistic, not knowing whether I would ever return, but also enjoying the sense of freedom which went with that uncertainty. I'd decided to make the most of the journey by travelling overland through Prague, Budapest and Belgrade. Mark escorted me to Friedrich-strasse, Norman came to see me off on the midnight train from Lichtenberg station in the East. We toasted each other's futures in a station bar where it was bafflingly possible to buy beer and sparkling wine together, but neither one on its own. I gave Norman a book on Buddhist meditation. He gave me a Trabant key-ring. We talked about Budapest, which Norman was keen to visit.

'Why don't you go?' I asked him. 'You can get a visa.'

He gave a sour, defeated look.

'Not for much longer. The Hungarians are planning to dismantle their border with Austria. That means visas will become very hard to get,' he smiled a little now, 'in case we all try to run away.'

Prague was still Prague. From outside the Stred station I stole one of the posters announcing the forthcoming forty-fourth anniversary of Czechoslovakia's liberation by the Red Army. It was a cartoon of a smiling Schweik-style Russian soldier, toting a cheery Kalashnikov in a cascade of pink and yellow flowers. Despite the imagery of spring, Prague too was still stuck in the cold.

It took less than an hour in Budapest to realise things were very different there. A friend of a friend, name of László, met me off the train at Nyugati station. It was the morning of May Day 1989. We stopped on the way back to his apartment and purchased the makings of breakfast at a private shop open even on this public holiday. Back at László's, a beautiful if dilapidated old flat on Bartók Béla in Pest, a black market currency transaction was discussed. László turned on the television and called up the day's official exchange rates on teletext. When I expressed surprise, he flipped quickly across several channels, explaining what each one was. We ended up looking at three fur-clad cavemen, pounding each other over the head with giant wooden clubs.

'And this,' said László, 'is Russian television – as you can see.'

While I took a bath, László tapped out a letter or two on a dated but still serviceable Commodore computer. A little later, in some nether part of Pest, we were looking in on an opposition party meeting. A crowd who, in the West, I would have earmarked as 'nice middle class' from their dress and demeanour, crammed an auditorium and stage.

From the few fragments of debate László, who gave the air of having heard it all before, could be bothered to translate, it appeared they were talking about liberal democracy. Before I had time to absorb much else, we were back in the car and speeding to another part of town. László told me that in Hungary there was now total freedom of speech.

'You can say to the President of Hungary, "Kiss my arse", and nothing will happen.'

At the other end of the drive was the Városliget park. Here we hurried round a muddy fete organised by yet more opposition parties. By now I was reeling. Private shops, teletext, home computers, opposition fetes, free speech. This was not the East that I knew. For the first time on this side of the Curtain, I felt the winds of change.

In contrast to the monolithic systems of Czechoslovakia or East Germany, the situation in Hungary had long been a slippery one. Here even the ruling Party had more or less given up pretending to believe in Leninism and after years of administering the most liberal regime in the East, had started initiating further reforms at least in part because they could no longer see any reason why not. Opposition parties had then been in existence only for a matter of months and the radical loosening of the restrictions on private enterprise had only just begun, but a small private sector of the economy was already some twenty years old, and the informal 'second economy' was estimated to involve a fifth of Hungary's population.

It took me a few days to figure Budapest out: the place was really two cities. Not the hilly Buda and flat Pest of the guide books, facing off across a muddy brown Danube, but command-economy Budapest and free-market Budapest, all mixed up together on both sides of the river. The first, much the larger, was full of the old state-owned department stores. The second was composed of new private boutiques, fashionable bars and restaurants. Each had its own population. The drab state-run cafés of the first Budapest were frequented by the same kind of citizens, dressed in their simulated leather jackets and polyester casuals, gulping back the local variant of Victory Gin, whom one would see anywhere in the East. The bright nightclubs of the private Budapest, places like the Rock Café or the Club of Young Artists, were inhabited by a younger and more cosmopolitan crowd in Hungarian versions of Western street fashions, dancing to Anglo-American pop music and drinking Scotch whisky or Austrian beer. In that time of transition, the place was perfect. You could poke around for Eastern crap in the daytime, go out and actually get a decent meal at night.

László was a citizen of free-market Budapest. The eagerness of his commitment to the virtues of capitalism bordered on the absurd. One evening we went swimming. Instead of buying our tickets at the desk, he insisted we sneak in through the out-door and bribe the attendant in the changing room. The cash saved was minuscule but for László it was a matter of principle: better to pay the individual entrepreneur than give money to the state. My assertion that Western swimming pools were also state-owned and that, if they weren't, there would undoubtedly be nowhere for people to go swimming didn't dent his conviction one millimetre. And thus, in countless small ways, the Hungarian system was being undermined from within.

In his late twenties, tall, bearded, balding and owlish, László was a good-humoured bundle of manic energy, involved in every scam he could think of and apparently incapable of sitting still for longer than it took to bolt a meal or dash off a couple of postcards. His flat was full of books but if you asked him about one, he'd always reply that he'd never had time to read it. That first time I met him, he was finishing film school and beginning to work as a stringer for CBS news. He was a classic fixer. A friend of his told me this story: László was producing a film. The director wanted to shoot at a certain location, but was saddened because a tree, some eight kilometres down the road, would have been perfect for the scene. The next day they turned up to start work. László had somehow moved the tree.

Now, just as the division of Budapest was more subtle than that created by the Danube, so Hungary was split along lines less obvious than 'left' and 'right', liberal and authoritarian. Here there were also the 'urbanists' and 'populists'. The former were cosmopolitan, democratic, urban, Western-looking. The latter were nationalistic, cherished the traditional folk values of the countryside, looked towards the agrarian heartlands of Transylvania.

This line was clearly visible in Laszlo. He was well-travelled, conversant with modern popular culture, spoke both English and Russian, saw the only future for Hungary as the arrival of multinational capital and integration with the Western system. On the other hand, he was comically proud whenever you liked something about his country, and if you got on to Hungarian history, particularly the centuries-old Magyar–Romanian contest over Transylvania and its Hungarian minority, he would become almost tearful. One minute he would be making nicely cynical cracks about how the IMF would in time make that damned waitress move more quickly, the next he would be wondering rhetorically, with a catch in his throat:

'Who cares about we poor Hungarians?'

'Budapest is a really happening city.'

I was saying this at a London dinner party more than three months later. Things in Greece, for a variety of reasons which belong in some other story, had worked out badly. Meanwhile things in the East had been working out well. Tiananmen Square had happened, Erich Honecker was ill, Imre Nagy had been reburied in Budapest, the opposition had won their landslide victory in the Polish elections and Jaruzelski had agreed to a Solidarity-led government, 600 East Germans had picnicked in Hungary near the Austrian border and then all calmly strolled across it, 3,000 had rallied in Wenceslaus Square to commemorate the Prague Spring, the West German embassy in Budapest was closed because of overcrowding and I was on my way back to Berlin.

London seemed very distant from all this. The others at the dinner table that night were people with jobs in and around the fashion business, all buying property, all feeling the pinch of rising interest rates. Thatcherism was beginning to stagnate. For the first time, I felt glad that I had never bought a flat, that I was on the move, a free agent.

'You're living in a dream world,' snapped one of the other guests, a builder and decorator with a designer suit and some glamorous clients. 'What are these communist countries? You're simply clinging on to something that's finished, over and done with.'

I was about to reply that it was precisely the sense of movement and change that had made Budapest so interesting, when one of the other guests spoke up.

'Where is Budapest, anyway?' she asked.

'It's the capital of Hungary.'

'Hungary?' She gave a small, supercilious laugh. 'Does it still exist?'

It was September when I got back to Berlin. Weekly demonstrations were just beginning at the Nikolaikirche in Leipzig. Twelve thousand East Germans crossed the Hungarian border in one seventy-two-hour period. The Party sat down with democrats at a Budapest Round Table and in Poland the communists changed their name. In Czechoslovakia a petition called 'A Few Sentences' – launched in June and calling for freedom of assembly, the respect of religious beliefs, the release of political prisoners and an end to media manipulation and the persecution of independent movements – had by now gathered 27,000 signatures. I walked into the Pinguin on my first night back – and saw Torsten at the bar.

'Are you surprised to see me here?'

I was speechless, utterly incapable of any hearty congratulations, any drinks all round. One or two regulars waved in my direction, surprised, in their turn, to see me. I nodded back, abstracted. Torsten gave a warm smile, the twinkles from the mirror ball sweeping across his face. It wasn't that I was shocked into silence. It was more that there, in the West, in my local, among so many others that I knew in so many other ways, I simply did not know how to talk to him.

For Torsten, too, that winter following his interrogation had been cold and inert. In March he'd been sacked from his job driving the hospital van. At work, as in his dealings with any facet of the East German regime, Torsten had decided not to compromise. He refused to drive the worst of the hospital vans, refused to work more than seventy hours a week. Not only was it too hard, it was also dangerous. He did it a couple of times and then said no. There was no longer any reason to placate the bureaucracy: he was finished with the DDR.

Over the next months he drifted into church activities. There was work taking over from others like him who had already gone West, making a few scratches in the political permafrost. They discussed green issues and he'd hear news of events and demonstrations all over the East. Following the May 'elections' in the East, he became involved in organising a demonstration against the invalidity of the electoral process. This was to take place, although it never did, on 6 June, at three o'clock in the afternoon.

On the morning of 4 June, Tina got a call at work. It was the department of Pankow Town Hall where they had filed their application to emigrate. Tina and Torsten must be there in one hour. She rushed back to Pankow and blurted out the news. She and Torsten looked at each other across the living room, knowing what it must mean but not quite daring to believe it. They hurried around to be told they had two days to leave the country. Two days? Normally it was more like two weeks. Not in this case. Torsten and Tina must leave on 6 June, before three o'clock in the afternoon.

There was no time to think about it, no time for emotions or goodbyes. At the Town Hall they were given a list of everything they had to do. They spent the rest of that day and all of the next waiting in line at all the offices and departments they were suddenly obliged to visit, settling up electricity bills, formally handing back their apartment, notifying the post office of their change of address, visiting a branch of every damn bank in the DDR to collect proof that they owed no money to the state. Once they'd collected all the paperwork, the Town Hall took away their ID cards and passports, gave them papers which declared that they were now stateless persons and allowed one exit from the DDR.

That last night, they didn't sleep. Torsten sifted through his belongings, wondering what to take with him. It reminded him of a fairy tale: in passing through the looking-glass he was allowed only that treasure he could carry in his hands. The next afternoon, amid crowds of Western day-trippers, the two of them walked out through Friedrichstrasse, seeing the bowels of the station for the first time in their lives. Torsten's sister Kerstin was waiting on the other side and they caught a U-Bahn in the direction of her flat. Changing trains on to the elevated line which runs through Kreuzberg, climbing from the tunnel into the afternoon air, Torsten noticed something strange – something he'd heard about but never believed could be true, not so close to the Wall. But there it was: the air smelt different, fresher. He took a slow, deep breath. It was the scent of the West.

I moved into a new flat, just down the road from Trevor's, sharing with friends of friends from London. Mark had bought a piece of the Pinguin Club. Spud had left the army and moved back to the USA. Norman was still in East Berlin, still dealing with the Russians, still scouting around for the kind of dodgy ephemera that might interest Mark or Trevor or prove saleable to someone else. Back in the winter, I had tried to talk him out of this. After the trouble with the Stasis and the Ivan Jirous petition, I had begun thinking about responsibility. Our thoughtlessness and tendency to push a thing too far had already helped Norman into trouble once. To do it again, by encouraging him to take crazy risks for nothing more than a bundle of flea market tat for us, a handful of West marks for him, seemed the worst kind of irresponsibility. But Norman was deaf to any argument. Once he'd got over the shock of the interrogation, he slipped back into enjoying the buzz of danger and recklessness. On our side of the game, we had initially been put in the position of taking stuff from him, not because we'd asked him to procure it, but because we'd worried about him having it and stashing it at home. What if the Stasi decided to turn the place over and discovered things like a Third Reich ID card, a people's policeman's hat, a Russian army jacket, an album of photographs from the 1933 Olympics and some Nazi Party badges? When it became clear that Norman would insist on accumulating such stuff, it seemed the lesser of two evils to help him get it off his hands. Having gone along with him once, the whole thing quickly became routine again.

Before I went to Greece, Norman had already begun devising elaborate procedures both for handing this kind of crap over and receiving the sometimes equally dodgy bits and pieces we were bringing him. Our meetings began to resemble scenes from some corny spy thriller. We'd arrange to rendezvous at, say, Centrum by Ostbahnhof (that winter being refurbished and renamed Hauptbahn-hof – another small episode in the East's attempts to claim centrality for their side of divided Berlin). While the GIs waited in the car, Mark and I would carry some battered hold-all into the store and hang around by the fake fur hat counter. In would stagger Norman with a conspicuously huge parcel wrapped in paper and string. We'd all put down packages to shake hands and try to simulate the kind of ten-minute chat one has with a friend unexpectedly encountered. There would be scores of shoppers around. Any number could have been Stasi. Norman's eyes would flitter nervously around and sometimes it could be difficult to keep a straight face. Presently we'd say goodbye. Norman would pick up our hold-all and we'd walk off with his outsize parcel. Into the car it would go and out into the West would sneak another bundle of finest totalitarian kitsch.

There were never any problems with this kind of exchange, but if anyone had been specially assigned to keep an eye on us, then our transactions would have been completely transparent. What precautions we did take were wholly inadequate given the danger of jingling a chain of contacts that stretched from American military personnel at one end to Russian soldiers at the other. But something seemed to be working. By the time I arrived back in September, there had been no further trouble.

After a meeting in a village outside East Berlin, Neues

Forum was founded and published its manifesto. The Hungarian Free Democrats organised a petition protesting at the timing of planned presidential elections. Two hundred thousand people signed. In Prague, over a thousand East Germans crammed into the West German embassy. Either something would soon snap or else there was going to be the great-grandmother of all clampdowns. Norman was torn by indecision. He equipped himself with visas for Hungary, Poland and Bulgaria. To join the growing exodus he simply had to pack a bag and board a train. Now's your chance, we told him. Take it before this window of opportunity comes slamming down. But even though his life was still meandering in hopeless circles, even though he had been talking of leaving ever since I had first met him, somehow he couldn't bring himself to go. The reasons he gave were nothing better than excuses and we set about dealing with them. He needed more money? We gave it to him. He needed to get the last stuff out of his mother's flat? Fine, we set up a day to go over with Salman.

I never found out what was in that last package – it had all been arranged between Mark and Norman – but whatever it was made Norman even more paranoid than usual. Instead of doing our usual exchange in the hat department, Norman was to leave the package in a left-luggage locker at Hauptbahnhof and meet us outside Centrum to hand over the key.

It already seemed a bit stupid to me as I hurried with Mark across the Centrum Hauptbahnhof car park, the street-lamps and Trabant headlights gleaming against the last of a smoggy day. It was too complicated. This was no Len Deighton novel. Shoppers swept in and out of the department store, a train pulled into the station, lights were going on in the flat blocks all around. Business was superficially as usual but a heightened tension was in the air – the result of events over the last few months.

Norman was nowhere to be seen. We scouted all the entrances and exits. Half an hour passed by, the dark descended. Our meeting simply had to take place today. Salman was about to go off on two weeks of field exercises in West Germany.

'Maybe,' sighed Mark, 'he's gone to the other Centrum.'

'Why would he do that?'

'We had an argument about which one we should meet at. Maybe Norman thinks it's the one in Alexanderplatz.'

My impatience now swelled into sudden anger.

'If we're going to play these bloody spy games it would help if you could take the time to get the fucking rendez-vous right.'

'I told him Centrum at Hauptbahnhof.'

'Obviously not in language clear enough for him to understand. You stay here in case he shows. I'll get Salman to drive me to Alexanderplatz and see if I can find him there. What's in this fucking parcel, anyway?'

Mark shook his head as if to say: You don't want to know. I hurried back across the car park.

Salman pulled up opposite the Stadt hotel. I dodged through the Trabants and hurried round the corner, through the passage that led into Alexanderplatz. There was Norman walking in front of me. I shuffled up behind and put my hand on his shoulder. His whole body jerked in fright.

'It's only me. Come on, let's get out of here. Mark's waiting at Hauptbahnhof.'

'But I told him to meet me here.'

'It's quite obvious the pair of you couldn't organise a blowjob in a whorehouse. Come on, Salman's in the car.'

Of all locations in East Berlin, the well-patrolled area around Alexanderplatz was one of the most foolhardy for a citizen of the DDR to run across the road against the lights, jump over the chain bordering the parking area and clamber ostentatiously into a car with US Army plates and a uniformed GI at the wheel. I was past caring. Let's just get this business out of the way.

'So the name's Bond, is it?' I asked as we skirted the fountain at Strausberger Platz. 'Norman Bond?'

Mark was still pacing around outside Centrum. We picked him up and parked down a deserted cul-de-sac behind the station. Mark and Norman took ten minutes to come back with the parcel.

'That was ridiculous,' breathed Mark. 'All the lockers

were watched by cameras. Even if I had got the key as arranged, it would have been bloody dangerous to use it.'

'What did you do?'

'Oh, Norman got the package. I just hung around pretending to look at the timetables.'

Norman looked abashed.

'That was the last dirty job,' he said.

A little more relaxed now the package was safely under the protection of the US military, we went off to eat in the plush Haus Moskau, joking about parcels From Norman With Love. When the time came to say goodbye we dropped Norman off in a side-street near Marx-Engels-Platz. He said he'd be leaving for Czechoslovakia in just a few days' time. We smiled and wished him luck and said we'd see him in the West.

The tension in the city washed right over the Wall. You could feel it as you moved around West Berlin. In the café where I took breakfast, people seemed bent over their morning papers with more than usual intensity. In the Pinguin at night, there was less local gossip and more political debate. But these were only symptoms. The atmosphere was something almost elemental: a crackle in the air, a mounting pressure, the fears and aspirations of a city and a nation bubbling up below the surface of normality. Though neither I, nor anyone else that I knew, would have dared to predict how far it would all go, it was clear things were in flux all over this half of the continent. West Berlin was now less an island than the eye of a gathering hurricane.

On 1 October, television news showed the first special trains leaving for the West, packed with those East Germans who'd been sheltering in the embassies in Prague and Warsaw. Altogether 14,000 people were to leave this way over the next few days, formally handing back passports and renouncing their East German citizenship as the trains travelled through the DDR to the West. I squinted at the screen, trying to spot Norman among the elated crowds boarding the train in Prague. Like him, most of the crowd wore the same Golden Rifles marbled denims. Unlike him, most of the young faces bore moustaches. Suddenly I saw Norman, darting past the camera in the crush. He was wearing the Luftwaffe jacket he'd been given by Mark, knapsack over his shoulder, hopping on the train without so much as a look back. I rang Mark and told him. Thank God for that, we breathed. Norman was out.

A night or two later, on the day the East German government announced that visa-free travel to Czechoslovakia had been suspended, Mark rang Norman's mother about something. Norman answered the phone.

'What the fuck,' shrilled Mark in surprise, 'are you doing there?'

'I didn't go yet.'

Obviously I hadn't seen him after all.

With the same mix of anger and impatience I'd felt on the Norman Bond afternoon, I rang him up, arranged a meeting, dropped my work for a few hours and went over the Wall to kick him up the arse. In the West, I told him, we had acquired a new word. To mess about and leave something until it was too late we now called 'to norman'.

Although Czechoslovakia was now impossible, Norman reckoned he could still go transit to Hungary and make his escape from there. To make it look even less likely that he was on the run, he was buying a train ticket to Bulgaria and a flight back to East Berlin from there. Otherwise there might be some way to get out through Poland. I gave him the hundred marks I had in my pocket. I also gave him the addresses of both László in Budapest and a friend of a friend in Warsaw. Back in West Berlin I had contacted both, asked them to expect him, shelter him, give him money if he needed it, which I would reimburse.

On the morning of 6 October, a small van-load of friends from London was passing through town on its way to Poland. As some of the party had never been to Berlin before, I whisked them off on a small guided tour. First stop: the famous Brandenburg Gate.

The suspense in Berlin had been mounting with the approach of the DDR's fortieth anniversary. That morning was the beginning of the celebrations. It was an ominous,

overcast day. There was a powerful tension at the Brandenburg Gate – strong enough to have attracted various
oddballs. An intense old lady, with a bicycle and a bag full
of groceries (we were miles from any supermarket),
stopped and asked if it was true that the border had been
closed (we were also miles from any border post). Down the
middle of the road by the Russian memorial strode a man
with beard and bulbous glasses, long blonde wig, stockings
and sequinned frock. He waved a pole on which were
strung small, tattered flags of various nations and leered at
us with an unsettling glint in his eye.

Some East German army officers – I could just make out
the red and yellow braid on their olive drab uniforms –
were standing on the top of the Gate, looking West through
binoculars. As we walked down towards the Wall which
blocked off the road maybe fifty metres in front of the
Gate, a US Army helicopter swung in over the trees of the
Tiergarten and hovered on the Western side. There it
stayed, watching the watchers, the nagging thwack of its
rotors winding up the atmosphere another notch. The
drag queen leaned his flags against a bench, unlocked the
door of a Volkswagen van, pulled off his wig and threw it
inside. His real hair was short and grey. He took out an old
army greatcoat, slipped it on over the sequinned frock and,
with another mad leer in our direction, tottered off down
the road again, high heels peeping from below his coat.
The old lady came back in the other direction and stopped
to shout over the noise of the helicopter: it was true, the
border was closed.

At Checkpoint Charlie a small crowd had gathered on
the Western side of the line, all asking each other just what
was going on. A gaggle of Scandinavian students returning
from the checkpoint confirmed what we had heard: the
border was closed. This was quite unprecedented. The
DDR government were obviously taking every precaution
to ensure that nothing disrupted their jamboree. The
Londoners and I retreated to a café on the corner.
Someone jokingly proposed a 'grand stratagem': take the
van on the transit road to Hamburg, then double back
illegally into East Berlin. While the others were laughing

about that idea, I picked up the phone at the end of the bar and dialled Mark's number. To my surprise, there was no reply.

Mark had been going on about it for weeks. After our thwarted attempts to make the thirty-ninth anniversary, there was no way he was going to miss the fortieth. Over the last winter he'd acquired a new piece of paper: a *Lichtbild-bescheinigung*. Issued by the West Berlin Senat, this gave resident foreigners the status of a Berliner. You could use it to travel beyond East Berlin to anywhere in the DDR from which one could return by midnight and, if arranged in advance, could also make overnight stays. Mark knew someone – the sister of a friend of Torsten – whose birthday was on 6 October and, with that as pretext, sorted out the paperwork to stay overnight.

It didn't make any difference at Friedrichstrasse. The only people being allowed through that morning were East German old age pensioners on their way back home and Mark was turned away with the rest of the crowd. He knew it would be the same at Checkpoint Charlie, but his *Licht-bildbescheinigung* allowed him to use any of the border posts reserved for Berliners. He caught the U-Bahn down to Kreuzberg and tried the one at Oberbaumbrücke. Apart from a couple of old ladies, the place was deserted. The guards were intrigued by Mark. It wasn't often they had to deal with anyone either young or British. Where was Mark going? To a birthday party. He brandished presents as proof. Whose birthday? Mark told him. The guard went off to make a phone call. Right up until that moment, Mark was sure he'd be turned away yet again, but the guard came back and gave him his papers: 'You may proceed.'

It still seems incredible that they let Mark through. I have never heard of anyone else getting over that day. Mark couldn't believe it himself, emerging into the East on the corner of Warschauer Strasse to find himself the only civilian on a street full of green-uniformed *Volkspolizei*. Nervous – all eyes were upon him – he stepped off the kerb to cross the road. A siren started in the distance. Mark looked up to see a black Lada, huge red and blues rotating on top, screaming down the road towards him. A cop stopped him on the traffic island. The Lada careered around the corner, four Stasis inside. It was followed by two enormous limousines, red flags fluttering in the head-wind as they hurtled towards the junction.

There was a figure at a back window of the first one. Mark smiled, recognising an image familiar from a thousand news reports: a dark red blotch of colour on a balding white head. Mark's hand jerked up in an almost involuntary motion. Mikhail Gorbachev, General Secretary of the CPSU Central Committee, Chairman of the Presidium of the USSR Supreme Soviet, from his back seat next to Erich Honecker, General Secretary of the SED Central Committee, Chairman of the Council of State of the German Democratic Republic, peered out of the window to see what must have passed for an ordinary member of the masses: a funny little chap with a hat on, grinning and waving hello. Gorbachev raised a hand, started to return the greeting – then lurched to grab hold of something as the limousine turned the corner too quickly.

The motorcade vanished in the distance. Mark looked around to see the cops all still watching him. The look in their eyes said: You crawling little shit.

Mark watched the parade the next day from the corner of Alexanderplatz. It was a horrible day and the crowds were thin. Everyone had clearly been expecting trouble and only three kinds of people had turned out: loyal citizens with children, disloyal citizens waiting to partake of any trouble should anyone else have the presence of mind to start some, and secret police. A few hundred metres down Karl Marx Allee, cordoned off in the drizzle behind several battalions of police, was a reviewing stand stacked with an assortment of dictators and soon-to-be-yesterday's men: Jakeš, Zhivkov, Jaruzelski, Ceauşescu, Ortega, Honecker. Yasser Arafat was up' there. And Gorbachev, of course, looking bored and impatient with the tanks and marching soldiers that trailed so remorselessly across his line of sight.

After the parade fizzled out – loudspeakers ordering everyone to disperse – Mark turned into Alexanderplatz. Maybe two hundred market stalls had been specially set up for the celebrations. All but half a dozen were deserted. On one side of the square was a podium full of officers from the East German forces. Some big-shot general down the front was introducing a smart young naval officer, specially chosen to deliver an anniversary address. It was clearly a great honour. The young officer stepped up to the microphone, back straight, bearing proud, and began reading from a paper. Productivity . . . protecting the Fatherland . . . the achievements of socialism . . . his voice faltered and dried. Mark could read the sudden doubt on the officer's face. Halfway through this important speech, this proud pinnacle of a brief but distinguished naval career, the sailor's conviction had fled. It had belatedly struck home that all these words he was supposed to declaim, all the ideals to which the whole of his young adult life had been spent in service, were nothing but the most miserable kind of bullshit.

He paused.

A thrill of expectancy lifted the crowd. Perhaps this guy would say something different. Perhaps he was going to break down and tell the truth. Perhaps, for once, someone might say out loud, in public, that the whole damn fortieth anniversary celebration was nothing but a fraud, that all the self-congratulatory speeches in the world couldn't disguise the fact that, at this point in history, any member of this crowd would sell out their socialist fatherland for a bunch of bananas and the keys to a serviceable secondhand Volkswagen without even stopping to think about it.

The general elbowed the officer to continue. He coughed and glanced about and resumed in a rush, rattling off the rest in a flat, embarrassed monotone. There was silence when he finished. No one applauded. When he turned back to face his colleagues, not one of them would shake his hand.

Later that night, Mark emerged from a backstreet near Marx-Engels-Platz to hear the noises of an angry crowd. In the car park outside the Palast der Republik a few thousand people were trying to chant 'Gorby! Gorby! Gorby!' but never quite hitting a rhythm. Trucks were pulling up.

Uniformed cops were jumping out of them. Flashing blue lights homed in on the scene from various directions. Here, then, was the trouble everyone had been expecting.

This was the first major demonstration in East Berlin. Although the rallies in Leipzig were already five times the size, and demonstrations in East Berlin would eventually reach a peak when half a million marched on 4 November 1989, at the time this was the biggest anti-government protest since the 1953 uprising. Mark cut across the park on the other side of the river, frightened of getting caught up in it. As he hurried over the grass towards Alexander-platz, cops started appearing out of the dark behind and in front of him, forming into cordons that soon ringed the whole area. Mark worked his way through them, waving his British passport.

We found out later what happened to at least some of those the police managed to catch that night. It was a chilling story: a clue as to what might have happened to thousands of people had not the hard-line faction in the regime, those who had publicly congratulated the Chinese leadership after it shot down the students in Tiananmen Square, not been outmanoeuvred in the days ahead.

The Gethsemane Church in Prenzlauer Berg had become a focus for dissident events. Mark had been there the previous night, with others from the birthday party. There was a gentle, candle-lit protest which made Mark feel as though he'd been transported back to the 1960s – except that all the streets around were lined with trucks full of waiting police and further patrolled by leather-jacketed Stasis in groups of three.

On the night of the 7th, a group of people, including a friend of ours, was making its way to the church. Some police popped out of the shadows and clubbed them to the ground. It was as simple and as brutal as that. The men, half a dozen of them, were separated from the women, bundled roughly into a van and driven off to a police station. In a long, white-tiled room they were stripped, searched and made to sit naked on wooden benches. Their feet were chained to the floor, their hands were chained to their feet and they were told to stare at a red spot of paint before them. No looking up, no talking, no falling asleep. If anyone disobeyed they were beaten.

After an indeterminate length of time, they were dressed, transported to another police station, and there stripped, searched and chained up again. From time to time there were questions. No sophisticated interrogation, just stupid, basic questions: Who are you? Where do you live? At one point they were given some vile-looking broth. One refused to drink it, fearing poison. He was clubbed. Presently they were dressed, moved, stripped, searched and chained up a third time. They had no idea what was going on in the world outside. For all they knew, this was the final clampdown.

Once more they were told to dress. This time they were driven into the countryside near Berlin. The police prod-ded them into a clearing in the woods, made them strip their clothes off again. There were four of them now: quaking with cold and fear. The cops pulled out handguns, held them to heads. This was it, then. Pistols were cocked, the triggers squeezed. Click. The guns weren't loaded. The cops all laughed out loud.

In the end the four were kicked out of the van, each in a different location, and left to find their way home without money or papers. When they finally got back to civilisation it was to discover they'd been gone for three days. Only the day before, Honecker's intention to use live ammunition on the demonstrators in Leipzig had been thwarted in the Politburo by one solitary vote.

'Will you please ask this Mark to stop leaving messages on my machine?' It was László, ringing from Budapest. 'I have seen nothing of your friend Norman.'

We were worried. It was nearly two weeks since I'd gone over the Wall to boot Norman into action. He appeared to have left East Berlin but hadn't yet even shown up in Hungary, let alone in the West. The demonstrations were gathering strength in Leipzig: 30,000 people . . . 50,000 . . . 100,000. On 18 October, Erich Honecker fell or was pushed from office. Trevor called me in the afternoon.

'We've got a visitor,' he said. I didn't even have to ask who it was. 'I'm bringing him round to see you.'

I was cooking in the kitchen when Trevor dropped Norman off. His story was simple enough: he'd caught a train out of East Berlin on 6 October, which was norman-ning things indeed. Apart from the usual thorough search, he had no trouble at the Czech border but was a little scared of one guy, a carpenter in his early thirties, who sat opposite on the train. Norman maintained the fiction that he was off to Bulgaria on holiday. The carpenter said he was doing the same. Later, meeting again in Budapest, they had dinner together, both still talking about their Bulgarian holidays. Norman went round to László's flat. No one was there so he slept in the station. After contacting the West German embassy, he caught a train to Vienna and then on to Frankfurt, ending up at the Giessen refugee camp. He met the carpenter there too, and finally they could talk without suspecting each other. After three or four days, sleeping in a dormitory by night, queuing up to sort out paperwork by day, Norman was given a hundred West marks and a free flight to Berlin.

He was glancing around the kitchen as he talked. I followed his gaze, trying to look through his eyes at the things laid out on shelves and surfaces. What struck me was the diversity of geographical origin: an Italian coffee pot, a flat loaf of Turkish bread, French apples, Indian mango chutney, a jar of Indonesian satay sauce, a Chinese wok, Spanish olive oil, glass noodles from Thailand, a box of English tea bags, Danish butter, a packet of Lebanese falafel mix, Japanese soya sauce, two small bottles of Korean sake, Dutch cheese, a carton of Greek yoghurt and a big jar of American peanut butter. The only familiar things among these products of the global market place must have been those packets of herbs and spices I had bought on the cheap in East Berlin. Norman had not just moved from East to West, from one half of a city to another. He had journeyed from the modern to the postmodern.

On the table between us stood a carton of milk, the packaging decorated with line drawings of West Berlin landmarks.

'Look, Norman,' I picked it up. 'Here we have the Gedächtniskirche, the Funkturm, Schloss Charlottenburg, the Seigessäule . . . but no Fernsehturm.'

Norman picked up the carton and examined it intently, as if hoping it would yield up some meaning from the confusion all around.

'Actually,' I said, 'you can see the real thing from the window.'

'Show me,' said Norman. 'I want to see.'

We got up and looked out together. Peeping just above the flats opposite was the familiar ball and spike, red lights on top winking a warning against the early evening sky. I wondered what was going on tonight in the troubled streets below.

'Just think,' sighed Norman, turning back from the familiar landmark to this kitchen packed with evidence of a steadily shrinking world. 'To move halfway across this city I have just had to travel about two thousand kilometres.'

10.
A MOTOR TOUR OF THE COLLAPSE OF COMMUNISM

Drewitz was different this time. The guard glanced at our papers, asked whether we had anything with us we intended to sell, nodded at our negative answer, saluted and indicated that we should proceed.

'That was funny,' said Trevor as we pulled out once more on to the transit road. 'No control. Do you think it's because we're heading for Poland and not Czechoslovakia?'

'Nah,' said Mark. 'It's because they don't know who they're working for anymore.'

It was the early hours of the morning of 8 November. Earlier in the evening I'd been packing a bag when a flatmate rushed in with the news: the entire East German Council of Ministers had handed in their resignations to the Volkskammer. In recent weeks, every attempt by the government to stem the tide of East German opposition had simply made things worse. Honecker's resignation had prompted still larger demonstrations. On 1 November, the decision to close the Czechoslovak border had been reversed. A new torrent of refugees flowed through the breach. Two days later the government declared that people leaving for the West this way would no longer have to renounce their East German citizenship. The measure included an amnesty for those who had already left and was clearly meant to encourage vital workers to return. Fifty thousand more promptly left the country. On 4

November, half a million people had rallied in East Berlin. As we motored towards the Oder–Neisse line, I looked at darkened houses in villages by the road and wondered what the people inside them could possibly be thinking. The process of change in the East now had the momentum of an avalanche, yet it was impossible to see quite where it might all end.

It was a strange time to be leaving town but our trip had been planned and largely paid for fully two months in advance. It had seemed to us after Czechoslovakia last year that if we were going to have another crap holiday, then we might as well go the whole way: to Ceauşescu's Romania. Dracula's castle at Bran near Braşov had been settled on as the furthest point of our navigation. After two mornings at Trevor's, arguing over maps, brochures and visa regulations, we had agreed a route that would take us to Transylvania through Cracow in Poland and various towns in the east of Czechoslovakia and Hungary, passing through Budapest, Bratislava and Prague on the way back.

Norman wasn't coming this time. It wasn't just that, as an illegal émigré, it was difficult for him to travel through the DDR. 'You lot, in Romania?' He'd shaken his head in horror at the thought. Even those with less direct experience of our collective behaviour in foreign parts were convinced we must be crazy. 'See you in fifteen years, then.' This was the most common crack in the days before we left. 'Don't end up in the last gulag.' It became quite tiresome.

Not that we were without apprehensions of our own. Ceauşescu's Romania was the worst kind of hellhole: a potentially wealthy land bankrupted by disastrous Stalinist policies, alternately starved and bludgeoned into submission by what was certainly the most brutal regime in Europe. While 90 per cent of all food was being exported from a land once known as 'the bread basket of the Balkans' to pay off foreign debt incurred on stupid industrial development projects, the population was cowed by the largest proportion of secret police per capita in any Eastern state. Even if the efficiency of the Securitate was widely overrated – a system incapable of providing a regular supply of toilet paper clearly wasn't up to the task of running a network of five million informers – its brutality was a matter of record. If they weren't afraid of manhandling the British ambassador (they had done this in Cluj, one of the towns on our itinerary, when he had tried to visit the dissident Diana Cornea), they would doubtless allow themselves considerable latitude in any dealings with a bunch of anti-social elements like us.

Mark was anxious enough to visit the dentist shortly before we left, remarking with complete seriousness that if he got thrown in prison, then at least his teeth would be all right. I had sharpened my own fears with a reading of Ion Pacepa's *Red Horizons*, the memoirs of Ceauşescu's former head of intelligence. According to this, citizens were required to report any conversation with a foreigner to the police. Possession of typewriters was illegal without a government licence, and a sample of the type from every machine was held by the Securitate along with handwriting samples for the entire population. Every telephone in the country was equipped with a microphone. Some hotels were run as 'intelligence factories' with every last member of staff a security agent, every vase or ashtray the site of a concealed monitoring device.

No, a country where the dictator had fifty members of his own family in positions of power, demolished and resettled whole communities on a whim, and was fond of poisoning his opponents with radioactivity was clearly no happy holiday resort. No one took their vacation in Romania. Torsten and Norman had escaped into the Free World and here we were heading as far as it was possible to go in the opposite direction.

We had been joined for the trip by John: was a friend of Trevor's from way back and someone who, for Mark and me, was an unknown quantity. He'd lived in West Berlin for years until the bar he part-owned went bankrupt and the bailiffs began taking such an intrusive interest in the contents of his flat that a retreat to London and a desk job in a newly privatised utility company had become expedient. He came back to Berlin especially for this holiday.

Mark and I shared doubts before his arrival. What if the chap was another Trevor? One was quite enough.

Whatever we'd expected, John was something different. He cut a huge and improbable figure in the tweed blazer, grey flannels, white shirt, tie and wide-brimmed gangster hat he always wore. Although in his early thirties and possessed of a wit both gruff and cynical, despite his girth and a set of sharp facial features which could at times acquire a menacing cast, John had about him a preternatural innocence. In his wide-brimmed hat, he reminded me less of a real gangster than of the movie *Bugsy Malone*, where all the hoods had been played by little children. Like a child, that first night, he was full of annoying questions. What's that over there? Why is this like that? How long are we going to have to wait here? Mark and I exchanged a weary look, the kind that passes between old hands in any area of human experience, humouring the naive new arrival.

We were somewhere near Wroclaw on the old Nazi-built autobahn to Upper Silesia when dawn broke. The black of night faded into the grey of dawn and stopped right there. It got lighter but no more colourful. The cars and lorries, even the grass in the fields, were all of the same monotonous shade. We passed exit roads which appeared to deteriorate immediately into muddy dirt tracks, signs warning us to beware of horses and carts. There were villages where all the roofs looked like they had been bashed in by some giant spoon. By mid-morning we were steering through the outskirts of Katowice, looking for somewhere to change money and eat breakfast. The steady advance of morning still had not dispelled the elemental grey. Streets and houses, shops and factories, everything looked about one stage up from utter dereliction. This was the industrial heart of Poland. As factories creaked into life for another day of pumping out poisons and products that nobody wanted to buy.

Later that morning, we went to Auschwitz. More shades of grey, smoke against the sky, parties of schoolchildren disgorging from grubby coaches. I knew right away that I couldn't handle any jokes in this place. When the others stopped to take snapshots by the 'Arbeit Macht Frei' gate, I hurried on ahead into the camp. If I was going to have to look at this at all, I would look at it alone. Rooms full of human hair, rooms full of shoes. I paced from one low brick building to another, staring blankly at the exhibits, skimming the captions on the walls. Mass murder, genocide, unspeakable cruelty, suffering without end – these are just words, like the shoes were just shoes. I was numbed, unable to relate what I saw to such history as I knew. Rooms full of spectacles, rooms full of suitcases, rusty cans that once contained Zyklon B, lids torn off in haste. One might 'know' the statistics, yet who can really comprehend the difference between ten thousand and a hundred thousand? Between one million and four million?

In one building was a long corridor, the wall covered in framed photographs of former inmates, former victims. Each was a mug shot of an individual. All were in hooped camp uniform, heads shaved. There were a few hundred such pictures, representing the tiniest fraction of the millions tortured, gassed and worked to death in this place, but even this number was too much to take in. Then I noticed that behind a few of the pictures, slipped between frame and wall, were single red roses – placed there, I supposed, by loved ones or relatives of the dead. I paused before one of them. The eyes of the subject, big and forlorn against emaciated features, looked out at me with the expression long ago directed at the guard who had operated the camera. The rose was fresh, the colour of blood. Someone remembered this person, loved them still. Something broke inside me and I started to cry.

I ran into the others on my way back outside. Anger mixed with my tears.

'Give me the car keys. I've had enough.'

There was nothing more to learn, nothing more to feel. Auschwitz made every emotion seem clichéd and banal. No one said anything as Trevor handed me the keys. I curled up in the car and closed my eyes. In time I stopped crying and dozed until the others came back. We drove in silence to the subsidiary camp at Birkenau, maybe half a mile away. I looked at the people on the streets and thought: How is it possible to have a normal life in this town, working, maybe, in one of the factories built by the Nazis for the exploitation of their slave labour, constantly in sight of this abomination? Through the gates of Birkenau we could see a perimeter line of watchtowers and barbed wire receding into monochrome mist. Mark got out to take a photograph. I shivered and looked away. It felt as if this place alone might be the source of all the grey, this monument to death that still cast its shadow: not just over Germany, over Eastern Europe, over the Middle East, but over the whole of this damned world.

It was already dark when we arrived in Cracow. The first hotel we tried was a big, square monolith called the Cracovia. We knew right away that we didn't want to stay there.

'Are there any other hotels in this town?' Trevor asked at reception. 'We want somewhere at least a hundred years old.'

'A hundred years old?' spluttered the clerk.

'Yeah,' Trevor sneered, glancing disdainfully around what was undoubtedly the most expensive place in town. 'And somewhere we won't get our luggage stolen.'

The clerk glared at Trevor, picked up a leaflet with a small city plan and scribbled the locations of various hotels, pleased to be getting rid of us so easily. Outside, as we climbed back into the car, a parking attendant ran up out of the rain and blocked our way while he spent about five minutes filling out a ticket. First he dropped it on the moving windscreen wiper. Then he bent over, picked it from the ground and shoved it through the window at John.

'It says 24 zlotys.'

'Here,' said Mark. 'Give him 50.'

John passed out the note. The parking attendant grew agitated, jabbed a finger at the note.

'Oh,' said John, looking closer. 'It's not 24, it's 240.'

'Fuck off,' Mark protested. 'He's not getting that. We've only been here about a minute. Give him a hundred.'

Another note was passed out of the window. The attendant hesitated for a moment, rain dripping from the peak of his cloth cap, then shrugged and disappeared into the dark. We were about a hundred yards down the road when Trevor spoke up:

'Hang on, how many zlotys were there to the mark?'

We all had to think about it. Eventually someone answered.

'About 2,400.'

'Oh no,' groaned Trevor as the meaning of this sank in. The attendant had been asking for less than the price of a box of matches back in West Berlin. We'd given him hell for it and handed over just half of that miserable sum.

We found a nicely shabby dive just off the main square. There were Donald Duck posters on the walls of the foyer and a telephone switchboard behind reception that looked like something out of Terry Gilliam's *Brazil*. Having dumped our bags, we walked across the square and into the first restaurant we saw: a place called Wierzynek, hundreds of years old with a beamed ceiling, ornate brickwork, axes and shields on the walls and a menu that offered 'Boiled Truth By The Weight' and 'Rump Steak "Metallurgic" Style'.

The ancient city of Cracow had, like the Poland of which it was once capital, been repeatedly invaded, plundered and occupied by Swedish, Russian, Austrian and German armies. While the Nazis had murdered the Jewish population, shipped treasures back to the Reich and tried to expunge everything Polish about the place, Cracow had remained a centre of the resistance. Under communism its population had quadrupled and a city placed high on UNESCO's list of the world's most precious historical objects had acquired the capacity to manufacture 58 per cent of Poland's iron, 45 per cent of its steel, 42 per cent of its cigarettes, 27 per cent of its medicines and enough industrial pollution severely to damage many of its venerable churches and famous old houses.

We were not the kind of tourists to waste much time on museums and churches, but it was hard not to enjoy the sense of history which infused everything. The mood of the old architecture was bolstered by the state of general disrepair, crowds that included monks and nuns and soldiers who, in their gaiters and hats, looked like they had stepped straight from the First World War. As the Solidarity government made its first legislative moves towards a free market economy, Florianksa Street teemed with individuals doing business. A row stretching half across the road offered gold chains and jewellery. There were stalls selling pirate pop cassettes and individuals offering zlotys that were still slightly cheaper than those purchased at the now nearly realistic official rate. Something about this primitive street trade – odd items individually imported or manufactured, newly open transactions that had nothing to do with the old state system – seemed almost medieval. As such, it suited Cracow perfectly.

I came out of the shower that evening to find Mark and Trevor busy with one of the pictures in our room. It was a collage: a building, mother and child holding hands, some aeroplanes, all floating in a white void. Mark had removed the thing from its frame and, with a meticulous pencil, added angel wings to the mother and child, machine gun turrets to the planes.

'The kid looks like he's holding something,' he said. 'What can I put in his hand? Something Polish . . .'

'The Pope's dick,' proffered Trevor. We were, after all, in the home town of Karol Wojtyla, whose election in 1978 as the 264th successor to St Peter in the See of Rome and the first non-Italian Patriarch of the West for 455 years, arguably marked the beginning of the end for the whole Eastern edifice.

Mark sketched exactly what Trevor suggested, a convincing Pope attached. We spent a moment admiring the results – you had to look closely to spot that these additions were not part of the original work – then hung the thing back on the wall. Just after it was safely back in position came a knock at the door. I opened it expecting John and found instead two Polish boys, both with lank black hair, one trying very hard to grow a moustache, the other with a cannabis leaf badge in the lapel of his cheap denim jacket.

They turned out to be students Mark had met that afternoon. He asked them to wait for us in the hotel bar.

'Why on earth did you tell them our room number?' I
asked when they'd gone.

'One of them's got some weed,' he said. 'I thought you'd
be interested.'

'Well, that's something, I suppose.'

Half an hour later, in a dark alley behind the Marian
Church, enjoying that special feeling of doing something
naughty in public, we smoked a couple of pipes of their
home-grown grass.

'Can we go somewhere with lots of girls?' asked Mark as
we zig-zagged across the square.

'You want girls?' asked the one with the cannabis badge.

He stopped the first two he saw in the street and engaged
them in conversation. They glanced over at this strangely
dressed bunch of Westerners – John in his gangster hat,
Trevor looking like a seedy insurance salesman, Mark like
an off-duty pilot and me in a coat that resembled a monk's
habit – exchanged a look, shrugged and joined the party.
Now we were eight. Cannabis Badge led us all round the
corner, through an unprepossessing doorway, down some
narrow stairs and into a low cellar that contained what
appeared to be a half-deserted youth club. We sat on
orange stacking chairs around a long formica table and
descended immediately into an absurd argument with the
waiter because we wanted vodka on its own and he insisted
it could only be served with cola. When finally he did bring
us neat vodkas, Trevor amused himself by protesting that
he'd wanted cola all along.

The girls were in their late teens or early twenties. Mark
was taken with one of them and concentrated his energies
on her. The other girl chatted to the student with the
moustache while I quizzed Cannabis Badge about life as a
Polish student.

'How much money do you get from the government?'

'It is very difficult. 296,000 zlotys a month.'

I did some mental arithmetic. The contents of the money
belt which held up my trousers amounted, at the official
exchange rate, to more than a year's Polish student grant.

Trevor pulled a hundred zloty note from his pocket, grinned at the student and calmly blew his nose on it. For a moment I thought Cannabis Badge might take offence, but as Trevor screwed the note up and tossed it into the ashtray, he started to laugh.

With eight drinking on our tab, it eventually dawned that our zlotys would run out.

'How much have you got, Mark?' asked Trevor.

'About 27,000.'

'It's a damn sight more than I've got,' said John.

'And,' I added, 'it's a damn sight less than the bill.'

I left Mark on the corner by the hotel, still chatting up the girl, the other three Poles in a knot nearby, and went off to sleep on the spare bed in John and Trevor's room. Mark would have privacy, should he wish to exploit it. In the morning I opened my eyes to find John's broad, hairy back directly in my line of sight. Dreadful snoring filled the room, the smell of sweaty socks. I was still in my clothes from the night before. Mark answered the door immediately when I tapped upon it. He was awake and alone. On the table stood an empty bottle of Polish vermouth, a couple of empty cigarette packets and a pile of confectionery wrappers beside it. I'd bought a family pack of chocolate-covered muesli bars before leaving Berlin which, along with a bag of apples, were intended to supplement my diet in those areas where vegetarian food was hard to obtain. Whoever had been in here had scoffed the lot.

'What happened?'

'Oh,' Mark groaned, 'all four of them came up here. They asked if I could get some booze so I went down and woke the night porter who sold me that horrible stuff,' he nodded at the Polish vermouth, 'for, like, ten dollars. When I got back they said: "Thanks for the chocolate."'

'They seem to have smoked most of my cigarettes too.'

'Yeah, the other three sat on your bed smoking and drinking while I was talking to the girl.'

'Just talking?'

'Well, she got into bed with me for a while, but she wouldn't take her clothes off. It was hard to do much else with the audience over there.'

He paused and sighed.

'When they'd finished the vermouth they all fucked off.'

'So they drank up all our zlotys and some of your dollars, ate all my chocolate, smoked all my cigarettes and when there was nothing left they popped off home.'

'Yeah, it was like, "Thanks, bye!"'

We looked at each other and burst out laughing.

'Serves us right, I suppose,' said Mark.

We drove down from Cracow and hit the Czech border in the mountains south of Zakopane. Crossing took ages. The guards gave us hell about everything and only lightened up when they opened Trevor's attaché case to find several sets of joke shop Dracula teeth.

'We're going to Romania,' Trevor explained.

The guard toyed with a set and smiled, making the incisors open and close.

The first night in Czechoslovakia we stayed at the Grand Hotel Praha in Tatranská Lomnica, the place where we'd run into the mining union conference last year. The luxury was wasted on me. Sick with what was probably a mild case of food poisoning, I went straight to bed while the others dined and discoed. In the morning we tried to find a copy of *Neues Deutschland*, the DDR newspaper, to see what was happening back home, but for reasons which only became clear later, there were no East German papers to be had. We went for a walk and found the ski lift closed again.

That day we motored south and east from the mountains. It was a nice drive, the first day on the road when it wasn't either black night or else grey and foggy. We'd been able to see the sights: rubbish tips, medieval castles, tractor factories, picturesque valleys, the occasional patch of dead forest. A gypsy encampment on a hillside, shacks built from old doors and bits of scavenged metal, made us all gasp with the sheer filth and destitution of the place.

'Now *that*,' whistled Trevor, 'is poverty.'

Košice was a town we'd heard absolutely nothing good about. Marek had mentioned it in Prague last year. 'Now that's a terrible place. Full of gypsies, really rough. It's a

233

wild town.' We'd resolved right then to visit the place and found it fitted perfectly on to this year's itinerary. Some girls Mark and Trevor had met in the disco the night before had reinforced the bad impression. We were going to Košice? They'd shaken their heads in amazement and disgust.

Our expectations were high, then, when we drew up outside the Hotel Imperial, having booked rooms by telephone the day before. The first thing they did at reception was warn us to remove everything from the car. It was still mid-afternoon and we went straight out for a walk.

'The four large windows on the eighth storey,' read the typewritten guide to Urban's Tower on the main street Leninova, home of a permanent exhibition on The Art of Bell-Founding in East Slovakia, 'provide the visitors with an unforgettable view of the beauty of old Košice, as well as the rapid building development of the present.'

So we climbed to the top and looked out of the window. The old town below was indeed very pretty. Then we raised our eyes. Rapid building development had covered all the hills around with rows of off-white flat blocks. Back at ground level we heard a distant chanting: the unmistakable sound of a crowd of football hooligans. On the streets everyone stared at us as if we'd dropped from outer space. This was not a town that had much experience with tourists and it was nice to be so far off any beaten track. On a bit of a high, savouring an atmosphere charged with violence, we wandered around in the gathering dusk, looking, as usual, for somewhere we could drink a beer. After several places where the single word 'pivo' occasioned a curt shake of the head, we came upon a *vinárna*, a wine bar. In Czechoslovakia, wine bars sold wine and beer bars sold beer and never the twain shall overlap, but we went in and sat down anyway. Maybe they'd know of a place. If not, we'd admit defeat and drink whatever they had.

The waiter was smart and proud, with classic Slav features and abrupt, almost operatic, mannerisms. Mark flipped through his phrase book and popped the question: Did he know anywhere we could get a beer? Gesturing to left and right, the waiter started interminable directions to some place evidently miles distant. I was just about to ask him to start again so I could write it all down, when something seemed to sink in.

'You want a beer?'

We nodded.

His whole manner changed. But of course, these boys want a beer. He drew himself even straighter, snapped his fingers: 'Come!' We were ushered through a low doorway into a tiny stone room, windowless, just large enough to contain a table and some chairs. Whisking a curtain across the entrance, he disappeared as we all sat down. There was a long wait. Mark started getting nervous. Our coats and bags were still in the main room, out of our sight. Perhaps this was some elaborate rip-off: hide us in the stone room and rifle our belongings. The wait stretched out. Mark fidgeted. Finally he could stand it no longer. He whipped out of the room and came back with his coat and bag.

'Happy now?'

'Yeah,' leered Mark. 'How long can you resist getting yours?'

Trevor and I sat proud and still, but in truth Mark had sown a little apprehension. Who would be the next to break? We sat in silence. John was growing visibly anxious. He shifted from buttock to buttock, eventually hauling himself up and fetching his coat too.

At that point the waiter returned, four bottles of Budweiser clutched close to his chest. He cracked tops and filled glasses to appreciative cries of 'cheers' and 'dobry, dobry'. At first he nodded in acknowledgement but as we span the routine out, making a mockery of the business of thanking him, he began tapping the table with impatient fingers. Trevor finally slipped him a couple of dollars and he swiftly disappeared.

'At least we made him work for it,' I said.

There was silence as we drank. It was uncomfortable in the windowless room, as if we were some privileged caste to be concealed from the view of ordinary mortals, the only ones, in this land of brewers, permitted to drink a beer.

When we got up to leave, the weight of Mark's leather

jacket and tiny knapsack was found to have bent the metal coat hook halfway off the wall. Ah, Czechnology.

Mark, Trevor and I stood waiting for John in the foyer of the hotel. The latest round of biscuits was coming on and we all lapsed into separate daydreams. I gazed at the dark wood veneer on the wall, watching the lines of the grain, like weeds in a stream, wave gently from side to side.

A blinding flash from above sent us reeling in surprise.

'That's a bit blatant, isn't it?' said Trevor.

It took me a second to work out what he meant. Trevor actually thought it had been the flash of a camera, some secret policeman taking our picture.

I said: 'It was just Czechnology – the bulb burning out.'

'No it wasn't,' said Mark.

'It was.'

We all looked up. There was a circular light fitting, one bulb lit, several dark. Had there been two lit before? I couldn't remember. The foyer did look a little darker, but that could simply be the after-effect of the flash. Now they had me suspecting it too. I fought against it. That there were secret policemen here, I could believe. But that they would openly take pictures of us with a flash camera in the foyer of a hotel stretched the bounds of credibility.

'You idiots, this isn't Romania.'

'No,' said Mark, adding a mournful tremble to his voice. 'But we are in Czechoslovakia now.'

It was Saturday night. At reception we asked if there were any discos in town. The women there nodded but looked doubtful. One reached over and felt Trevor's upper arm, as if judging the strength of his biceps, then shook her head slowly. The meaning was clear: Košice discos were too rough for us. We were sat at the hotel bar, apparently the one place in town where beer was sold openly, wondering what to do when a man – maybe forty-five, gaunt, thick spectacles, tweed jacket and tie – approached and addressed us.

'You are speaking English. How lucky for me. Oh, I love to speak English but there is always so little chance. My name is Stanley. Stanley Walkbridge. There was a story about me in your English newspapers. "Stanley of the Castle," they called me. Oh yes, "Stanley of the Castle".'

We eyed this apparition with some surprise. The routine formality of his dress, the soft excitability of his voice – everything about him reminded me of an ineffectual schoolteacher.

'"Stanley,"' repeated Mark doubtfully, '"of the Castle"?'

'Yes of course. But what about you English boys? You are English boys, yes?'

Suddenly the air was full of insistent questions. What were our names? Where had we been? Where were we going? What were we doing here in Košice? The kind of questions a secret policeman would ask. The background menace we had been feeling in this town suddenly crystal-lised into sharp paranoia. Stanley persisted, a smile on his face: What were our professions?

'I'm a musician,' said Mark.

'I'm a graphic designer,' I said.

'I'm a salesman,' said John.

'And I am a spy,' said Trevor, enunciating his words very clearly. 'I work for the British government.'

Mark spluttered at my side. Stanley's smile was replaced by a look of consternation. Here we go again, I thought, and tried to change the subject.

'What we're doing in Košice is looking for a disco.'

'Oh I know a place,' said Stanley. 'There are many places. Come with me, English boys. Come with me.'

We followed him out and round the corner into Len-inova, Stanley still brimming with questions. We looked at one place. Our hotel receptionists had been right. None of us had big enough muscles to handle the fierce-looking crew in quilted anoraks who stood on the stairs outside and shot us a look that said: What the fuck are you lot doing here? We backed off short of the door. A second place was just as unwelcoming. As we walked down the street towards a third, Stanley quizzing Mark about why he lived in Berlin, Trevor murmured to me:

'How did he get on to us so quick? Do you think it's because we booked the hotel in advance?'

237

'I don't know. You'd think they could have found someone better than this.'

'Perhaps he was the only one they could find on short notice who spoke English.'

The Slovan was the town's obligatory modernist four-star hotel. The nightclub was huge: a dance floor at one end, low tables at the other, a band playing Abba songs, people kicking pennies, everything dark red and black. Stanley was still asking questions: What did we think about Czechoslovakia? Did we go often to East Berlin? How long were we staying here? What time would we leave? Trevor leaned forward and looked him in the eye.

'Are you a spy, Stanley?'

Stanley's mouth fell open.

'Are you a spy?' Trevor insisted, a grin creeping over his face. 'Come on, you can tell us. We don't mind. We're spies too.'

'Those girls,' Stanley leant over to me, changing the subject, 'they are very interested in you.'

I looked where he was pointing. Two girls, one chewing gum, the other an unnatural blonde, were staring into space. They didn't look very interested in anything.

'No they're not.'

'Don't you like girls? Are you married? You are very good-looking. Surely you must have many girls?'

Only then did it strike me that Stanley was gay. I'd been so preoccupied with the question of whether or not he was a secret policeman that this other interpretation had until now eluded me. Of course, the matter of his sexual preference didn't mean that he wasn't some kind of spy. On the other hand, if he was really checking us out for the authorities, would he spend quite so much time insisting that we get up and dance?

He'd now turned his attention to John. Why didn't he ask a girl to dance? Was he too shy? Stanley would ask for him, handle all the negotiations. It was Saturday night. John must dance. Stanley must insist. John was uncomfortable.

'Stanley,' he growled. 'Do you understand English? I do not fucking want to dance. None of us want to dance.'

Still Stanley went on. Nothing could divert him. Where

did he live? In Bratislava, but come on, Trevor must dance. What was his job? He worked in the Hotel Carlton and Mark – surely Mark liked to dance. What was he doing in Košice? Visiting some relatives and what about it, David, now is the time to dance.

'Listen, Stanley,' said Trevor. 'We're driving to the Hungarian border tomorrow. As one spy to another, can you tell us if there are any good military bases on the way? We want to take some photographs.'

Stanley stared at Trevor for a long moment. It was as hard for him to know what to make of us as it was for us to decide about him.

'Ah,' he cried in sudden understanding. 'I think you are players, yes! You are artists!'

'I wouldn't go that far,' I said.

On the way back to the hotel, he announced that I must be his friend. I was a graphic designer. This was very interesting for him. We would write to each other, such fascinating letters. We would discuss art and literature. If I would just give him my address . . . At reception he was distracted for a moment. I grabbed my key and dodged into the lift. It was a creaky old thing and the concertina doors took an age to slide shut. Just as it finally began to lurch off, Stanley appeared in front.

'David, where are you going? But I thought we would be friends . . .'

His voice faded out below as the old lift rattled upwards.

A wall is no permanent feature of any landscape, just a line drawn by humans across a piece of the earth, following some natural features perhaps, but always arbitrary. That line might mark the limits of an influence, the boundary between one person's property and another, the edge of a vast and powerful empire. But yesterday's bricks and mortar are always tomorrow's picturesque ruins. The odd remaining fragments of Hadrian's Wall, marking segments of an old line that passed through Newcastle only yards to the south of the room where I was born, were a reminder of what happens to empires.

The Berlin Wall had fallen down.

We'd known things were changing, known this would probably be our last holiday full of *Schwarzgeld* and secret policemen, but the following lunchtime, in the dining room of the Hotel Bodrog, Sárospatak, Eastern Hungary – an obscure corner of Europe by almost any measure – none of us was remotely prepared for the news.

The Berlin Wall had fallen down.

The diners kept on with their chatter. The waiters in their red embroidered waistcoats carried on moving between the tables. But for us, at that moment, as Mark read out the story, the compass wheeled and everything changed. In the middle of a journey, we learnt that the point to which we would return was no longer the same as our point of departure. In the middle of our lives, we learnt that the world we grew up in had just shifted shape. It was hard to know whether to look forward or back. It was hard to know where to look in the present.

It already seemed strange, as the truth sank in, ever to have considered that state of post-war armed truce, that forty-five-year-old face-off across a line drawn through Europe by three old men in Yalta, as constituting any kind of certainty. Yet right up to that moment – damn it, fully three days after the event – it had been quite inconceivable that the process of change in Europe might go that far, that quickly. The evidence had been all around us, but we were so used to the Wall, both as historical fact and as local landmark, that it had come to stand for incontrovertible fact.

In those first few days without it, we felt lost. All the life seemed to drain from our holiday. The trip was supposed to have been an adventure, an escape from the dull certainty of daily routines. Yet back home daily life had turned upside down, while here in Eastern Hungary the landscape was flat and the towns were boring. We looked around Tokaj, around a Polish market outside Nyíregyháza, around the bars and nightclubs of Debrecen and all we could think was: what are we doing here? Looking back, we could only imagine the scenes that must be taking place. Hints came through Trevor's phone calls home: Trabants everywhere, queues outside every bank and supermarket, new border posts opening to cope with the flow, people dancing on the Wall at the Brandenburg Gate, scenes of joy and jubilation. Looking forward we could imagine only . . . Romania.

Romania. The word rang like an ominous chord. Ever since the jokes had started back in West Berlin, a sense of fear and foreboding had been building. Every time our spirits rose too high, it seemed that some small thing would remind us of where we were heading and – Romania! – like a nasty little arpeggio on a movie soundtrack, warning that the killer is at the door. The closer we got to it, the worse our apprehension. On our last night in Hungary, in Debrecen, just short of the border, every time we thought of the morrow, conversation would falter and our hearts would sink.

Back in Berlin we'd talked to a Romanian exile and made our preparations. Not only was the car packed with spare car parts and food – mostly American MRE packages – we had also stocked up on ballpoint pens, condoms, chewing gum and disposable lighters. These were all unavailable in Romania. You could sell them, give them away, use them as bribes. We also had several cartons of Kent cigarettes, which constituted a virtual second currency in Romania. Mark had forbidden me to smoke any of them.

'Remember, if you smoke those, you are literally smoking money.'

The problem was: what to do with the biscuits? Having blithely carted them across every other border, here was where we drew the line. It wasn't just that we'd been warned to expect the worst search of our lives. Nor just that should we be caught, the penalties would be especially draconian. It was also that, if we behaved in Romania the way we behaved anywhere else when we'd been eating them, trouble was sure to ensue. On the other hand, we did want our biscuits for the rest of the journey. I thought of posting them to László and rang him in Budapest to discuss it, keeping hazy about the details, saying only that we had some things we didn't want to take with us. It turned out his girlfriend's sister was a student in Debrecen, would be going up to the capital the next day. Mark and I spent the best part of that evening following a trail that led through a women-only student hall of residence where no one spoke English or German, and ending up in an evening of Hungarian folk music and dancing. There we found the sister and handed over a bag full of biscuits, my notebooks and various other crap we thought it best to be rid of.

In the restaurant later, we realised that not one of us was actually looking forward to the next part of our journey.

'It doesn't feel like a holiday, does it?' said Mark. 'It feels like we're going on a fucking mission.'

'Be careful,' said László when I rang him from the hotel the next morning. 'Be very careful. Remember, you are going beyond civilisation now. Really. Beyond civilisation.'

His words rang in my ears all the way to the border. We stopped at a café a few miles short of the checkpoint and there Mark produced six biscuits. He'd kept them behind for this moment but we would have to eat them now. One and a half each. This was a heavy dose. We looked at each other, sighed, shrugged and washed them down with a bottle of beer. A heavy-looking guy on the other side of the room was looking in our direction. I wondered if he might be Securitate, nipping over this side of the border to see who was coming their way, then dismissed this as pure paranoia. Outside, as we climbed into the car, I turned back to see the same guy standing beside a Dacia with Romanian plates, his keys in the door, watching us draw off for the frontier. He must have been Securitate. No one else was allowed to leave the country. On the last stretch of well-kept Hungarian road, two Romanian trucks passed us coming the other way, one trundled ahead of us, going back.

'There they go,' said Trevor. 'Taking the cheese and tomatoes out, bringing the handcuffs in.'

The border was ridiculous. A hundred metres short of the checkpoint, we came to a guard handing out customs declaration forms. Before he would give us any, we had to bribe him with a disposable lighter. Every last thing had to come out of the car and be piled up on a stone table, every last object was examined. The junior officer stole some pistachio nuts and a carton of sterilised milk. The senior officer examined every recess in the car, tapped all the panels, felt behind the seats and then stole the batteries from our torch. We had, on the advice of our Romanian exile, left a couple of packets of Kents lying around where they could take them. These offerings, too, were duly pocketed.

'Have you got any bibles?' asked the senior officer, surly and aggressive. 'Are you journalist? Are you detective, eh? Are you detective?'

No, just tourists. Trevor showed him the Dracula teeth.

'Have you got gun?'

He slapped at the breast pocket of my jacket, as if expecting to find one.

'What is in here?'

Nothing, I showed him. It was where I normally kept my notebook, but I'd shoved the one I'd just started in a discreet side pocket of my bag. The officer finally looked at all the boxes of food and made some comment to his colleague. We had to laugh. Though none of us knew a word of Romanian, it was obvious what he'd said:

'What are they going to do, open a restaurant?'

An hour and a half had passed by the time we'd put everything back, bought some petrol coupons and changed the required amount of hard currency into Romanian lei. The notes made Polish zlotys look clean and crisp. They were shrivelled and threadbare, filthy and furry and horrible to touch. An hour and a half had also been time enough for the biscuits to take effect. As we finally motored into Romania, steered beyond civilisation, we were all feeling very stoned indeed.

Beyond civilisation. It felt like that immediately, as if we had just passed from the known universe into some semi-mythical badlands.

No one said a word as we bumped a few miles along poorly surfaced road, to either side of us the overgrown waste-ground of what was presumably some border no-go area. Silence still reigned as we drove through the town of

243

Oradea, a slighty shocked silence now. The roads were pitted and potholed, half the buildings looked to be falling down, there were as many horses and carts on the streets as there were grubby little cars and everything appeared to have been dipped in mud. The only splashes of colour were the metal signs emblazoned with inspiring slogans.

'CEAUŞESCU – ROMANIA – PACE!'

The queues of people at the bus stops, dressed in what anywhere else would have been thrown away as rags, looked lean and hunched and defeated. The buses were covered in grime and had ungainly propane tanks on their roofs.

'ROMANIA COMUNISM! CEAUŞESCU EROISM!'

We juddered along a road out of town that appeared to have been surfaced with corrugated roofing material. To one side was a concrete gully along which flowed a narrow river, shaded a chemical green.

'CEAUŞESCU – P.C.R!'

We emerged into bleak countryside cross-hatched with pipelines and ducts. Most of the few vehicles on the two-lane main highway were olive-drab tankers. Trees to either side, in lieu of proper roadmarkings, had their trunks splashed with whitewash.

'EPOCA NICOLAE CEAUŞESCU!'

On the verge ahead a uniformed cop had pulled up his car and was hassling a small group of gypsies. He was raging and shouting and waving his arms in their faces, forcing them to cower away. One of the gypsies sprinted away across a field. Just as we drew level with the scene, the cop started off in pursuit, pulling a gun from his holster as he ran.

For the first time in the East, I was truly appalled. A sign beside a giant chemical works read: 'Welcome to Stina for a Beautiful Visit'. Great stretches of country were nothing but bulldozed expanses of mud, mist and chemical smoke. Hills were chewed away by quarries and open-cast mines. Peasants wrapped in sheepskin cloaks sat on ancient, rotting carts pulled by weary old horses. It was like medieval serfdom married to everything terrible about the twentieth century.

We made the odd, nervous joke but mostly stayed silent. At one point Trevor slowed slightly as we passed through a village in which every house seemed to be leaning at a different angle. There was a drab, dark café, outside which stood a row of brutish-looking peasants in knee boots and strange traditional hats, arms folded, watching the traffic.

'Shall we stop here?' Trevor asked.

A chorus of negatives. No one could handle it yet. It was as if the car was a small, safe bubble and once we stepped outside, anything might happen. Trevor touched the accelerator, just as happy to keep moving. We had to make it to Cluj, having registered this at the border as our first night's destination. As dusk fell, the driving grew difficult, with nothing but the whitewashed trees to give us any bearings. Soon the blackness was absolute. Even in the villages there were no lights anywhere and we had to crawl along in fear of bicycles and carts without headlights or reflectors, ridden by peasants in clothes as dark as the night. Coming into the blacked-out suburbs of Cluj, the hulks of unlit flat blocks dimly perceptible to either side, felt like entering a city depopulated by some science fiction disaster.

In the centre of town there was a little light: maybe one street lamp in ten was working, a faint glimmer came from certain windows. In West Berlin we had been obliged to purchase Romanian hotel coupons at fifty marks a night, so now we steered around looking for the most expensive place in town. The Transilvania Hotel, on a hill just over the river from the centre, was the usual tacky concrete block. We walked into a dim foyer with bulbous plastic decorations on the ceiling and 'Human' by The Human League playing in the background. The receptionist made us fill out a two-page form. Name . . . date of birth . . . home address . . . profession . . . where we had come from . . . where we were going . . . what we thought we were doing there . . . parents' first names . . . Parents' first names? Suppressing a smile, Trevor discreetly showed us his entry. He had written: 'Dick and Dora'. Immediately it became a game. Down on the other forms went Philip and Elizabeth, Jack and Jill, Antony and Cleopatra.

While we were working through these, lined up along

the reception desk, one of the many people hanging about in the lobby came up to me and asked me in a loud, clear voice:

'Would you like to change money on the black market?'

From all I knew of Romania – indeed, from all I knew of common sense – the chances of anyone even remotely kosher coming up in the foyer of a hotel used by foreigners and asking a question phrased in such perfectly incriminating terms, simply had to be some kind of rotten, if rather incompetent, provacateur. I looked up at him: a burly man in an anorak, my second Securitate of the day.

'No, I most certainly would not.'

Before going out for a walk, there was just time to poke around our de luxe accommodations. The door had been made so badly that light from the corridor leaked all around the frame. The tap wouldn't turn off in the bathroom and thin trails of black slime trickled down the pipes from somewhere above. Mark turned on the television and got a fuzzy image of Ceauşescu making a speech. The phone had no dial. Both the earpiece and mouthpiece were glued to the rest of the handset so it was impossible to unscrew them – presumably to protect a bug within.

We made it into town just in time to inspect a department store. It was called Central. 'Central Services,' muttered Mark. Inside one strip light in four was burning. Such stores in the East were normally full of crap but this place was nearly empty of anything at all. There were some dismal clothes, a few shabby toys, nothing to hold even our interest. On the streets outside, silent crowds waited for infrequent buses. We looked in a video arcade. A few antique Space Invader machines stood like a row of rotten teeth, all blacked out or bashed in save one, which was surrounded by scruffy kids. We looked in St Michael's Church, a vast Gothic edifice on the main town square. Inside there were absolutely no pews or seats, just a stone floor in poor repair. A lone old woman knelt before the altar, praying.

There was a restaurant with a picture of a mushroom outside. The place was just closing when we walked in but the waitress indicated she would serve us, if we were quick.

The one dish on offer, served with or without 'meat', was a tepid, murky stew of salty but indeterminate composition garnished with a pale mush of potatoes that had been cut like chips, dipped into fat just long enough to turn soggy and then allowed to go cold and congeal. We all took one mouthful and put down our forks.

'Joking apart,' I said, 'I mean, we say it all the time, but this really is, without one word of exaggeration, the worst fucking meal I have ever tasted in my life.'

Mark smiled. 'Well, it's what we came for.'

The waitress looked sad and apologetic when she saw the four untouched platefuls. The bill, on the other hand, at the official rate of exchange, came to about the price of a full meal in a decent West Berlin restaurant. It was the first money we'd spent here. Romania, we realised, was not only a vision of hell on earth, it was also about as expensive as Switzerland.

Without much heart for the task, we set about the usual search for beer and disco. It soon became apparent there was nowhere to go. Eight o'clock in the evening and everything was closing down. We did find one open café. The furniture was decaying, paper peeled from the walls. A bunch of bad-tempered locals were drinking some viscous, ochre-coloured liquid that might have been whipped-up egg yolk – had eggs not been so rare in Romania that, like Kent cigarettes, they virtually functioned as currency. Whatever the stuff was, none of us were tempted to try it.

Cluj was as miserable as our worst imaginings. Still in a state of mild shock, we walked back up to the hotel. The bar had just closed but at reception they were selling Lebanese beer, sixty-five US cents a bottle. We bought all they had – a shrink-wrapped pack of ten – and sat at a table in the lobby. The background music was 'White Rabbit' by Jefferson Airplane. ' . . . And you just ate some kind of mushroom.'

Within minutes we had attracted a small group of young men in anoraks, clean and well-dressed by local standards. While the bulk of them engaged in some badinage with Trevor and John, one sat down next to me.

'You are English? I have a girlfriend in England.'

'Oh yes? Where in England?'

247

'In Cambridge.'

'Oh. I have a brother in Cambridge.'

'Oh yes,' he said. 'I have a sister in Italy.'

'Really?'

'And my father is a lawyer.'

'What do you do?'

'I am training to sing at the opera.'

Which, though it was mildly interesting, was not quite interesting enough to puncture the guarded formality of our exchange. I couldn't think of a single thing to say to him. I had questions – too many – but they were not about things I felt comfortable discussing in a hotel lobby with someone I didn't know who, even if he wasn't another Securitate, was still obliged by law to report this conversation to the police. Suspicion poisoned the air between us.

The background music had changed to Scott MacKenzie: 'If you're going to San Francisco, be sure to wear some flowers in your hair . . . '

'I met my girlfriend when she was here with a dance group,' he offered, then drew a breath. 'If I give you a letter for her, will you post it for me?'

A sharp twinge of guilt accompanied a memory of Jachym's petition. To be caught taking out any evidence of contact with a Romanian citizen was to risk the worst kind of trouble for everyone concerned. On the other hand, why not help him if I could? If it didn't seem worth the risk I could always throw the thing away later, or else take the girl's address and call her up. My suspicion gave way to sympathy.

'OK,' I shrugged.

He went up to reception and borrowed paper, then carefully began printing a short note. Trevor, Mark and John were still talking to the other boys. The conversation had steered its inexorable course towards the subject of changing money. The opera boy looked up and shouted at them in Romanian.

'I want to stop this business,' he told me. 'I do not like this business.'

He shouted some more. They all shrugged and smiled and drifted away. We were a bit pissed off that he had dispelled them so quickly: after our experience in the restaurant it was clear our official lei wouldn't last five minutes, assuming we found anything to buy.

'I do not like this business and I do not like this system. This . . . this . . . ' he spat out the word, '*Ceauşescu* system!'

His anger surprised me. The degree of his hatred and the precise nature of his grievances about the system were exactly what I most wanted to ask him about, but by uttering the name of The Creator Of The Epoch Of Unprecedented Renewal so loudly and so abusively, he had only rekindled my distrust.

The boy caught the look on my face.

'It's all right. My father is a lawyer and my sister is in Italy.' He repeated this, a litany to ward off evil. 'My father is a lawyer and my sister is in Italy.'

I took his letter and slipped it in my pocket without looking. Later I read the thing. It said: 'Dear Linda, I am sitting in the Hotel Transilvania with some English boy. I hope you are very well. Love Petre.' He obviously didn't really know the girl. I decided it wasn't worth the risk, tore it up and threw it away.

While the others went down to the garage to bring food up from the car, I saw one of the young men who'd been at our table disappearing into the toilets. I followed him in there. Raising an eyebrow but not saying a word, I showed him some dollars. He leered and produced a roll of Romanian lei. A rate was negotiated in silent sign language, currencies were quickly exchanged. I walked back out into the lobby, feeling pleased with myself.

We asked at reception for more beer. They said room service would bring some. It was cloudy stuff, in unmarked bottles, a dollar a throw. Something about the taste of it reminded me of farmyards. We asked the guy who delivered it what number to call if we wanted some more. He pointed to the phone without the dial.

'Just call Central.'

Television had closed down for the night. We ate cold MRE baked beans from the camouflage sachet, flavoured from a jar of brinjal pickle Mark had been imaginative enough to bring. Our conversation was halting. We still didn't know what to think or say – especially with someone listening from the dial-less, glued-up phone. When we'd finished our food, we went to bed. There was nothing else to do.

Next morning, as we walked across the lobby to the restaurant, 'If You're Going To San Francisco' was playing again.

'This background music,' I said, 'is unfailingly surreal. Have you ever been anyplace where you felt less like wearing flowers in your hair?'

Breakfast was included on our hotel coupons. In the otherwise deserted restaurant we asked for a menu. The waiters shook their heads: no menu. What did they have then?

'We have . . . butter,' they announced with pride.

Yeah, yeah. Butter. What else?

'Sausage.'

John and Trevor ordered that.

'Omelette.'

Mark and I put our hands up.

The waiters slowly laid out a repast that was the height of local luxury: omelettes that tasted like they had been fried in hair oil; skinless sausages so foul that Trevor, who normally shovelled anything down, managed only half of one and remained in a bad mood about it for the next three hours; butter; a saucer of 'jam' that looked like a curl of black dog shit and might well have tasted that way too, had any of us been brave enough to try it.

The waiters moved to and fro, their movements choreographed to a song by Black: 'It's a wonderful, wonderful life . . . '

'ROMANIA! CEAUŞESCU! PACE!'

Another long day's driving, measuring the passage of miles with the slogans of Ceauşescu. We passed through three or four checkpoints. Every vehicle was being stopped. Each time a uniformed cop took our papers and we had to wait for ten minutes while he went into a hut to check them out. Once or twice we also had to stop for flocks of sheep.

'P.C.R. – PACE! CEAUŞESCU! ROMANIA!'

The town of Turda was full of people wheeling primitive barrows containing three turkeys or two pigs. A man ran for the bus holding a turkey under his arm, dodging his way through the horses and carts. Every third window was broken along the front of a large, primitive-looking factory.

'EPOCA CEAUŞESCU! CEAUŞESCU P.C.R!'

We were the only car driving down a stretch by some military base. A guard at a corner tower followed us all the way through binoculars. We passed several agricultural compounds, also with watchtowers and barbed wire perimeters. In places where the countryside hadn't been totally ruined, it was actually quite beautiful.

'PARTIDUL COMUNISTA ROMANIA!'

Outside Braşov, heading south to the village of Bran, a level crossing by a tractor factory held us up for a while. Mountains loomed ahead.

'Maybe,' Trevor grinned, 'we should throw away the MREs and see what it's *really* like.'

'Over my dead body,' said John.

There was a small market in the car park at Dracula's Castle. Apart from a coach of schoolchildren, we were the only ones there. I prowled around the stalls, looking at woollen pullovers and wooden toys, then turned when I heard a commotion. John, hat on head, a look of real fright on his face, was being forced backwards by a great clamouring crowd of children, all trying to grab the packet of chewing gum he held high in his hand. He'd offered some to one child and then been set upon by all. Shouting and leaping and pushing his stomach, they shoved him slowly across the car park. John was panicked, no idea what to do.

'Throw it away from you,' laughed Mark. 'Throw it away and they'll all run after it.'

John tossed the pack of Juicy Fruit over towards the coach. The kids chased off. One boy got there first and picked it up. The rest immediately tried to mug him.

'The poor bastards,' said John. He reached in his pocket and dug out all the chewing gum he had, threw it all over

251

into the scrum. One big fight fragmented into several small ones. He shook his head sadly. 'The poor little bastards.'

The woman at the ticket office asked us for coffee. The man at the gate wanted Kent cigarettes. As we walked up towards the castle, a couple of mongrel dogs started following us. Even they knew we were the ones to scrounge from.

Commanding the pass through a dramatic ravine, towers and turrets rising up through woods against a backdrop of jagged mountains, Dracula's Castle (actually a fourteenth-century fortress built by someone else entirely) was impressive from the outside. The interior, though, was a major anti-climax. Most of the place was being renovated and the couple of rooms that remained open contained only a few old bits of furniture and a couple of suits of armour.

'We can't get anything right, can we?' I said. 'We leave Berlin just before the Wall falls down, arrive in the Tatras when the ski lift is closed for the second year running, get to Tokaj before the wine is ready and turn up at Bran when they've just started renovating the castle. We're always too late or too early.'

This turned out to be not entirely true. It was 15 November 1989, the second anniversary, as we worked out later that evening, of the Braşov uprising. On this day in 1987, spontaneous protests about a rise in food prices had culminated in workers from two factories ransacking the town's Party headquarters. Thousands had been rounded up in the aftermath, many never returned from their interrogations, many of those who did later died of cancer and other diseases accountable to Ceauşescu's fondness for treating any disease in the body politic with massive doses of radiation. Braşov was that night like a town under siege. We hardly had a chance to notice the pretty Gothic centre of this old Saxon town. All our attention was taken by the armed patrols, standing at intervals along the main street. Each was a group of three: two soldiers and one uniformed police officer. The soldiers had machine guns, the cops had muzzled attack dogs. Pedestrians walked past with eyes fixed on their feet.

One such group stood right outside our hotel, handily

located just a block away from the Party headquarters. The mood in the foyer was tense as we filled out more two-page registration forms. We rushed back out to catch the shops before they closed.

In another sparse Central store I bought an atlas which had scores of Romanian maps but absolutely nothing about any other country. There was a frontispiece of Ceauşescu, smirking as if he owned the place. Mark, juggling with the phrase book, was pointed to a girl who could speak English. She looked about eighteen and was mopping the floor when Mark strolled up and said hello and asked if she knew where there was a disco. The girl stiffened in fear, mop clutched to her breast, eyes scanning the store from left to right. She couldn't speak, was terrified of being seen in the company of a foreigner.

The store closed. So, as we walked around the narrow cobbled lanes, did everything else. There were patrols on every corner. On the big, bleak main square the 'wine cellar' of the old Saxon Merchants' Hall still seemed to be open. We walked downstairs into a long, dingy room full of rough crowds around tables. Everyone was drinking an orange liquid that looked like paraffin. We waited ages for the waitress but she wouldn't even look in our direction. The place was closing, there was nothing for us.

'How do they put up with it?' wondered Mark sadly. 'I don't know how they put up with it.'

Mark talked to the two waitresses in a quite nice-looking but firmly closed restaurant next door, and learnt that everything closed at nine o'clock, which seemed to mean they stopped serving at eight. One waitress suggested the bar of the Hotel Carpati, open until ten. A few flakes of snow were beginning to fall as we walked down the dark street she indicated. Along the opposite pavement staggered a drunken old man, shouting at no one in particular: the first person we'd seen who didn't look totally cowed. He got as far as the patrol on the corner, and was then bundled away in a van.

The Carpati bar was, of course, 'being renovated'. We walked back to our hotel and made enquiries at reception. Where could we sit down and have a drink? 'Hotel Carpati.'

We told her it was closed. 'Open tomorrow,' she shrugged. In Romania it was never jam today. Was there anything at all in our hotel apart from horrible Lebanese beer at sixty-five US cents the bottle? Nothing, except for room service, but that didn't start until ten. It was not yet nine. Perhaps, she suggested, we could get something from the restaurant on the first floor. Up the stairs we went – and then straight back down when we discovered you could only get to the restaurant by lift. Up in the lift. The restaurant was closed, but said room service would bring us something.

'It's mad really, looking for any kind of normal entertainment in a place like this,' I remarked as we trudged up to the rooms. So far the thrill of the chase for beer and discos had remained funny in a grim kind of way. Now it was beginning to get to us. Trevor rang down to room service and ordered a bottle of red wine, a bottle of white wine and bottle of mineral water. We sat waiting for an hour, our sachets of MRE baked beans waiting for some liquid to wash them down. Nothing came. Eventually Mark went for a walk and discovered a trestle table set up in reception, serving wine and sandwiches and mineral water to patrols coming in off the street. This was the extent of nightlife in Braşov: a glass of disgusting wine with the riot police.

We played Botticelli for a while, wondering what the secret police would make of that. The rooms were so cold that we rang central services to complain. A man came up, felt our radiators, walked out again and returned with extra blankets. Yeah, we sighed, fair enough. Once more, there was nothing to do but go early to bed.

The next morning, we were again the only ones in the restaurant. Biting into a forkful of hair oil omelette, I felt something hard in my mouth. I picked it out, expecting eggshell, and found a piece of broken glass. As I stared at this, Trevor loosed a loud, perfectly loathsome fart.

'Oh no!'

He shifted in his seat and stuck a hand down his trousers.

'Look,' he said, waving a finger under my nose, 'I've just gone and shit myself.'

I pushed away my plate. Breakfast was over as far as I was concerned.

'CEAUŞESCU! ROMANIA! PACE!'

'There even seems to be a shortage of slogans,' I noted. We pulled into a filling station. The woman at the pump had clearly never seen a petrol coupon before. She took it over to consult a man sitting in a parked white Dacia at the side of the forecourt. The Securitate said our coupon was all right.

'ROMANIA COMUNISM! CEAUŞESCU EROISM!'

We decided to stop and look at Sibiu, another beautiful old Saxon town, once known as Hermannstadt. A sign outside a theatre read: 'Comedia Feudaluj'.

'Look,' said Trevor. 'There's a feudal comedy.'

'The whole damn country is a feudal comedy.'

Snow was falling in the main square. An old woman with no legs was trying to pull herself along the uneven pavement, her stumps, on a trolley, bound in dirty white cloth, her hands wrapped around with soggy cardboard. She held them up to let the icy water drip off. John, as he passed, dropped some Kents in her lap. I reached in my pocket, found a lighter, dropped that too.

Round a corner maybe two hundred people were queuing in the snow for eggs and butter. I suddenly felt bad about leaving my omelette, broken glass or no.

'I was in my local supermarket the other day,' said Trevor quietly. 'There were hundreds of Romanian tomatoes on sale.'

'PARTIDUL CEAUŞESCU ROMANIA!'

We drove on through more bleak countryside and drew up in a lay-by full of rubbish where Mark wanted to take a group photograph using a huge smoking chemical works for backdrop. As he was setting up the shot, trying to position the camera on the car bonnet so he could run round and join the picture, a Dacia pulled up beside us. There was a husband and wife, three children in the back. As Mark messed with the camera, they sat and watched us: not saying anything, not doing anything, just watching. It became quite unnerving. In the end, as we were getting back into the car, the man called over: Did we have anything he could give his children? We rooted around in the

255

boot, dug out some milk, chocolate and US Army MRE cakes. He took it all and drove off without a word.

The giant modern lobby of the Hotel Astoria, Arad – another concrete block in another old town – was full of silent men in coats, dotted around the plastic chairs and sofas. We were filling in the forms again.

The hard-faced woman at the desk spoke down to us like the kind of schoolteacher who clips you round the ear. John's form was illegible. How could she be expected to read that? He must fill out a new one. John sat down with a scowl and went through the whole two pages again. She sighed in exasperation. Lord save her from idiots.

'I still can't read it.'

'It's perfectly clear,' Mark protested.

'Listen, we can read it for you,' I said.

We recited in unison: 'Name – John. Born – London. Parents' first names – Ron and Nancy . . . '

'No, no, no. It's no good reading it now. They won't be able to read it later.'

'Who won't be able to?' I asked innocently. The woman busied herself with her papers.

Mark grabbed a new form and filled it out for John, copying the replies from his last one. She inspected it with haughty eye.

'Yes, this is all right.'

We all clustered around, pretending to be schoolkids.

'Whose was the best, miss? Was it mine? No, mine was the best. Me, miss, me. Mine was the best.'

At that point, she actually smiled. It wasn't much of a smile: a faint but perceptible twitching at the corners of the mouth, quickly suppressed, but a smile none the less. We practically cheered. It was a famous victory: we had actually made a member of the Romanian secret police smile.

'The best at writing?' she asked, mouth corners twitched again. 'Or the best at talking?'

We absolutely howled. Not only had we made her smile, we had also induced her to make a joke of her own. The situation was becoming almost, well . . . almost human.

'You have to go to another hotel for breakfast,' she said, filling out a chit. 'The restaurant here is not working.'

'Did it ever work?' grinned Mark.

We all went: 'Ooooooh!' Back in the knife drawer. The woman glared at Mark.

'Uh, excuse me,' I said. 'Which hotel exactly do we have to go to for breakfast?'

She nodded at Mark. 'Get him to tell you, if he knows so much.'

The corridors were so dark I had to use a lighter to read the room numbers. The hall was so cold all the staff kept their coats on. But the Astoria had one signal virtue: it was the home of Arad's only video disco. The asking price, in a combination of dollars and lei, was so outrageous that Mark and I walked straight back out of the little office off the lobby where they sold the tickets. The woman called after us and we looked back in. Of course, she said, there was always the 'business rate'. So we slipped her some Kents and got the tickets on the cheap.

The video disco started later. First we wanted food. We didn't even consider looking for a restaurant, but we did want some wine to go with our MRE baked beans. This proved impossible to obtain in the hotel so Trevor, Mark and I went out to look. Up one side of the broad Bulevard Republicii, over at the lights, back down the other. An old woman pointed us to a 'supermarket', actually a dank hall, lit with a couple of distant bulbs, around which were scattered a few stalls staffed by people in coats and scarves. The biggest queue was for a stall selling fish heads, the second biggest for one selling pig's feet. I found out later that these last were called 'patriots': the only part of the animal that didn't leave the country. Another sold bread and, amazingly, one at the far end had wine and beer. We bought a couple of bottles of red, a bottle of sparkling, a few unlabelled farmyard beers and a loaf of bread. On the way back out I noticed, pinned to the wall, a special price list for the 'Nomenklaturul'.

We were more or less opposite the hotel. It was raining. Light-controlled crossings were a hundred yards away in either direction and down the middle of the road were tram tracks, fringed by shrubbery and trees. Where we were standing, there was a small pathway through the middle, although a sign clearly indicated that crossing here was forbidden. 'Oprita' – by now we had learnt the word.

'Hey,' I said. 'Let's cross here and see what happens.'

After three days in Romania we were beginning to get cocky. It was a measure of how much the place had got to us that this should seem like some great adventure. Trevor and I marched straight across. Mark, doubtful, hung back at first then scuttled after. Trevor and I got on to the little pathway, picked our way over the tram tracks and were halfway across the other side when a whistle blew and a frowning policeman stepped out from the shadows to demand our papers. He and I discussed the matter in French. We were sorry, I explained, struggling to find the words and not start laughing when I noticed, over the cop's shoulder, Mark hiding behind a tree in the middle of the road. Back in England, I continued, where we came from, it wasn't forbidden to cross where there were no lights and here, well, we simply didn't know the rules.

He gave me a sly, sceptical smile that said: I know your game. I met his gaze with equanimity. It was impossible to tell whether he didn't believe we didn't know, or didn't believe it wasn't forbidden in England. He held up his hand, rubbed thumb and forefinger together, muttering: 'Lei, lei.' Something told me we would get away with it. I patted my pockets and gave an eloquent shrug. The cop gave up and handed back our passes. He would let us off this once.

Mark and I laid the food out like a buffet, composing arty arrangements of olive drab sachets, a pyramid of apples, fans of carrots and plastic spoons. Thus we made the most of our meal, watching footage of old Party conferences on the television: Ceauşescu speechifying, delegates clapping in rhythm, a montage of factories and flat blocks and combine harvesters, Ceauşescu again, his name captioned in pretty flowers, another standing ovation.

I scooped up the last of my US Army baked beans.

'You know, the most damning indictment of this whole sad country is that it actually makes these MREs taste good.'

At the video disco there were dancing girls, struggling to make their best of routines choreographed to Madonna songs. Occasionally the power would go off and they'd freeze until the lights flickered back and the music started over. There was a mournful old conjuror, doing leaden versions of corny tricks with playing cards, string and top hats. No one applauded him. He was still halfway through his last trick when his music ran out and segued into the introduction of the next dance number. He picked up his table and shuffled off the stage, head bowed, a broken man. The best was a bearded compere who gave an unintentionally hilarious performance miming to a tape that kept speeding right up and slowing right down.

The bar was covered with plastic flowers and arrangements of Arad tourist leaflets. The word 'video' was written everywhere, as if in itself this guaranteed something special. We had a long conversation with the waiter when we sat down, trying to get him to remove various sickly-sounding ingredients from one of the cocktails on offer and thus leave us with a simple vodka and orange. They brought vodka mixed with what tasted like the syrup from a can of pineapple rings. Later the waiter sat down and conversed with Mark.

'Are you here officially?'

'What do you mean? Of course we're here officially.'

'No but are you here . . . *officially?*'

'Yes, we're, like, official tourists.'

'But you are from the British army, aren't you?'

We'd decided long ago not to take any food back out of the country. Anything left over, save perhaps a couple of vegetarian things for Mark and me, we would give away. This wasn't thought through very carefully. After Sibiu there floated a vague notion that maybe we'd find a queue somewhere and hand the stuff out. That morning in Arad we decided to look for a village before the border, unload it on whoever we found there.

In the car park in front of the Astoria, Trevor had his

head in the bonnet, replacing a malfunctioning fan. Mark and I were at the back, sorting out the crap, putting the food to be given away into a couple of boxes. An old woman in a headscarf stopped to watch, then came up and asked me for something. I gave her a couple of MRE cakes. A man in a raincoat stopped at the front, pestering Trevor.

'Give this fucker something, will you, so he'll leave me alone.'

John handed him some food from the box. Two young guys in anoraks started badgering Mark. The first woman was tugging my sleeve again. The man who'd been at the front started pleading: 'Deesko, deesko?' An Italian disco cassette we'd bought in Cracow was sitting on the dashboard. John reached in and offered it to him. Mark handed out cakes to some children who ran over. The first woman also started pleading: 'Deesko, deesko?' There was another Italian disco tape so I handed her that. She threw her arms around me and gave me a slobbery peck on the cheek. A man walked to the front and begged for the broken fan Trevor had just replaced. Trevor nodded: take it. Some more children scampered up . . .

Earlier that morning we'd stopped at a kiosk and bought four copies of a magazine because we liked the cover illustration of Mr and Mrs Ceauşescu in socialist realist pose, showing the workers the way. That alone had been enough to attract a small crowd, jostling to see what we had bought. Now that we were handing out food, right in the middle of Arad's main street, every passer-by seemed to join the crowd. Soon there were twenty or thirty around us, begging and pleading, pushing and shoving, waving rolls of lei in our faces, snatching things from our hands, desperation mixed with resentment in their eyes. I was beginning to panic. The crowd heaved and swayed. Any minute now and the police would arrive. Trevor finished working and slammed the bonnet shut.

'Come on, let's go.'

We crammed the last of our bags into the back. The crowd was still growing, pressing closer. I could feel hot breath on my cheek. We pushed our way around to get into the car, shoving people back just to pull the doors shut.

Trevor started the engine but still couldn't drive away. A gang of scruffy children had thrown themselves at the car, pushing their hands through our open windows, waving them about, their grubby faces, streaked with tears, pressed close to the glass. John shoved some cakes into the imploring hands. The kids snatched them from each other, begged and cried for more, still clutching through the window. We flung a load of stuff out the other side. The kids all let go to run after it. Trevor gunned the engine and at last we were out of there.

'Those poor fuckers,' said John. 'Those poor little fuckers. Did you see their little faces? Their poor little faces? The poor fuckers.'

He was almost in tears. We were all very shaken.

There were still two big boxes of food in the car. On the road towards the border, we started throwing stuff out whenever we saw children. Apples and oranges and MRE cakes thudded down in front of kids making mud pies, landed among them in the backs of horse-drawn carts. This part was fun, watching faces light up in amazement as presents seemed to fall from the sky. Before we knew it we'd arrived at the tail end of a long line of trucks and realised this was the queue for the frontier. A gang of children were hanging about and scrounging from the truck drivers. As we slowed and stopped they all came running. John shoved out the first box. The nearest child grabbed it and ran. John shoved out the second box. Another kid grabbed that one and hared off in a different direction. The rest of the kids pursued one or the other, sprinting away across snow-dusted fields.

As we drew up to the checkpoint and a female guard approached the car, Trevor muttered a curse, reached in a pocket, pulled out some piece of paper, crumpled and dropped it on the floor. He showed us later what it was: a postcard of Auschwitz, addressed to Nicolae Ceauşescu and scribbled full of complaints about Romania and comparisons with the institution pictured overleaf. He'd forgotten to post it in Arad.

The search of baggage and car was mercifully light. We

were then ushered into a room with a table. On book-shelves were the complete works of both Ceauşescu and Lenin. On the walls were portraits of Ceauşescu, quotes from Ceauşescu, graphs of rising production figures. The officer who searched our pockets was polite but thorough, poking into every last pocket, examining every little scrap of paper, even feeling around John's hatband. He would have found Trevor's postcard in five seconds. He came last to Mark, who produced an incredible amount of rubbish from various recesses: money, chewing gum, condoms, paper handkerchiefs, three lighters, a packet of Fisher-man's Friends, several pens, packs of Kents, a large bunch of keys, screwdriver, sunglasses, a phrase book . . . It was better than the conjuror in Arad. We were all cracking jokes and our officer was soon laughing along.

'Can you tell me what you were looking for?' asked Mark, as he put all the crap away again.

'Yes,' said the officer, and pointed at the Fisherman's Friends. 'Can I try one of these.'

'Sure,' said Mark. 'But be careful, they're hot.'

The officer popped one in his mouth.

'What was I looking for? You see, it is very difficult –'

He gasped and spluttered as the Fisherman's Friend hit home. Right at that moment one of his colleagues came in, showed him a Marlboro packet with a small lump of hash-ish at the bottom.

'Ah,' said our officer, rubbing his hands with pleasure. 'You must all now excuse me.'

As we filed out of the room, we saw him leading away one very frightened hippie.

A few hundred yards further on, our passes were checked through the car window by two young Hungarian guards, one with a tray full of rubber stamps. We were playing some Puccini and they asked us to turn it up, then shook their heads. No good. Had we heavy metal? Trevor put on a Motorhead cassette we'd bought in Cracow and cranked the volume louder still. The two young guards started tapping their feet, stamping our papers in time. Louder, they motioned, louder still. Romania was only a stone's throw behind us, but already we were in another world.

But Romania stayed with us all the way to Budapest. It stayed with us as we sat around László's living room, discussing what we had seen, László answering our questions about the Braşov uprising, the Hungarian minority, Transylvanian history. It stayed with us as Mark and I went over to meet some Romanian exiles on an eight-day hunger strike, shivering in a tent opposite the embassy. It was a pathetic little protest. They told us of exile organisations infiltrated and destroyed by Romanian agents. They had just started a new one. It had only twelve members but they were quietly optimistic: something would change, there would be pressure from the rest of the communist world, the army could overthrow Ceauşescu, but change would be bloody.

We were not so optimistic. When we told László of our games with parents' first names, he clasped his forehead and groaned.

'Now you can never go back to Romania!'

'I never would go back to Romania,' I swore, 'until Ceauşescu and his wife are both dead and buried and all his family are in prison.'

Which was to say: never. Not for one moment did I imagine that the hunger strikers could be right, that Ceauşescu could be overthrown from within. It seemed to us that the lid was on too tight, that change could only come if some foreign army invaded the place. At that moment, on that first afternoon back in civilisation, so much was Romania still with us that if someone had walked in to announce the formation of a United Nations task force for an Operation Stuff Ceauşescu, we would probably have all joined up.

I kept wondering what had happened next in several of those stories which had brushed with ours. Had that gypsy escaped from the 'cop with the gun? Or been shot in the back, gunned down in the field? Had the woman with no legs been able to make any use of the lighter and packet of Kents? Or had someone stolen them the minute we walked out of frame? Had the kids with our boxes of food got clean away? Or had others of their gang caught up and redistributed that sudden wealth? And the fightened hippie, the one who hadn't been sensible enough either to bake his stash into biscuits or else leave it behind – had he been kicked back over the border? Or flung into some unspeakable jail?

Yes, Romania stayed with us that first Friday night in Budapest, the memories and emotions of all we'd just seen still vivid and unsettled inside us. It stayed with us through a couple of relaxed beers in a bar off Váci Utca, through a decent meal in a private restaurant. It stayed with us through a hysterical drinking session in the Club of Young Artists where a young man called Attila was wound up so tight by our cracks about Romania, our deluge of in-jokes, our dogged refusal to give a sensible answer to any straight question, that he lost control and punched one of his friends and we had to break up the fight.

It stayed with us as we moved on to a disco and joined the heaving crowd on the dance floor. I was up there for hours, dancing with rage and dancing with joy, dancing until I was drenched in sweat, until I could hardly walk any more, until I loped over to a chair and sat down with a beer and, in the sweet exhaustion of that moment, felt I had finally flushed Romania from my system.

In contrast to the days before, that long weekend in Budapest was simple fun: eating, drinking, shopping, exploring a city that often seemed, as Trevor put it, 'like a half-price Germany'. But Hungary was not yet the West. We developed a game called Catching Budapest Out, savouring those moments when the city revealed its Eastern side. A mug of beer costing fifty-one forints? Yes, we were still in the East. A woman tearing tickets at the funicular railway up to Castle Hill, standing right next to a new machine that was supposed to do the job. We were still in the East. Walking into the McDonald's off Váci and seeing so many uniformed employees behind the counter that they hardly had room to work. Caught it again: we were still in the East.

Meanwhile, there was news. László hunched over his radio, shouted out reports of the latest developments. On the very day we slipped out, Romania had closed its

borders for the run-up to the Fourteenth Party Conference. There was something almost hallucinatory about the
idea of all these frontiers opening and closing just after we
had crossed them. Everything was negotiable, nothing
solid or sure. First the Hungarians had opened their
border with Austria. Then the Berlin Wall had been
breached. Now the whole Eastern house of cards was
coming tumbling down. László called out news of big
demonstrations in Sofia, of bigger ones in Prague. There
was trouble behind us and struggle ahead. The world was
changing and we were right in the middle of it all. One
afternoon I found myself on the Chain Bridge, virtually
skipping across the Danube, caught up in a mood of
absolute elation. I was high on history.

The officials on the Hungarian–Czech border were in an
uncommonly good mood. One grinned as he took our
passports, called out our home town football teams in place
of our names as he handed them back. Another made a
joke out of opening the back of the car, glancing at the
contents for a derisory five seconds, then slamming it shut
and waving us a cheery goodbye. As we drove off, a Czech
customs man was picking up a female Hungarian colleague
by the waist and swinging her around in the air. Both were
laughing out loud.

In Bratislava we looked for Stanley and found him just
where he had said he'd be: behind the information desk of
the Hotel Carlton.

'It took you so long,' he said. 'Where have you been?' He
lowered his voice and shook his head. It was 20 November.
At that point it was still rumoured that four had been killed
in Prague. 'You must be careful. It has been very bloody
here. Very bloody.'

It took us about five minutes to run into our first
demonstration. There was no room at the Carlton, so we
drove on to the Hotel Kyjev. Its flat glass and concrete face
loomed high above as we pulled out our bags and paid the
parking attendant. A chanting rose around the corner:
'Gorby! Gorby! Gorby!' The policeman in a parked car
nearby honked his horn and the colleague who had been

stretching his legs hurried back to the passenger seat. Down the street streamed a crowd of maybe five hundred, most of them young and carrying candles. We stood still as the procession swept by, felt the brush of its soft, tentative exuberance, and then ran into the hotel. If we checked in and dumped our bags quick enough, we might just catch the end of it.

We missed the end of the demonstration. It wound up in the square outside the Carlton and by the time we got there, all that was left were the candles, slowly burning down around a statue. Later, deep in the warren of the old town, sitting down with Stanley in a wine cellar, I reached over and lit the candle in the bottle on our table.

There were folkloric violinists singing songs. People at other tables joined in. When the musicians took a break, members of the public sang songs of their own. The mood even passed over our table. I found myself breaking into, of all things, 'Jerusalem'. Mark and John took it up. We really began to enjoy singing. Only Trevor didn't join in and I'd wondered if he thought it was stupid, until later he shrugged: 'Nah. I just didn't know the words.' The local drinkers, Stanley included, looked on in some surprise and when we finished there was a small, startled silence followed by much laughter and a few saracastic handclaps. Then someone struck up another Slovakian tune and we were forgotten.

The mood was still relaxed as we walked back to the hotel, despite the secret policemen on every corner. We knew now for sure that Stanley wasn't one of them. He was just one of those sad people whose lives had stopped back in 1968. As we said goodbye and shook his hand, it was clear that in Stanley's part of the world, life was once more on the move.

In Prague, at Moskevská station, I saw something new. People were queuing to buy newspapers. On this fifth day of the revolution, things had already changed so fast that, after decades of censored reports, official speeches, photographs of Party big shots, the papers now contained enough real substance to have a hundred people standing in line, eager for a chance to read. Here and there, taped to the tiled walls of the underground, were sheets of type-written text. People gathered also to read these.

We'd stopped long enough at Smíchov for Andrea to fill us in on events. A student demonstration on Friday – commemorating the fiftieth anniversary of the funeral of Jan Opletal, a student killed by the Nazis – had snowballed from 15,000 to 50,000 and ended up rolling into Wences-laus Square. There the crowd had been encircled by riot police with shields and truncheons, anti-terrorist squads in red berets that no one had ever seen before. The demon-strators handed out flowers. The police bludgeoned them to the ground. Reports of the violence spread on Saturday. 'Voice of America' announced that one student had been killed. This brought more people out on to the streets. By the time it was discovered that reports of the student's death had been greatly exaggerated, events had acquired their own momentum. That afternoon as we arrived, the third big demonstration was already gathering in Wenceslaus Square.

We caught the train to Mustek. Many in the carriage had Czech tricolour ribbons, small splashes of red, white and blue, pinned to coats and jackets. As the escalator moved closer to street level, so a certain mood was building. We emerged at the bottom of Wenceslaus Square and felt it grow stronger still. The crowd which stretched up the half-mile towards the National Museum, decked with ribbons and banners and candles held high, was the biggest I had ever joined. More were arriving by the minute: maybe 200,000 were there that day. People shinned up lampposts, passed along notes, leaned out from balconies all along the square. The mood pulsed around us as we inched through the crush. It was something special, something I had never felt before: a mixture of hope and exhilaration, tinged with fear that was in turn balanced by a determination to beat that fear away, to banish it by staring it straight in the face.

The Velvet Revolution was still young and the crowd didn't quite yet believe in itself. Chants would begin some-where far up ahead, ripple their way down through that huge mass of people, pass across the lips of those around us and then fade out further down on a note of poignant uncertainty. People around us, hearing our English voices, translated one or two. That chant, tailing off on the fringes by Mustek station, that one was about freedom of choice. This one, starting up near the statue of St Wenceslaus, this one was asking the miners to join the revolt.

In contrast to the crowd around us, our confidence was unshakeable. They spoke of Tiananmen Square, murmured that the police were ready and waiting. We said: don't worry, it's going to be all right. They said we didn't understand how things were in their country. We said that maybe we knew a little more than they might suppose. Much of that confidence, though in retrospect not misplaced, certainly came from the feeling of finally landing in the right place at the right time. We were on a roll. As tourists, we were also free from any fear of ending up in the firing line, should the clampdown suddenly come. Yet there was more to it than that. Over the last two weeks we had toured the East, tasting the change in Berlin and Poland and Hungary, gagging on the bitterness of Romania. All we had learnt, all we had seen, all we had felt or turned into a joke – all this informed our intuition about the situation that day. This was the moment. On a balcony in the distance, Václav Havel was speaking. We didn't even know who it was, couldn't understand a word of any speech, on any banner. All we could do was feel the mood, and that mood felt powerful and strong.

The last chant tailed off, the last words of the last speech echoed away across the square. There was a pause. Hats were doffed, victory signs hoisted, sparklers lit, and the crowd began singing the Czech national anthem. Despite our rendition of 'Jerusalem', I have never been big on patriotic hymns. But these were the beginnings of a revolution. Wenceslaus Square was hosting another great moment in the history of the nation. So strong were the emotions tied up in that singing – the hope and the exhilaration, the fear and the strength – that water welled into my eyes. When silence fell and the enormous crowd began quietly filtering away, I looked around and noticed even Trevor's lip was quivering.

The next morning, for what we knew might be the last time ever, we commenced a time-honoured ritual. We made a black market currency transaction, divided the proceeds into four piles, ate one biscuit each and went out shopping. It was a fantastically strange morning, wandering about in the middle of a revolution, trying to spend all our money before we left for Berlin. Outside galleries and cafés, people gathered to read the notices taped on walls while we scuttled in and out of record shops and department stores, using up our black market income on cheap alloy garlic presses, postcards with Czech recipes on them, Sparta Praha towels, and paint boxes with rockets on the lid. I was particularly pleased to find a secondhand *Mayhew's London* and 'Gems of Russian Classics' on three cassettes.

Thick snow was falling as we set off for David and Andrea's. It was around two o'clock. As the day had worn on and the next demonstration approached, more and more ribbons had been appearing on lapels. Not enough, I kept thinking. A little doubt had crept in from somewhere, undermining the confidence of the day before. The thought of the revolution being crushed, at this moment of sudden hope, here in this city where we had so many friends – most now working behind the scenes of the uprising – was too horrible for us not to be anxious. We caught a taxi on Wenceslaus Square. It was a few hours before the start of the demonstration but already there were several hundred waiting. The statue of St Wenceslaus was draped with flags and banners, surrounded by flowers and candles. As the taxi whisked us away down a side street, I craned my head around to catch a last, quick look and imagined the crowd that would soon fill the square. Maybe there would be enough after all.

First, there was white.

An hour north of Prague, I slipped 'Gems Of Russian Classics Volume 3', a selection from Rimsky-Korsakov, into the cassette machine. Outside, snow continued to fall. Slow and mournful, the first piece billowed from the speakers: 'The Song of the Indian Guest from Sadko'. Like all great Russian music, something in the scale of its melancholy evoked immense spaces, vast silences lying somewhere just beyond the sound. Mist was descending from the sky to meet the snow laid over fields unmarked by tree or stone. The car was enfolded in a seamless white from which only the road ahead stood out. It felt as if we were driving on a bridge over the void.

Later, there was black.

Just south of the Czech–DDR border at Zinnwald, Mark put on a cassette of the Pet Shop Boys. Outside it was black night. No moon, no stars. The foundations of the sound were computerised speed and precision with some urban clutter and climax, textured on top. The song was 'It's Alright', an English treatment of a black American piece. Some words Neil Tennant had added as an extra verse to Sterling Void's original danced out of the speakers to command our attention:

Forests falling at a desperate rate
The earth is dying, desert taking its place
People under pressure on the brink of starvation
I hope it's gonna be alright

These lines, which might have seemed trite in other circumstances, gathered all our emotions together. We were passing through the dead forest. Poisoned trees were keeling over in the dark outside. 'People under pressure on the brink of starvation' – Romania. And having left Prague in those first uncertain stages of the revolution, all we could do was hope that it *was* going to be all right.

Eventually, Berlin.

One last time, we pulled into Drewitz in the small hours. Trevor slowed into one line of traffic, reconsidered, got out of the car to look at the sign for the lane, decided he'd made a mistake and started to edge the car over into the queue on our left.

A passing guard snapped: 'What are you doing?'

'Trying to get into the right lane.'

'It doesn't matter which lane.'

'Look,' snarled Trevor, 'I've always had the utmost respect for German correctness.'

A bright blue Trabant came up to take the place we had just vacated. Everyone looked over at this unfamiliar sight: a little Trabi, casually rolling into West Berlin. It was no great shock. That both its occupants appeared to be gay leather clones was more of a surprise than the car itself standing there. We watched them wave their papers at the guard, and move off into town. For them this was probably a beginning, their entrance to a new world of possibility. For us this was most definitely an ending; not just of a holiday, but of a chapter in our lives. The guard now ambled towards our car as another Trabant drew into line. The tides of history had caught up with us. Forget Russia, forget America: this was Germany now. I handed my passport through the window to the guard. He looked at me and I looked at him. There was no longer any looking-glass between us. Nothing would ever again be the same as it was, once upon a time in the East.

II.
EPILOGUE:
AFTER THE FALL

Sometime in spring 1990, I keyed the SAVE command on my computer, thus transferring from memory to disk one of the first few fragments of this manuscript, sighed, stubbed a cigarette and, picking between piles of books and clothes, took the three or four steps to the mattress in the corner. The noise of traffic, heavier in the months since the Wall came down, sputtering Trabant now mixing with throaty Mercedes, rose up three floors to vibrate through my window. I stretched out and closed my eyes and drifted away into another of those afternoon dreams, another divided city of the soul.

In this dream I was in Beirut, alone on a bus, travelling through the rain. My stop was the one before the bridge, but when I got off there, mingling with the crowd on the pavement, I looked down at my bare feet and realised I had left behind my shoes. I jumped back aboard as the bus set off over the river. The buildings on the banks were a hot, sandy colour; the river a deep, iridescent blue. I knew it to be the Danube, dividing the two halves of Beirut. As I scrabbled around to find my shoes, the bus carried me over to the other side. . .

Sometime in summer 1991, I put down my pen after cutting a few more words from the final draft of this book, strolled out in the sun to the S-Bahn station and caught a train to Friedrichstrasse. Where once had been armed guards, control cubicles, metal barriers and customs officials was now only a boring tiled concourse, sprinkled with citizens changing trains. I stood where the border post used to disgorge its clientele into the East, mapping memories on to the scene. There, where that woman with the shopping bag was walking, was the site of the old money-changing booth. And there, by that souvenir stall offering pieces of Wall and toy Trabants (lately available everywhere), had stood the machine they once used to X-ray my cigarettes.

It was jolting to be back there. I'd been avoiding our old Eastern haunts, partly because there were few reasons to visit them any more. This side of town was no longer cheap, no longer so very different. The only new thing happening was the systematic demolition of any evidence that communists had once run the show. That and a wave of brutal racist attacks. Guest workers and asylum-seekers now cast as the villains and victims. I'd also been staying away because I hadn't wanted to disturb my recollections of how the East had been until I had written them down. Now the book was nearly finished, one nagging question remained.

Had Norman been a Stasi?

As our world had been changing, so had our lives. Mark was in love, had a smart new flat, owned a piece of the Pinguin Club and was launching a dance label for the recently privatised East German state record company. Torsten had separated from Tina, was living in Mark's old flat and studying at the Free University. Salman had got married and, only a few days before, returned to the States to seek his fortune. He was the last of our tame GIs to leave town, Buttle having been demobilised the year before. Trevor had been seriously ill and, on doctor's orders, given up drink and drugs. His wife, who for years had given him hell for staying out late and coming home drunk, had found she liked it even less to have him home all the time, stone-cold sober. One day she'd upped and left him. Trevor was now a responsible single parent and happier than I'd ever seen him. In Czechoslovakia, Jachym's magazine was selling from news-stands across the nation. Andrea had got the job of private secretary to the Czech ambassador to Germany, and she and David had moved to Bonn. Down in Budapest, László was doing PR work for American multinationals. We were all still in touch with each other. All except for Norman.

He had not lasted long in the West. We'd found him work helping renovate a friend's new restaurant. One day he hurt his leg and decided he couldn't work but never thought to ring and tell his boss. That was the end of that job. Mark then employed him to decorate his new flat. In return Norman would get both money and Mark's old place. Halfway through painting the main room, having neglected to put anything down on the floor and thus ruining the carpet, he vanished without contacting any of us ever again. Only a few nights before, at Salman's farewell party in the Pinguin, I had seen him for the first time in eighteen months.

We'd all felt betrayed by his sudden disappearance and gossip and rumour had rushed in to fill the vacuum. How had Norman, for example, got out of his interrogation so much more quickly than Torsten on the thirty-ninth anniversary day? Why had he never got into trouble for being unemployed? Had he only befriended Torsten after learning of his contact with GIs and Westerners? Torsten remembered the class book at school. Norman's father had been a Stasi. Norman had always known about demonstrations long before Torsten did, but couldn't account for the source of his information. Had Norman really got out through Budapest? László claimed to have been home that weekend. Another time, in December 1989, Norman told me he was going to London. I gave him an address where he could stay but he never turned up there either, told me he'd lost the piece of paper and stayed with someone he met on the train. Had he, we wondered later, weighing up this and all the other circumstantial evidence, been somewhere else instead? Had he been some kind of spy all along?

This was all mere speculation, the kind of lingering suspicion that was poisoning relationships all over the old East. Against it I placed my memory of Norman's fear and anxiety on the day I went over with Ed the American.

Paranoia like that would have been hard to fake. But long before Norman turned up at Salman's party – Mark having rung his mother's on a whim, found Norman there and invited him along – I knew that some day I would have to ask him straight. So there I was, in Friedrichstrasse station, at our old rendezvous, waiting for Norman one final time.

'Write that I was a Stasi,' Norman insisted. The question had insulted him but he wouldn't deny it directly. 'Write it in your book. Then when you've accused me I'll be able to see my file.'

We were walking along a Friedrichstrasse full of construction sites. Down the road was a new branch of American Express. Round the corner in Unter den Linden, the Bulgarian Cultural Centre was holding a closing-down sale.

'But were you?'

'What do you think?'

'I don't know. That's why I'm asking.'

'It was like a Hitchcock film,' he said. 'Arriving at the party and everyone saying I was a Stasi. Exactly Hitchcock.'

We sat in the sun outside the Opera Café. The tables now sheltered under Marlboro umbrellas, passing buses bore adverts for Western furniture stores, our cans of Coke had 'Keep South Africa Tidy' embossed on the lids.

'It was because you disappeared without contacting anyone that the rumours began to fly.'

'You could have called me.'

'We didn't know where you were.'

'I was at my mother's the whole time.'

'But you were the one who disappeared without saying anything.'

Norman sighed.

'I just couldn't stand it. I was completely disappointed. About the flat, about the life.'

'Well, what did you expect? We warned you often enough: how awful Mark's flat was, how life could also be hard in the West. I remember you saying one time that the main reason you wanted to come over was to see Mark's flat for yourself.'

'Yes, but I couldn't have lived in it.'

'Mark always said you'd go straight back to your mother's.'

'It was like I always used to say to him about the East: you had to live there to understand. It was all horrible. Not just one part of it, not just the flat, but all, it was shit here before and now it's shit from the West.'

He was spitting out the words.

'Everything is shit.'

Norman paid for the Cokes because I had no money and we walked on towards Alexanderplatz. There was a fun fair in the car park of the Palast der Republik, now closed and awaiting demolition. Few Trabants were still on the street, few people were still dressed in the old marbled denims, fewer male faces wore moustaches. The only way left to spot an Eastie was by a certain cold glint in the eye, a look of insult and resentment.

'Did you ever read E.M. Forster?' I asked as we walked across an Alexanderplatz now filled with croissant stalls. Centrum had changed its name to Kaufhaus and was filled with Western crap. A neon sign for Panasonic had appeared over the buildings opposite the Stadt hotel.

Norman shook his head. He was still angry.

'He once said: "If I had to choose between betraying my country and betraying my friend, I hope I should have the guts to betray my country."'

'You hurt us, Norman. Don't you see? It doesn't really matter whether you were a Stasi or not, but we counted you as our friend and you ran off without saying anything. Everything might be shit but friends are important. You don't let them down because often they're all that hold you up. This wasn't all just about East and West, it was about friendship.'

We stopped at the entrance to the U-Bahn, just near the World Time Clock, the base of which was now plastered with posters for concerts. Norman had to go off to work, as a hotel night porter.

'If you've got no money,' he said, 'would you like me to give you back that hundred marks you gave me when I left for Budapest?'

'I don't even remember giving it to you.'

'You did. Do you want it back?'

'If you can afford it,' I admitted, 'it would help. Times are hard. I've scarcely earned a pfennig since last October.'

He proffered a note and I pocketed it gratefully.

'Give me a ring,' I told him as we shook hands goodbye.

'Maybe,' he said. 'I'm not sure. I have to think about it.'

As the bus swept across the bridge that spanned the Danube of my dream, I was too busy tying my shoes to notice where we were going, passing into the other side of the city, twisting and turning through a maze of backstreets before finally pulling up in a sunny square. There I got off, knowing only that I was stranded on the wrong side of the city, miles from where I'd started, no idea how to get back. But then, looking at the road, I realised that my bus had actually been a tram. There, embedded in the asphalt, gleaming in the sun, were its polished metal tracks. I smiled. Here was my trail of crumbs. Past grand country houses with gardens and orchards, I started to follow them home.

ACKNOWLEDGEMENTS

I have many to thank, not only for the usual sorts of things – advice and encouragement, sending me books, buying me lunch, helping out in foreign parts – but also just for being around in difficult times when often there seemed nothing else to get me through but the love and the kindness of friends.

Penny Herman, Dennis Kelleher, Don Macpherson and Neil Tennant read earlier drafts of the manuscript and made invaluable suggestions. All four also helped in many other ways. Mark Reeder was a friend indeed and should know I'll always love him for it. John Fitzsimons, Edison Lagos, Raoul and Caroline Orzabal, Pete Robertson, Jane Taylor and Trevor Wilson were also there when it mattered.

I am also indebted to Thekla Ahlrichs, Rolf Amann, Wolfgang Doebeling, Tracey Drew, Petra Elkan, Gosto Babka von Gostomski, Chaos Franck, Lynne Franks, Norman Hannert, Alistair Gray, Volker Hauptvogel, László Horváth, Torsten and Tina Jurk, Jane Kidd, Andrea and David Kopelent, Julia Krings, Ingo Lamberty, Mihal and Magda Olszanski, Adrian Palka, Pie, Hilary Potter, Tim Randall, Paul Raw, Elisabeth Recker and Peter Krause, Dick and Lorna Rimmer, Martin Rimmer, Pru Roscrow, John Stokes, Tony Swann, Pol Ferguson Thompson, Jachym Topol, Steve Tuttle, Kassim Visram, Elaine Wangford, Ed Ward, Ellen Wenk, Jana Wolff . . . and naturally also all Pinguin Club trunk guests, same if our humour was often two pairs of shoes.

Berlin-Schöneberg, September 1991